Mahesh Dattani

His Stagecraft in Indian Theatre

Mahesh Dattani

His Stagecraft in Indian Theatre

Vishwanath Bite

AUTHORSPRESS

Worldwide Circulation through Authorspress Global Network
First Published 2013
by
Authorspress

Editorial
Q-2A Hauz Khas Enclave
New Delhi-110 016

Marketing
E-35/103, Jawahar Park
Laxmi Nagar, Delhi-110 092

e-mails: authorspress@rediffmail.com; authorspress@hotmail.com
Website: www.authorspressbooks.com

Mahesh Dattani: His Stagecraft in Indian Theatre
ISBN 978-81-7273-737-5

Printed in India at Krishna Offset, Shahdara.

Dedicated to

Mahesh Dattani

My Inspiration, who taught me

to write plays.

Preface

The most exciting thing in the book Mahesh Dattani's Interview is included which will help researchers, scholars, academicians and teachers to understand dramatic world of Mahesh Dattani.

Vishwanath Bite in his well researched article *Thirty Days in September* analyses the play through different perspectives. N. Anisha in her insightful article, recterates Representing the Other in *Seven Steps Around the Fire*, that Mahesh Dattani's hand touches the heart of the third gender through his vivid portrayal of the hijra community in his play *Seven Steps Around the Fire*. She further says that Dattani explains the term 'hijra' through the words of Uma Rao, a research scholar in sociology, by taking recourse to the *Ramayana*, and also tries to explore the misery of the marginalized sections of the society.

V.B. Chitra & T. Sasikanth Reddy's paper regarding Sexuality, Alternate Sexualities and Gender in Dattani's *Bravely Fought The Queen*, highlights the place of modern Indian theatre that is predominantly urban, manifestly influenced by Western traditions even as it tries to find its own feet, still evolving and searching for a distinctive identity. They state that drama is part of the larger 'Indian theatre', decidedly influenced by, and drawing inspiration from many of its traditional forms.

Kaustav Chakraborty in his article, The Inconsistent World of Gays: A Psychoanalytical Approach to *On a Muggy Night in*

Mumbail Mango Soufflé, discusses the homosexual bond between the gay characters that seem to be fraudulent, as revealed through Dattani's play *On a Muggy Night in Mumbai.* He further says that we stigmatize the gay characters in Mahesh Dattani's plays/movies with polygamous infidelity; we must do it keeping their psychological struggle in mind as well as should not exclusively evaluate their appeal on the sole basis of their sexual behavior.

Dipanita Gargava in her well-research article, "Mahesh Dattani's Plays: a Mirror of Contemporary Society", states that Dattani's plays are a reflection of the contemporary society. According to her, Dattani not only deals with common and ordinary people but also the common problems of people in realistic terms. In many of his plays, he deals with various issues like homosexuality, gender discrimination, communalism and child sexual abuse. Dattani manages to delve deep into the hearts to recreate characters with authenticity and a sense of liveliness.

Anisha Rajan in her article highlights the theme of gender discrimination in Mahesh Dattani's play *Tara*. She says that gender inequality is a form of inequality which is distinct from other forms of economic and social inequalities. It stems not only from pre-existing differences in economic endowments between women and men but also from pre-existing gendered social norms and social perceptions. Through this play Dattani brings out the root of gender discrimination by making the woman, the destroyer of another woman's life.

Shiv Kumar in his research article, Child Abuse and Its Psychological Repercussion in Mahesh Dattani's *Thirty Days in September,* portrays the psychological drama of a character who suffers from sexual abuse which happened when she was young. His paper will mainly concentrate on the figure of the protagonist of the play, Mala, around whom the entire play revolves and who occupies the major space in the play. The paper will attempt to examine the consequences of child abuse and how the solution is provided within the world of the play.

In her article, The Noesis of Otherness in Indian Society: Mahesh Dattani's *Seven Steps Around the Fire* and *Dance Like a Man,* M. Preetha throws light on the discourse of otherness in Indian society that has resulted as an outcome of the socio-psychological perceptions of the Indians. According to her, the playwrights who follow the tradition of social realism ruminate on the contemporary social problems like intercaste marriage, untouchability, sex, power and wealth. Their plays are more panoptic in scope and add a new colour to the Indian drama.

Rashi Sharma in her insightful article, (Re)Framing Present through Past: Dattani's Synchronization of Discord in *Dance Like a Man,* seeks to contextualize Dattani's endeavour to harmonize conflictual sensibility of the characters in *Dance Like a Man* where past seems to dominate the present and yet tends to shape it. In addition, the paper also attempts to map out and challenge how the play strives to synchronize multiple dissonances among the fissured characters.

Pinaki Roy in her article, Mahesh Dattani's *Final Solutions*: A Brief Rereading, states that Mahesh Dattani has always been concerned with truthful depictions of the Indian society in his plays. She further points out that in *Final Solutions,* he gets to grips with the sectarian tension and mistrust between two major communities of India. The tense interface between the two communities of India in the aftermath of Partition provides the context for the basic situation.

Archana Bhattacharjee & Bhairaban Borah in their contributory article regarding Marginalization and Identity Crisis in Mahesh Dattani's Play *Seven Steps Around The Fire,* reveal that

Indian traditions are preserved in Natyashastra, the oldest of the texts of the theory of the drama. The play *Seven Steps Around the Fire* claims for the drama divine and a close connection with the sacred *Vedas* themselves. They state that the play beautifully deals with the pathetic plight of the *hijras,* their ways of life, their ardent sense of individual identity in a callous and cruel atmosphere where a minister had a young *hijras* burned to death.

M.S. Raj Sree in her research article, Opening the Discourses on Incest and Child Sexual Abuse with Reference to Mahesh Dattani's *Thirty Days in September,* observes that Dattani belongs to the tradition of avant-garde feminists who present women as the centre of their fictive world. His themes reflect upon the ordinary and everyday conflicts of urban people who may be living in transitional periods of history, caught between the firm undertow of tradition and modernity. She also mentions that his characters struggle for some kind of freedom and happiness under the oppressive weight of tradition, cultural constructions of gender, and repressed desire.

Umesh S. Jagadale's paper about Speech Situations in Radio Plays: A Pragmatic Approach to Mahesh Dattani's *Seven Steps Around the Fire,* highlights that *Seven Steps Around the Fire* by Mahesh Dattani is characterized with the typical radio-play features like the use of sounds, silences, pauses, voice-over etc. The playwright sets the play in a stark reality of the socio-cultural ethos in the contemporary world. The play candidly uncovers the problems of gender identity of the *hijra* community, their sexual exploitation and social isolation. He analyses the play through pragmatic perspective.

Yatri D. Dave in her research article discusses the gender issues in Mahesh Dattani's play, *Tara.* She states that in this play Dattani focuses on the nature of typical Indian bious society. Tara is protagonist in the play. She is a victim of social prejudices. She has all the quality of an emerging new woman ready to defy age-old prejudices and compulsions. Here emergence as a new woman is reflected in her ability to take decision and assert her identity. M. Anjum Khan in his insightful article, Decrypting Symbols: A Symbolic Reading of Mahesh Dattani's *Ek Alag Mausam,* explains that Mahesh Dattani's *Ek Alag Mausam* is a sensitizing play articulating the unheard voices of HIV positive patients and prejudiced society. The play projects emotional, psychological medical and social ordeal of patients infected with HIV. In addition he also says that social hostility, prejudice and lack of awareness are also symbolised through characters in the play. In her well-researched article Grishma Khobragade examines the gender discrimination and social consciousness in Mahesh Dattani's *Tara.* Her paper is also an attempt to scrutinize his drama to show how he is conscious of the social system and that have come up in the contemporary India. The study is based on the hypothesis that his drama effectively depicts the gender discrimination and social consciousness of modern India.

R. Manjushree in her article, Political Exploitation through Communalism in Mahesh Dattani's *Final Solutions,* tries to say that the play *Final Solutions* is about the cultural hegemony how Hindus had to suffer at the hands of Muslim majority like the character of Hardika/Daksha in Hussainabad. And how Muslims like Javed suffer in the set-up of the majority Hindu community. It disturbs the normal social life and also it is a hindrance for the national progress. The play also presents different shades of the communalist attitude prevalent among Hindus and Muslims in its attempt to underline the stereotypes and clichés influencing the collective sensibility of one community against another.

Sophia Jaychandran in her insightful article, studies the tragic elements in Mahesh Dattani's *Tara.* She further discusses that *Tara* is an emotional play about a boy and a girl who are joined together at the hip. Their predicament is that they have to be separated surgically, which will mean the death of either of the two. Injustice is promulgated by Tara's own mother, Bharati, whose preference is to the male child. This issue makes the play more compelling signifying that it is woman who perpetrates preferences.

Sanjeev Kumar's article, Spivak, Subalternity and Mahesh Dattani's *Final Solutions*, seeks to investigate representation of subaltern in Mahesh Dattani's play *Final Solutions* in the purview of postcolonial theory particularly from Gayatri Chakravorty Spivak's interrogation of the voice of subalternity. He also states that while highlighting multifaceted vibrations of contemporary psyche and its distortions, especially in the postcolonial set-up, Dattani unearths how the subaltern seeks to speak against a background of multiple oppressions—religious, social, familial, gender and, more importantly, psychological. M.K. Rukhaya in her article, *Tara:* The Other Side, says that Mahesh Dattani's *Tara* comes across as a play that deals with twin aspects that are two sides of the same coin. It also presents the conflict between illusion and reality as echoed by the multi-level set. She also examines the title 'Tara' that is symbolic of a shooting star that is a temporary guest of a small fraction of time as the protagonist is. The idea also brings to mind the concept of the binary star systems that consist of two stars that are gravitationally bound, and generally move around each other in stable orbits.

Sanchita Das in her well-researched article, *Tara*: The Star That Never Shines, observes the miserable life of the protagonist Tara. She also states that the play can be approached through the issue of simple man-woman relationship, or it can be responded to in terms of the disabled children's struggle against a variety of odds, which have been put in their way by nature, or chance, or accident of their birth. Or one can respond to the text through the positioning of the girl-child in Indian culture and society.

Nidhish Kumar Singh in his article, The Significance of the Play within the Play: A Study of Mahesh Dattani's *Brief Candle*, discusses the technique of play within play. With the help of this dramatic device, Mahesh Dattani indicates to his audiences that suffering, tragedy and death are inescapable human conditions but there is a possibility of reducing the sting and pain of these with the help of art, which in this case is dramatic art. Further, he says, Dattani endeavours to show that life is not as bland as people usually think it to be. Life is full of joy and variety. The device helps Dattani in the representation of these two aspects of life.

The present anthology has strictly followed blind peer-review procedure while selecting the papers. I am thankful to Dr. P. Madhurima Reddy, Asst. Professor in English, Chaitanya Bharathi Institute of Technology (CBIT), Hyderabad-500075, Dr. Anita Singh Professor in English, Department of English, Banaras Hindu University, Banaras, India., Dr. Rambhau Badode, Professor, Department of English, University of Mumbai, Vidyanagari, Santacruz (East), Mumbai for reviewing, selecting papers, making suggestions and sharing with me critical arguments.

I must record my deep sense of indebtedness to Mr. Sudarshan Kcherry, Managing Director, and the whole team of Authorspress, New Delhi for pursuing me to edit present volume. I must not forget to express my deep sense of gratitude to my respected father, Shri. K. S. Bite, my beloved wife, Madhuri Bite, for her help in editing and her constant support in my literary activities. I must thank my brother, Ramdas Bite, for his love, affection and constant support.

Dr. Vishwanath Bite

Contributors

Anisha N., Aneesh Bhavan, Anad P.O, Nedumangad, Thiruvananthapuram, Kerala.

Anisha Rajan, TC-9/1035, Kripa, Sasthamangalam P.O., Thiruvananthapuram, Kerala.

Anjum Khan M., BC-16, ACC Colony, Madukkrai P.O. Coimbatore, Tamil Nadu.

Archana Bhattacharjee, Associate Professor, Department of English, Kakojan College, Jorhat, Assam.

Bhairaban Borah, Lecturer, Department of English, Kakojan College, Jorhat, Assam.

Chitra V.B., Assistant Professor of English, Department of Humanities, Jawaharla Nehru Technological University, Anantapur.

Dipanita Gargava, Lecturer, Shri G.S Institute of Technology and Science, Indore, Madhya Pradesh.

Grishma Khobragade, Assistant Professor, Department of English, Birla College of Arts, Science & Commerce Kalyan, Maharashtra.

Kaustav Chakraborty, Assistant Professor in English, Southfield College, Darjeeling, West Bengal.

Manjushree R., Assistant Professor in English, Alva's College Moodbidri, Karnataka.

Nidhish Kumar Singh, Research Scholar, Department of English & MEL, University of Allahabad, Allahabad, Uttar Pradesh.

Pinaki Roy, Assistant Professor of English, Malda College, West Bengal.

Preetha M., PhD Research Scholar in English, Avinashilingam Deemed University for Women, Coimbatore, Tamil Nadu.

Raj Sree M.S., Research Scholar, Institute of English, University of Kerala, Trivandrum, Kerala.

Rashi Sharma, Assistant Professor of English, Ramgarhia College Phagwara, Punjab.

Rukhaya M.K., Expert writer at Brighthub.Com

Sanchita Das, Deahbandhupara, Siliguri, Darjeeling, West Bengal.

Sanjeev Kumar, Department of English, Govt. P.G. College, Karnal, Haryana.

Sasikanth Reddy T., Academic Consultant in English, YSR Engineering College of Yogi Vemana University, Proddatur Town, YSR Dist, Andhra Pradesh.

Shiv Kumar, House No. A40, Block 10, Trilok Puri, Near Mayur Vihar, New Delhi.

Sophia Jaychandran, Assistant Professor in English, Vanita Vishram Women's College of Commerce, Athwa Gate, Surat, Gujarat.

Umesh S. Jagadale, Assisstant Professor in English, Sangamner College, Sangamner.

Vishwanath Bite, Assistant Professor in English, Government of Maharashtra's Ismail Yusuf College, Jegeshwari (E), Mumbai.

Yatri D. Dave, Lecturer, Nirma Institute of Technology, Nirma University, Ahmedabad.

Contents

1

Interview with Mahesh Dattani

Vishwanath Bite

Vishwanath Bite: Will you tell us something about yourself (place of birth, school and anything in between)?

Mahesh Dattani: I was born in Bangalore to a middle class Gujarati family in 1958. My parents were keen that my sisters and I receive our education in English and so they sent us to good 'convent' schools! I studied in Baldwin Boys' High School, which was considered in its time as one of the top schools in Bangalore.

VB: What motivates you to write? And why did you choose to be a dramatist?

MD: I guess I am sensitive to my environment and perhaps perceive things a bit more openly than most people. Writing is a wonderful medium to express one's concerns and also to recount human behaviour as perceived. Drama offers a tighter focus—an extreme close-up if you may—of human relationships. Of all that I perceive, it is the human being in conflict with other human beings that interests me the most.

VB: When did you start writing?

MD: In the mid-eighties after I had established by theatre company Playpen in Bangalore.

VB: Which books did you find yourself reading whilst growing up, and which are you currently reading?

MD: Growing up, I loved reading Enid Blyton and Arthur Conan Doyle along with James Hadley Chase, Harrold Robbins—all popular pulp amongst teenagers in my time! Right now I am reading *God's Debris* by Scott Adams, the creator of Dilbert. The one I just read was Thich Nhat Hanh's *Cultivating the Mind of Love.*

VB: Which writers have influenced your writing?

MD: I think earlier on Tennessee Williams, Vijay Tendulkar and Mahesh Elkunchwar were clearly my influences. I deliberately kept away from reading great writers in my formative years as a playwright to discover my own voice.

VB: How would you describe your plays?

MD: Modern Indian theatre.

VB: How much time do you take to finish a book?

MD: Varies. I took two years to write *Final Solutions* and six weeks to write *Dance Like a Man.*

VB: Which play of yours do you like most? Why?

MD: I really can't say. I like them and dislike them from time to time.

VB: What's the best thing a reader ever said to you?

MD: More an audience member really. I remember after a show of *Final Solutions*, a young man came up to me and said his name was Bobby but originally Babban. After the play in which a character does something similar, he was inspired to change it back. He found pride in who he was.

If a play can transform even one life it has done more than what is expected of it.

VB: **How do you see the literary scene in India? Is it progressing or retrogressing?**

MD: I really cannot comment. I have no idea whether people are reading more than before or not. What is good to see is that there are more publishers today than every before. I guess that is a good sign.

VB: **Are there any new playwrights who have grasped your interest?**

MD: Anuvab Pal, Ramu Ramanathan, Anupama Chandrashekar to name a few.

VB: **Did you learn anything from writing your books? What was it?**

MD: I learnt a lot about myself. I actually discovered my concerns only after I began writing.

VB: **What are the most important elements of good writing? According to you, what tools are a must-have for playwrights?**

MD: I think it is very important to understand dramatic action. Characters want something and the consequences of their actions to attain what they want should help them grow or destroy them completely. Good writing, whether for stage or for the page, must reveal character and take us through a journey of transformation.

VB: **What identity are you comfortable with—dramatist or director?**

MD: I think a dramatist, because it includes many aspects of theatre.

VB: **What are your current projects?**

MD: I am working on a new play that I hope to direct by the end of the year.

VB: **What was the hardest part of writing your book?**

MD: The sheer fact that it will be published and be read by scholars. That is as nerve wracking as facing a first night audience!

VB: **How will you judge the body of Contemporary Indian Writing in English?**

MD: I can only say it's very slim compared to other languages!

VB: **What message would you like to give to readers?**

MD: Enjoy the book or play. Appreciate it and succumb to the charm of the story. Let the critiquing come afterwards.

VB: **What message would you like to give upcoming writers?**

MD: Follow your heart and discover your own voice. The craft will come along the way.

VB: **What is the role of the Central Sahitya Akademi in popularizing the Indian English Literature?**

MD: It can play a huge role as they are bound to translate all award winning books to other Indian languages. However, they need to take that work a lot more seriously and produce translations of world quality, especially of writers whose writings have a strong local flavour.

2

Mahesh Dattani's *Thirty Days in September*: A Critical Study

Vishwanath Bite

Mahesh Dattani's latest play *Thirty Days in September* was first performed at the Prithvi Theatre, Mumbai on 31 May 2001. A play about silence and betrayal, it treats the sensitive and generally taboo issue of child sexual abuse. The play was commissioned by RAHI (Recovery and Healing from Incest), a support group for women survivors of incest (RAHI was supported by the D. John and T. Caterine, MacArthur Foundation) a Delhi-based support centre for adult women survivors of childhood abuse. The play endeavours to lift the veil of silence which surrounds child sexual abuse and addresses the issue unflinchingly. The play is described as 'a silent scream ... on the issue of sexual abuse'. Dattani's much acclaimed play, *Thirty Days in September*, was organised on 7 April 2006 at FICCI Auditorium. Child sexual abuse is a heinous crime prevailing in society. The play aimed to sensitize the masses about this issue.

In the play, the focus is on an interior kind of story, with a lot of happenings inside the minds of the characters. Dattani personally feels that it is a kind of progression in his writing. The style is more sub-textual than overt text. He personally went to Delhi to research the play; visited and spoke to eight incest and child sexual abuse survivors for about a week. With intense interviews, they came out with their stories talking about what had happened to them; which was also a kind of therapy. Of course, with this material, Dattani could not write the play all at a stretch; it took him a little over a year. He says, "I need to be objective to look at the material and say now that's an interesting plot-line and work on a structure. But then I have to get subjective again to feel as these survivors felt and speak as they would. I need to bring their stories alive through the play." He has woven together many real stories to form this play.

Dattani feels that *Thirty Days in September* is his most severe play till date, contravening his usual design. The seriousness has to keep going throughout the play. It is by far the most melancholy of all his plays, with a weightiness that is maintained throughout the play. Given the seriousness of the problem that it addresses a malaise that can at no level be taken lightly, he tackles it with raw emotion and the stark realities are dramatized vividly. For want of space, the researcher would like to restrict the study of this play only with the thematic concern. He would like to explore the theme of child sexual abuse in the play *Thirty Days in September* and discuss how far Dattani becomes successful in his endeavour to lift the veil of silence that surrounds child sexual abuse by sensitizing the masses about this issue.

Thirty Days in September is a stage play in three acts. The stage is divided into four acting areas. The first area has a comfortable chair and a simple table with magazines and a double seater. The chair is reserved for the counsellor whom we never see. The second area, occupying the central portion of the stage, is the living room of Shanta and Mala's home in a suburb of Delhi. The dominant feature is a large picture of Shri Krishna. Here the family would meet and receive the people. The third area is the pooja room which is perhaps behind a screen so that it is visible only when required. The fourth acting area is the most flexible representing several locations—a party house, two restaurants and Deepak's home. During Mala's taped conversation, we see the back of a life-sized doll of a seven-year-old girl propped on a chair.

The play is entirely Mala's story, and Dattani uses very little sub-plot, dealing with the memories of the molester, visualizing him, and confronting those terrifying moments that will leave the spectator feeling sickened to the core. The play centres on a mother, Shanta, and her daughter, Mala, who was sexually molested by her uncle, Vinay, while young. The plot, however, is rooted in this very milieu, the final system that betrays the individual – a child called Mala – who will carry these scars into adulthood, and never trust it again. The story is about her recovery and survival, and the keen sense of betrayal she feels towards her mother. People, who are abused when young, go through a range of emotions starting from betrayal to anger, to guilt, to the feeling that their body is not their own and that it's a tool to attract attention. The story is told in retrospect through the eyes of Mala – the survivor. It is not true that child sexual abuse happens only in upper class households. In fact, many people receive it as a working class condition. Dattani says: "Actually, I would see the setting of *Thirty Days in September* as upper middle class. I chose this setting, because I did not want them to dismiss sexual abuse as something that does not happen to people like them."

At the opening of the First Act, Mala, the protagonist of the play, is sitting before the counsellor. She is under the treatment of a psychiatrist and now is improved. She is now much more confident and happy, as she knows that what happened in her previous life was not her fault and now, there is nothing to hide. Today, she doesn't hesitate to use her real name. Mala, when a girl of seven was sexually abused by her uncle continuously, till she grew up to thirteen. As a result, she has become fond of sex. It seems to her that she was made for it; she was born that way. She thinks that it is her born fault that she is like this—incest. Sex is a game for her and as she likes it, she thinks herself a bad person without character. She knows her fault, but she cannot stop herself doing that. She thinks that her mother is responsible for her incestuous behaviour. Mother could have prevented all this by telling her to stop all this. She could have prevented a lot from happening. Her mother, Shanta, never prevented her. It was her silence that took Mala towards the feeling of betrayal. So, Mala is always angry with her mother. There is a good deal of communication gap between them. There is no third person who could have taken care of her in this matter. She thinks that her father left the house as she was like this. Now, they were living in her uncle's house. Deepak, a young man from a good family wants to marry Mala. He wants to take her on good path of life. Shanta thinks that her prayers to Shri Krishna have been answered. All those years, she was waiting for this moment. But Mala is not ready to marry Deepak, saying: "I told you so. I know it won't work between us."

The Second Act too, starts with Mala's conversation with the counsellor. From her voice on tape, we come to know that her father sends them money every month, pays the rent, but never comes to see them. She tells that it's not just the men in the office, but much before she had seduced her uncle when she was thirteen. She slept with her cousin and anyone who was available. Now she requests the counsellor to help her stop this behaviour. She wants to smile as a little girl for the first time. Her uncle left her saying he was disgusted with her—her behaviour. She is attracted towards her uncle and now confused. She doesn't know what she feels for him. Shanta now tells Mala the truth that the money that they kept receiving after her father left them was from this uncle. This uncle has helped them so much after her father left them. Mala angrily says that Shanta was a failed wife and a failed mother.

In the Third Act, Shanta requests her brother to talk to Deepak about marrying Mala. At the dinner party, Deepak asks Shanta whether Mala was abused as a child. Shanta denies it. However, when uncle offers the legal documents of the flat to Shanta, Mala gets excited and reveals the truth that her uncle was giving his flat to shut her mouth. She was abused by this uncle, every day, during the summer holidays. In the end, it is revealed that her mother too was molested for ten years, since she was six years old. As a result, she looked at Shri Krishna for help and He helped her by taking away all her feelings, giving her only silence. Her tongue was cut off. At the end, Mala gains control over herself and as a fellow-sufferer understands her mother; asks for forgiveness for blaming her all her life.

Dattani has been appreciated widely for his use of naturalistic theatre to define the problems of the urban Indian bourgeoisie in the twentieth century. Naturalistic theatre allows for a discussion of complex and intricate matters with ease in the confines of the drawing room. In the hands of Dattani, naturalistic theatre lays bare the hypocrisies and the entrenched secrets of the middle and upper classes. But these secrets, when entrenched with silence, take the shape of a demon and leave the psyches of the sufferers scarred. Mala's voice on tape reveals her scarred psyche. As she was sexually abused in her childhood by her own uncle, she turned into whore-like woman from age thirteen. She knows that this is terribly wrong, but she doesn't know why she does it, why she behaves like this. She enjoys sex, timing it for thirty days, even marks it on her calendar and after that she moves on – as it is no longer satisfying to her. She enjoys it with the right kind of people, and the right kind of people are usually older men. Deepak, her fiancé, is only a few years older to her and loves her very much. She could stop all this vicious circle; but she thinks it is too late. She goes on visiting men after men and blames her mother for not preventing her from such misdeeds. Deepak is trying to understand her and is ready to accept her as his wife, in spite of all her blotted history. But Mala is not confident about herself, as she is aware of her adultery and thinks that no man can accept and live with such a wife. She wants to stop this vicious circle, but now she thinks that it is not in her hands to stop all this. As a result, she psychologically suffers a lot; transfers her resentment upon her mother who kept silent throughout her life.

Shanta, Mala's mother, too, is the victim of the same problem of child abuse. At the end of the Third Act, it is revealed that Shanta too, was sexually abused from her sixth year and it wasn't only summer holidays. For ten years she was abused badly and kept silent as if her tongue was cut off. She lost all her feelings of pain or pleasure. It shocked her so much that she got 'frozen'. Her husband left her saying, "I married a frozen woman" (36). She lost all her sensitivity and sensation for love and sex. Sex was neither a thing of joy, nor pain for her. She had no meaning for any feeling or relation. She was a 'failure as a wife and as a mother'. That is why she remained silent throughout her life. She remained silent not because she wanted to, but she didn't know how to speak. She could not save herself, then how could she have saved her child? Nobody could see the pain in her eyes. Her child was suffering the same agony, which she herself had gone. Suffering was stuck to their bodies because they were born female. When the close relatives, family members, do the black deed of sexual abuse, no girl has a way to escape and no mother has the tongue to utter. These incidents of child abuse leave their scars upon the psyche, forever. The pain these scars bear, cannot be cured in one's whole life. Mala became incestuous and Shanta became cool. Mala got burnt into the fire of lust and Shanta was frozen to ice. Both of them bear the scarred psyches. Asha Kuthari Chaudhuri commenting on this problem says: "Every other character is implicated and made party to the crime, even the mother's complicity through her silence that betrays her own child, affirms her guilt."

Lecherous hypocrites like the uncle are present in many families. They do what they want with the small girls and let them suffer their whole lives forever. They may provide shelter and money to their victims, but the scars on the tender minds will never get cured. These hypocrites make a show of their care and generosity in the society, as if they have done nothing wrong. It is very ironical when he says repeatedly:

> "Isn't she like my daughter also?" (38)
>
> "I shall play the dutiful uncle tomorrow at dinner." (38)
>
> "I have always been there like a father for her, in spite of everything." (42)
>
> "If I'm Mala's uncle I can be your uncle, right?" (47)

Under the veil of uncle's so-called pious relationship, he abused Mala. Under the veil of sister's pious relationship, he abused Shanta. Yet, both of them could not utter a single word against this hypocrite. Thus, the play reveals the silent screams of the sexually abused survivors.

People abused, when young, go through a range of emotions, starting from betrayal to anger, to guilt, to a feeling that their bodies are not their own and that it is a tool to attract attention. Mala suffered going through all these emotions. All the time, she was angry with her mother as if her mother was responsible for all this stuff by remaining silent. Once, Mala pleads with Ravi to take her to his room as she badly needs 'it' from him. Ravi is with his fiancée, Radhika, and when Mala was gets very close to him while dancing, Radhika pulls them apart. Mala stands humiliated and looks around at all the people who are staring at her. She is angry with herself and feels guilty too. Leaving the party area, she goes into the living room and angrily starts quarrelling with her mother for letting Deepak in the house against her wishes. Shanta tries to pacify her by saying that she will prepare 'alu-paratha' for her the next day. Mala angrily says, ".... that's what I got whenever I came to you hurt and crying. Instead of listening to what I had to say, you stuffed me with food.... Every time I came to you mummy, you were ready with something to feed me."

Mala angrily flings the painting of Krishna out of the door. When her uncle comes to her house after a long gap, she goes to Deepak's house and tells him that she likes to attract the people, wants them to come to her and allow them to do anything to her. Mala thinks that her body is the tool to attract the attention of the people. Dattani in one of his interviews says: "It's the silence and the betrayal of the family that affects me the most. Like in this case the mother knew that her daughter was being sexually abused by her uncle, but still chose to keep quiet. It's this silence that makes the abused feel betrayed."

The play, *Thirty Days in September*, is a voice against this silence and the betrayal of the family. Many times Mala dicusses the subject. But Shanta sometimes pretend that she doesn't remember anything, sometimes pretended that Mala is making up stories or seeing bad dreams, sometimes she changes the subject, sometimes starts praying and chanting before the portrait of Krishna to avoid Mala's questions and sometimes pacifies her by stuffing with food to shut the mouth. Mala recognizes all these escapes of her mother and is certain that her mother knows everything and that's why she is prepared to avoid the subject anyhow. Whenever Mala says something serious, mother takes it lightly, deliberately. After all, she tells her mother about the incidents glaringly. She tells her that she is speaking about the time when uncle Vinay would molest her, when she was seven, eight, nine, ten – every vacation. Mother is busy either in the pooja room or in the kitchen. Then she goes to papa and cries, but before she can even tell him why she is crying, he would tell her to go to her mother. Mother always hides herself behind Krishna's portrait. Shanta has seen Mala pushing herself on her uncle in the bedroom when she is thirteen. She has seen Mala forcing him to do things to her. She remembers the days when Mala's cousin, her father's nephew, came for holidays, Mala enjoyed sex with him. Shanta was praying to God, so He could send His 'Sudarshan Chakra' to defend Mala from the demon inside her. However, instead of praying God, she should have warned Mala. She should have told Mala that what she was doing was all wrong and she should stop at once. She should have been rebellious with her brother, nephew and Mala, long ago. If she had done that, Mala could have been reformed. She could have abandoned the filthy path of incestuous behaviour. Instead, she kept silent and prayed to God. Mala went on enjoying the pleasure of sex from anybody she could find. Free sex becomes her addiction. As her uncle said before, at thirteen, she turned into a 'bitch' – a 'whore'. Thus, the silence of her mother made Mala feel that she was betrayed. She thought that it was her mother's fault. So she went on taking the pleasure to forget the pain. In fact, it is no use totally blaming her mother. However, there is some sense in her words when she says: "I suppose it's these Western values, I wish I were more traditional then I would not behave like this.... no, no, that's stupid, I know, that's very easy to put the blame elsewhere..." Mala knows where the wrong is. But she is unable to put herself right. She needs help and surely, it is her mother who can help her in time before she turns to be addicted to the bad habit. Mala's family, as well as the social milieu too is responsible for spoiling Mala. Fear of disgrace and a sense of shame keep many women mum; but Shanta has gone through the same state of disgrace and out of resentment for the misdeed which happened to her, she should have revolted against her own child's exploitation. Instead, she prefers accepting money and other help from her brother. The following dialogue is telling:

> *Mala*: Yes you did. He didn't just buy a flat. He bought you!
>
> *Shanta*: That's not true! Oh God!
>
> *Mala*:He bought your silence. So that you can never tell anyone what he did to your daughter!

Mala is absolutely correct when she accuses her mother. Many questions arise in the mind of the audience, and haunt them as they haunted Mala. Where was Shanta when Mala was being molested almost every day in summer vacation, every year? Was it not her duty to pay attention to her daughter and be careful herself, when she had such bad experiences of sexual abuse in her childhood? Was it not her duty as a mother, to ask her daughter what was wrong with her? Wasn't there a bit self-respect and resentment in Shanta? Can a mother in India who has a great tradition of self-sacrifice for her child, sell herself off to a sick bastard brother? Why was Shanta's tongue cut off? Was it for the livelihood she received from him? Is character less important than bread in our society? Shanta should have known that instead of spending time in praying to Krishna for Mala, she should have given time to build Mala's character. At least, she should have fought against her daughter's sexual abuse. She should have abandoned her filthy brother for the sake of her daughter's future. Dattani doesn't give any sound and direct suggestions for the problem of child sexual abuse; but he hints at all these suggestions.

Dattani's plays capture the pulse of urban audience by reflecting the problems of its day. However, the problem that Dattani has handled skilfully in the play is related to all the classes of society. He has rightly mentioned that the audience needs to arrive at the "moment of truth". If we look around us with open eyes, and read the papers carefully, we come to the truth that this is happening around us, even in the working class, but was not articulated with such a focus by any other writer. Dattani should be thanked and praised for this unique contribution to the Indian Drama in English. He has successfully created a world-view by focusing on the issue of child sexual abuse. His use of naturalistic theatre leaves the audience thinking of such problems around them. They experience what Dattani calls 'a catharsis-like-situation' and will empathize with the characters, look into them and think about such problems with a critical mind. Lillette Dubey, the director of this play, notes down her experience in the following words: "After every performance, women have come back stage with their own traumatic stories writ large on their faces, grateful for the catharsis the play offers, but even more, I think, for the expiation of their own guilt which they have arrived as a heavy burden for so long .... For through it they believe, their silent screams have finally been heard."

The title of the play is unique and symptomatic of the climatic incident of the play. The abuser in the play, while abusing the child, asks her to sing the song learnt in school. It is 'Thirty days has September. April, June and November. February has twenty-eight. All the rest have thirty-one!' He asks her to keep on singing till he stops her. The song becomes the filthy rhythm of her life. She grows fond of sex as a game for enjoyment. She starts fixing people who she likes best for continuous thirty days. After thirty days, she moves on—in search of people older than her who are right kind of people for her. Whenever she sees a man, she gets stimulated, she remembers her uncle and then the song—'Thirty days has September…' Thirty days in summer holidays was a vicious circle in her life. She moves with this vicious circle singing the song. Thus, the title is symbolic and penetrating.

To conclude, *Thirty Days in September* is the most sombre of all his plays with a theme of child sexual abuse, rarely touched with such an intense devotion by any other playwright. This is Dattani's unique contribution in the field of Indian Drama in English. For the actors, who played the abuser—first, Darshan Jariwala and later, Amar Talwar—it was a process that took them into the heart of the darkness. Their reward was the passionate dislike they evoked in the audience for their superb portrayals. It evoked in audience amazing depth of emotion and strong outrage across the world from varied critics in India to Colombo, to the US and Malaysia. There is a lot of movement in the play in terms of time and space shifts. The dialogue is brief and to the point, pregnant with raw emotion barely held on leash. Dattani makes extensive use of monologues in the form of taped voices. This technique intensifies the empathy of the audience with Mala. The technique is used with great workmanship to show the victim slowly recovering from her abused and tortured past. The action is presented starkly and undiluted. The narration of the abused is as naked as possible, which literally drags the audience into facing the molester. With *Thirty Days in September*, Dattani pulls up one more 'invisible issue' from under the carpet and puts forth before the society. Dattani is indeed a creative genius able to deal with such complex, invisible issues with seriousness and insight. The play is Dattani's unique creation which reveals some intensely horrifying faces that haunt the society. As a dark piece, powerful and immensely moving, the commercial success and critical acclaim of the play were surprising.

Works Cited

Chaudhuri, Asha Kuthari. *Mahesh Dattani,* New Delhi: Foundation Books Pvt. Ltd. 2005

Dattani, Mahesh. *Collected Plays*: Volume Two, New Delhi: Penguin, India, 2005.

<http://www.MaheshDattani.com > 22/6/07.

<http://www. MaheshDattani.com.>

Santhanam, Anitha. "It's the silence that affects me most". *Mahesh Dattani on 30 Days in September*, a play about child sexual abuse.

3

Representing the Other in *Seven Steps Around the Fire*

N. Anisha

> Our eunuch dreams, all seedless in the light,
> Of light and love the tempers of the heart,
> ("Our Eunuch Dreams" by Dylan Thomas)

Mahesh Dattani's hand touches the heart of the third gender through his vivid portrayal of the hijra community in his play *Seven Steps Around the Fire*. The title of the play reminds us of the holy religious rituals associated with the Hindu marriages. Dattani tries to represent here the wide distance between the third gender and the 'normal'gender

Dattani explains the term 'hijra' through the words of Uma Rao, a research scholar in Sociology, by taking recourse to the *Ramayana*:

> A brief note on the popular myths on the origin of the hijras will be in order, before looking at the class gender based power implications. The term hijra, of course, is of Urdu origin, a combination of Hindi, Parsian and Arabic, literally meaning "neither male nor female". Another legend traces their ancestry to the Ramayana. The legend has it that god Rama was going to cross the river and go into exile in the forest. All the people of the city wanted to follow him. He said "men and women

> turn back"'. Some of his male followers did not know what to do. They could not disobey him. So they sacrificed their masculinity, to become neither men nor women and followed him to the forest. Rama was pleased with their devotion and blessed them....perceived as the lowest of the low, they yearn for family and love. The two events in mainstream Hindu culture where their presence is acceptable-marriage and birth-ironically are the very same privileges denied to them by man and nature (*CP* 10-11)

From time immemorial, the issue of the "other" has caught our attention. We have the character Shikhandi in *Mahabharata* who stands as an icon of identity crisis. Thus the issue of identity and the need for space is an innate plight which clinges on the shoulders of third gender. Transgendered people are wrestling with the society around them for building of alliances and to have an identity of their own. For the common, transgenders identity does not match the usual notion of male and female genders. According to *With Respect to Sex* a book on sexual and social difference in India written by Gayatri Reddy, hijras are believed to "be endowed with the power to confer fertility on newlyweds or newborn children"(26)

The hijras are treated as outcasts, and are forced to beg on street corners or rely on prostitution to survive.

In the play Dattani tries to explore the misery of the marginalized sections of the society. Uma, the protagonist of the play *Seven Steps Around the Fire* writes about hijras:

> Not for them the seven rounds witnessed by the fire god, eternally binding man and woman in matrimony, or the blessings of 'may you be the mother of a hundred sons'. (11)

The title of the play *Seven Steps Around the Fire* gains significance here. Jeremy Mortimer in his Introduction to the play writes:

> For the story he (Dattani) chooses to tell is no ordinary story. The murder victim Kamala, a beautiful hijra eunuch, had it turns out, been secretly married to Subbu, the son of a wealthy government minister. The minister had the young hijra burned to death and hastily arranged for the son to marry an acceptable girl. But at the wedding—attended of course by the hijras who sing and dance at the weddings and births—Subbu produces a gun and kills himself. The truth behind the suicide is hushed up, but Uma has been keeping full notes for her thesis on the hijra community. (3)

The whole play is centre on the murder of kamala, an eunuch. When we go through the entire play we get the feeling that this is not a murder of any human being because for the heterosexuals, the murder of Kamala has not been an issue at all!! None from the normal society wants to probe deep into the case except Uma Rao, the PhD scholar. She thinks deep about hijras:

> Nobody seems to know anything about them. Neither do they. Did they come into this country with Islam, or are they a part of our glorious Hindu tradition? Why are they so obsessed with weddings and ceremonies of childbirth? How do they come to know of these weddings? Why do they just show up without being invited? Are they just extortionists? And why do they not take singing lessons? (Pause) Is it true? Could it be true what my mother used to say about them? Did they really put a curse on her because they did not allow them to sing and dance at their wedding? Or was that their explanation for not being able to have children of their own? Or...a reason to give to people for wanting to adopt me? (*CP* 16-17)

The silencing of the minority class by the homophobic society is what Dattani tries to explore through this play. In the play 'silencing' works at two levels, both emotional and at physical level. Through emotional, what I mean is that the silencing of their desire—their desire to become a mother, a father, a brother, a sister or even a daughter. Their desires to be loved by others, their desire to love others—all are at stake.

"I didn't kill her, she was my sister"—Anarkali's words, the main accused in Kamala's murder, challenges the whole society by showing them that the third genders too have sisters. "Would you kill your sister?" is a question that Dattani throws to his audiences. The helplessness and the awareness of the isolation that society imposed upon them make Anarkali to speak to Uma in a heart-rending tone: "if you were a hijra, I would have made you my sister" (242)

Uma's consideration for Anarkali evokes in her a kind of fear to mingle with the heterosexuals: "Oh! You are only being kind—don't hurt my heart". (242)

Eunuchs are physically ostracized from the society. They are marginalized even in crime. Uma explains:

> The invisible minority, behind Russell Market, everyone knew where to find them, although I couldn't see any hijras on the streets. They only come out in groups and make their presence felt by their peculiar loud hand clap. (21-2)

The silencing of their identity is another core issue that Dattani puts before us. Munuswamy, the constable, asserts: "Sh! Of course it will talk to you. We will beat it up, if it doesn't". (CP 233)

> They knew. Anarkali, Champa and all the hijra people knew who was behind the killing of Kamala. They have no voice. The case was hushed up and was not even reported in the newspapers. Champa was right. The police made no arrests. Subbu's suicide was written off as an accident. The photograph was destroyed. So were the lives of two young people… (42)

The story of the love affair between Kamala and Subbu shows the impossibility of the marriage between a eunuch and a man in Indian society. Their love doesn't bloom, for Kamala is a eunuch. "Marry! Who would want to marry…? Tchee! What kind of people are there in this world?" (263)

She pays this love with her own life. Thus her love is silenced by the cruel political hands of Subbu's father... who wants to see his son married to a person from a heterosexual community. It makes us feel that politics and society determine one's sex.

"One hijra less in this world does not matter" (35); the refrain goes, "Back! Beat it! Kick the hijra" (7)

The play opens with the chanting and mantras of religious rituals. What rings paradoxical here is that we need the blessings of hijras during marriages and at the time of children's birth, yet we can't accept them as an individual of the same flesh and blood as the heterosexuals have. Society often marginalize them, even fail to recognize them as human beings. Their life goes on unnoticed by the other world. An example:

> *Champa*: Oh! So you are a social worker. Say that.
>
> *Uma*: Yes. I am a social worker.
>
> *Champa*: Please excuse me, madam. I didn't know that...you see us also as society, no?

Since Dattani's play throws light on the plight of the eunuchs, the play reminds me of Kamala Das's poem "The Dance of the Eunuchs" where she tells about the misery of eunuchs. They dance and make other people happy despite knowing that they cannot reproduce and lead a simple, happy life.

> It was hot, so hot, before the eunuchs came
> To dance, wide skirts going round and round, cymbals
> Richly clashing, and anklets jingling, jingling
> Jingling... Beneath the fiery gulmohur, with
> Long braids flying, dark eyes flashing, they danced and
> They dance, oh, they danced till they bled...

The play ends with these words:

> They have no voice. The case was hushed up and it was not even reported in the newspaper…Subbu's suicide was written off as an accident. The photograph was destroyed. So were the lives of two young people…but Anarkali's blessings remain with me…I did not want her blessings for a child. All I want is what they want…to move on. To love, to live. (282)

Gayatri Chakravorty Spïvak's words echoes here:

> We cannot speak…when we want to speak nobody listens. When we cannot speak…

Dattani reads the minds of these marginalized people—their quest of love and to live. *Seven Steps Around the Fire* represents the voice of the 'other'. The play is about the identity crisis of the third gender and their longing for social acceptance. The play questions our social constitutions, gender bias and prejudices. The voice of subaltern is omnipresent all through the play. John McRae acknowledges Dattani in "The Voice of India" and speaks about his plays:

> They are the plays of today, sometimes as actual as to cause controversy but at the same time they are the plays which embody many of the classic concern or world drama.

Through this play Dattani opens our eyes to look into the stark realities of contemporary Indian society where all gender divisions are visible. It is the time to rewrite the slogan "unity in diversity" as "no unity in diversity" as far as gender is considered.

> Mahesh Dattani frequently takes as his subject the complicated dynamics of the modern urban family. His characters struggle for some kind of freedom and happiness under the weight of tradition, cultural constructions of gender, and repressed desire. (Erin Mee, 'Note on the Play', *Collected Plays)*

In one of his conversation with Utpal K. Banerjee, Dattani states:

> I'm strongly affected by social issues, especially when it comes to power-play in class and gender. A lot of my plays deal with them and they remain the leitmotifs of my plays. I am, however, not a social activist. From my long experience in theatre, I know what will work in a play, that is, what will be empowered writing. My first service is to the story and I believe that the form should serve the content. Usually, there is something like coming to terms sat the end and the audience can experience a catharsis like situation. That's deliberate and is part of my craft! (*Indian Literature)*

Works Cited

Dattani, Mahesh, *Collected Plays*, New Delhi: Penguin Publishers, 2000.

Mortimer, Jeremy. "A Note on The Play". *Seven Steps Around the Fire. Collected Plays.* op.cit.

Multani, Anglie, ed. *Mahesh Dattani's Plays: Critical Perspectives.* New Delhi: Pencraft International, 2007.

Dalmia, Vasudha. *Poetics, Plays and Performances: The Politics of Modern Indian Theatre.* New Delhi: OUP, 2006.

4

Sexuality, Alternate Sexualities and Gender in Dattani's *Bravely Fought the Queen*

V. B. Chitra and T. Sasikanth Reddy

With its 15 national languages, and more than 800 dialects, the spectrum of India's cultural fabric is decidedly complex and difficult to encompass. Hence, when one talks of 'Indian theatre', one enters a vast and intricate arena, both idiomatically heterogeneous and polyglot in character. Although numerous strands show us the links, it is after all, an arbitrary term, randomly used to designate one or the other of the diverse performance arts practised in the country, belonging to diverse traditions. It is extraordinarily inclusive—encompassing the classical (like the Kathakali, or some Bharatanatyam pieces), the ritual (such as the Raas, the Ramlila, or the Theyyam), the devotional (many of the musically dominant performances), the folk (like the Chhau or the Therukuttu) and the modern, partaking of sundry traditions, forms and lore, sometimes unique, and sometimes bewilderingly intermingling with each other.

Dance, drama, mime, song, instrumentation, puppetry, the orally delivered narratives all combine happily, almost seamlessly in a performance by an ensemble of artists working simultaneously. Given such a situation, it is hardly possible to fit this convergence into neat categories of Western theatre and performance that a student of Western literatures is wont to do, although it is possible to find working categories within its own socio-historic-political ambit, as within its own traditions.

A closer look at theatre in India from the time of the emergence of Sanskrit drama and its traditions, or the folk performance art still current in rural India is, however, beyond the span of this study. Our attempt will be to assess the place of modern Indian theatre that is predominantly urban, manifestly influenced by Western traditions even as it tries to find its own feet, still evolving and searching for a distinctive identity. This drama, none the less, is part of the larger 'Indian theatre', decidedly influenced by, and drawing inspiration from many of its traditional forms. To narrow down our focus further, we shall look at the place of English language drama in postcolonial India, a genre that unfortunately, (until recently) retains a somewhat mongrel nature, especially so when one juxtaposes it with the flourishing tribe of Indian novelists who write in English.

Modern theatre in India is not a rural phenomenon. It owes its origins to the growth of large urban settlements like Kolkata, Chennai, and Mumbai beginning sometime in the eighteenth century, under the British, who had established secure centres of trade by the mid-nineteenth century. Around the same time, three major universities were founded in these three cities, and English education was firmly underway. An entire class of intelligentsia was thus initiated and exposed to Western literature and drama. By the last part of the nineteenth century, drama in Indian languages, but modelled on Western lines, began to be performed, particularly in Kolkata, catering to private audiences from the upper classes. A powerful political tool, theatre quickly began to make both overt and insidious attempts to subvert the existing oppressive political order. This drama also began to look inwards and often exposed the social injustices and corruption within the greater Indian society.

By the time India finally achieved independence, theatre was struggling to survive in the face of the tremendous popularity of cinema. Modern theatre in India has however, come a long way. Many forms of profit generating, commercially viable professional drama, a whole gamut of amateur theatre with varying degrees of commitment and competence, some experimental theatre of a very serious nature that makes radical departures from convention, and a host of dramatic activities that are seen in school and college campuses are some of the truly heterogeneous terrain of modern, urban theatre.

In a typically reactionary postcolonial situation, to write in English—the language of the colonial ruler—in newly independent India, came to be largely considered politically incorrect. While it still had its uses for the more run-of-the-mill administrative purposes, it was considered presumptuous for it to aspire to the territory of artistic or creative expression. However, it is one of India's recognized languages, invaluable as a link language between divert linguistic groups, the communicative tool for people from different states. It is also the language of the upwardly mobile middle classes—or those who aspire to be part of the middle classes—with some amount of snob-value still remaining as the trace of its earlier status as the language of the masters. English is also the language of higher education, and for any Indian with a college degree, a working knowledge of the language comes as a matter of course. It is still the language of officialdom, although great efforts have been made to change the situation. Hence a grasp over the language would open up employment opportunities in all sectors.

English is however, used as an everyday speech habit by only a fraction of the Indian population, mostly those living in the urban areas who are necessarily a minority. With early novelists writing in English like Mulk Raj Anand or Raja Rao or even R.K.

Narayan, the situation was extremely different and their work was received differently. In the 1960s, writers like Anita Desai, had to deal with tremendous suspicion, even resentment, in her own country. The situation we have today, especially in fiction, is vastly different, with contemporary Indian writers hogging the centre stage wherever English writing is read, not having to depend upon readership at home alone, which generally follows the international response. But to shift focus to contemporary drama in English by Indian writers, the problems become more intricate. Few Indian writers in English become playwrights. Fewer still are able to achieve literary/critical acclaim, and rarely find appreciative and faithful audiences in performances in cities and towns other than the metropolises. In the late nineteenth and early twentieth centuries there were English 'plays' written by Michael Madhsudhan Dutt, Sri Aurobindo and Harindranath Chattopadhyay which were hardly 'stage worthy', indeed, such attempts can be seen as mere literary exercises; not real theatre that would draw audiences. In the 1970s came plays of Dina Mehta, Snehalata Reddy and Shiv K. Kumar. Asif Currimbhoy, Partap Sharma and the poet Nissim Ezekiel all wrote a few plays that were actually staged but had little impact. The plays just failed to relate to the audiences, who were not yet ready to accept plays in English written by Indians. Also, English theatre seemed to become associated with light amusement for the urban elite. Significantly, this was also the time that the Theatre of Roots movement was making its impact felt in terms of using indigenous material for contemporary theatre, written and performed in vernacular Indian languages.

Writing is only one aspect of theatre; the other predominant one is the performance. These plays did not amount to anything substantial like a tradition of play writing, nor did their staging lead to the emergence of a tradition of Indian theatre in English.

The problems here are enmeshed with the reception of a play. A book is verily meant for the educated. Not so the theatre, because performances could be watched by anyone. Does English theatre then, exclude the majority of the populace, an audience that would otherwise have easily received a play in their own tongue? To write a text (fiction or drama) requires a degree of competence and prowess that most Indian writers possess. To actually translate the text into a living performance that a given Indian audience is to watch and relate to is quite another thing. This is the crux of the problem that posed and still poses the major obstacle for Indian dramatic performances in English. Whatever degree of comfort that an Indian, irrespective of the part of India he/she may belong to, feels in reading English, the same degree of ease would never be maintained in watching a full performance with the actors speaking in English. The reason is simple enough. The entire spectacle rings false. The great majority of Indians, rural or urban, still communicate orally with each other in the vernacular. Dramatic performances are generally seen as a slice of, an extension of that lived experience itself. Hence, the difficulty for the audiences to come to terms with English as the language of performance. This remains the major problem that must be tackled before the playwright begins to envisage a play in English for Indian audiences. It is only in the 1980s that such a movement seems to begin, albeit in a very small way. After decades of active urban usage and in a sense, homogenization of the English language, with the audiences becoming much more at home with the many varieties of Indian English that is internalized and spoken without premeditation, Indian theatre in English begins to emerge with a distinctive and vigorous identity.

Mahesh Dattani is in the vanguard of those who have made this happen; he is an actor and director with his own theatre group and has an innate sense of dialogue that is vital, stimulating, lucid and effective. Dealing with compelling issues rooted in his milieu, he has dispelled the perception about English theatre being just gratuitous fizz. His audiences have been large and responsive, both to the spectacle and the language. Theatre is not a mute and mechanical representation of social dynamics but it is a lively representation of social dynamics and the voices resounding in context of totality of human experience that consciously or unconsciously affect the existing dynamics of human sensibility. Mahesh Dattani, one of the exponents of modern Indian drama, thematically shows about the areas where the individual feels exhausted. Dattani in the process of engineering the current of Indian drama by bringing it closer to the real life experiences tried to articulate the voice of the oppressed sections of the society whose identity is shrouded in the cover of myths and social prejudices. They have been dragged in darkness, doomed to survive in perpetual silence bearing the oppressive burden of the hegemony of the elitist class.

Drama is the most wide-ranging, the most polyphonic of all the arts: it both represents life and is also a way of seeing it. It can never become a 'private' statement—in the way a novel or a poem can—without ceasing to be meaningful theatre. As a play is staged, a multitude of signs are unleashed for the audience to react to, requiring considerable agility on their part. The performance is forever in flight, and in the wealth of signs and the perceptive capacities of the spectator. Dattani within the framework of dramatic structure tries to investigate the identities of those who occupy no space in social order.

The social awareness, social discrimination in the name of religion, humiliation of humanity in the aroma of social pride, irrational acceptance of prejudices, sacrificing the ethical code based on human love, are brought to the stage through the dramatic vision of Dattani. The social conventions often hamper the growth of individual and do not acknowledge the call of human love. The perpetual clash of the commitments of an individual for social order and the force of personal derives makes life intolerable. Dattani with the fine balance of stage and performance imparts an exceptional vehemence to such situations. In the traditional society of India, the identity of gays, lesbians, hijjras and homosexuals has not yet been organized.

He dramatizes the crisis of those relationships that are not rigidly demarcated in terms of socially accepted gender constructions. All his works so far—plays, films, screenplays—focus on the marginalized entity.

Mahesh Dattani is responsible for successfully launching the Indian theatre in English. His plays emerged as 'fresh arrival' in the domain of Indian English drama in the last decade of the twentieth century. With the coming of the Sahitya Akademi Award, he is now considered an officially recognized part of the Indian literary establishment. Michael Walling, the artistic director of the multi-cultural theatre company, Border Crossings, in his introductory note to *Bravely Fought the Queen* writes:

> His plays fuse the physical and special awareness of the Indian theatre with the textual rigour of western models like Ibsen and Tennessee Williams. It's a potent combination, which shocks and disturbs through its accuracy, and its ability to approach a subject from multiple perspectives. Post-colonial India and multi-cultural Britain both have an urgent need for a cultural expression of the contemporary; they require public spaces in which the mingling of eastern and western influences can take place. Through his fusion of forms and influences, Mahesh creates such a space. This is in itself a political and social statement of astonishing force. (Dattani, ii)

In the larger context of contemporary Indian theatre, it is difficult to situate him as a part of a continuum in a given 'tradition' of Indian playwriting, or even as a break, within the larger framework of Indian dramaturgy. Dattani himself would locate himself as the 'change' in that strand, evolving out of his roots without needing to unnecessarily hark back to the past, or drawing from a milieu that no longer sustains him or his audiences:

> ... I do see myself as the change element of that thread. I'm not so sure even that I want to go back to my roots.... I don't need to revisit it. I'm more interested in pushing it forward.... I am pushing, and I'm pushing the audience. (Vardhan, 2)

Bravely Fought the Queen has been critically acclaimed all over the world, including Britain's prestigious Leicester Haymarket Theatre. The play is set in Bangalore of the 1980s and 1990s and charts the emotional, financial, and sexual workings in the lives of an urban Indian family of two brothers. The brothers are the co-owners of an advertising agency, married to two sisters—women who remain mostly at home and look after the men's old mother, Baa. The play dramatizes the emptiness and sham in the lives of its cloistered women and self-indulgent, unscrupulous men, blurring the lines between fantasy and reality, standing on the brink of terrible secrets, deception and hypocrisies.

The script is in three acts, titled 'Women', 'Men', and 'Free For All'. The claustrophobic 'female' world of Act I is pitted against the 'male' world of business of Act II and the characters stand exposed in Act III where the two worlds clash and collapse, with the home as the site for the battle. The fissure between conventional and current cultures having thrown up a new social landscape, the play races towards a brave culmination, laying bare the gruesome truths that lie behind the pretence of conservative Indian morality. Questions of gender, sexuality and identity are raised and the unspoken is voiced, the unseen made visible. These are issues that we shall deal with in greater detail in later chapters.

To focus here on the manner in which the setting coalesces with the themes, it must be noted that the trademark Dattani stage often uses the various levels to create theatrical resonance in a special way. For instance, the level where Baa is placed remains a constant in all the acts, and the time shifts that occur in terms of her memory carries the audience back and forth in time even as the present seems to parody the past. The men play out their part in the office in Act II, even as repeat performances of what has already ensued in Act I continue at the other levels. Such repetitive devices serve to undercut the issue itself, and reveal the facade for being just that—a facade. The prosperous business family, the Trivedis, is finally stripped of its veneer and everyone stands exposed to unpalatable realities of abuse, alcoholism, adultery and homosexuality as fallout of the war on the home front. The multi-layered reality in the play suggested by the split stage levels move constantly into an internalized reality, as it were.

Dattani writes with a dexterously veiled acidity, employing a language that uses both simplicity and serration, pressing the word to its limits, flanked by equally pungent, loaded silences. The play concerns itself with alternate sexuality, although the approach is more oblique and perhaps secondary to the more overt theme of gender differences and the rupture between the world of men and that of women.

While the play also looks closely at the politics of the Indian joint family as the setting, it constantly points at the gender divide and the dominance of the one over the other. This is made obvious in the names that Dattani gives to his three acts: Act I is called 'Men'; Act II is 'Women' and it is a 'Free for All' in the third act.

As usual, the performance space that is used is spare and functional; a useful and telling resonance is created in the *mise en scène* utilizing the same set structure split into multiple levels in all the three acts. The level occupied by the silhouetted, ever tortured/torturing presence of Baa is common to both acts. The audience is ushered into the women's world, with the mellifluous thumri by Naina Devi in the background and the focus is on Dolly who sits filing her nails abstractedly. Enter Lalitha, the emissary from the male world, and immediately throws Dolly into disarray as she (for the men) upsets Dolly's plans for the evening. After a tense argument, Dolly exits and Alka enters heading almost immediately for the bar. Lalitha has had to answer Baa's urgent summons and as she meets Alka, Dolly's sister/sister-in-law, they start a conversation and share a drink.

Dattani uses his very keen sense of dialogue to generate subtle undercurrents that now begin to slice through the tension-filled atmosphere as Dolly re-emerges, ready to go out for a party that has been cancelled. Dolly and Alka exchange hurtful words at times, each trying to score over the other and barely drawing the line at the dangerous zones in the references to Praful, their brother who manipulated Alka into marrying Nitin and Daksha, Dolly's daughter who turns out to be a spastic: a painful reminder of the violence wreaked by Jiten, Dolly's husband. Even as the bitterness in the sisters' relationship stands exposed through their apparent need to be one upon the other, Lalitha, the outsider, tries to discuss a masked ball that the men have arranged. Dolly resists the intrusion for sometime, warding off the pressures of the male world that bear down on and attempt to devour the women's spaces.

The other constricting reminder of the male world is Baa, who insistently rings the bell to summon her daughters-in-law, rupturing the slowly evolving sense of intimacy among the three women. Lalitha, the interloper begins to belong in this world, with her revelation of her own emptiness that she fills up with her obsessive love for her bonsais. Through the small talk that the women make, Dattani puts in an element of self-reflexivity—they make small talk *about* how to make small talk. The immensely significant semiotic referent—the bonsai—is introduced via this subtext and goes on to become the single most important metaphor in the play. The stunted growth, the bizarre shape, the grotesque reality of the bonsai becomes resonant in the existence of all the characters that people the play. This is especially torturous for Daksha's mother—Dolly—to whom Lalitha actually presents a bonsai. All the three women try to escape the confines of their claustrophobic world in various ways: Alka with alcohol, Dolly with her fantasizing about Kanhaiya and Lalitha with her obsession with bonsais.

After Dolly's chagrined acceptance of Lalitha's presence, the women discuss the masked ball. The connotations of the mask is impossible to miss—the introduction of the world of make-believe, of untruths, of paste-on realities and of the need to hide behind a facade to survive. "Khoob ladi mardani thi woh to Jhansi wali Rani thi..." The analogy straddles both worlds; underscoring however, that it is the female who fights braving all odds, but behind the garb of the male—a 'manly' queen. The phrase will acquire unexpected connotations at the end of the play when the latent homosexuality of Nitin (and Praful) is revealed. Once again Dattani points towards the spaces that are shared by the concerns of the female and the gay male.

Act II 'Men' transforms the sets into offices with the common component of the bar and Baa, and in a sort of parody, the entire sequence is enacted again, this time from the perspective of the men. With Jiten dominating the scene with his overbearing, egotistical and corrosive presence, Nitin seems almost ineffectual while Sridhar tries to be assertive in various ways. Apart from the repeated motif of the cancelled party, Baa's delirious ravings provide a sense of movement back and forth in time. Meanwhile, the men discuss the psyche of women and the 'ReVaTee' brand of lingerie that they are to market. Even as Jiten argues for a male perspective on the item they are trying to sell—women's underwear—Sridhar tries to argue for the female. One set of stereotypes is contested by another. Jiten forces Sridhar to fetch him a prostitute. Sridhar gets back at him by giving him his 'leftovers'. Nitin remains neutral, always. The reference that is made to Praful creates a matrix of significant suggestions that carries forward the play with increasing tension towards the 'Free for All" of Act III.

The men too, would escape: Jiten seeking to hide his weaknesses behind violent aggression, Nitin concealing his homosexuality behind the sham of his marriage, with Praful as his collaborator, and Sridhar, who covers up his own chauvinism with a politically correct exterior that he projects. While the women do it to create their own spaces, the men use escapism as a means to avoid unpalatable disclosures. Baa, the mother, partakes of both situations—she is both the persecutor and the victim. Abused by her own husband, she goads her son to hit his pregnant wife; but selectively—"No! Jitu, hit her on the face but not on the... stop it Jitu! On the face, only on the face! Enough! Stop!" (Dattani 311). Naturally, her escape is into senility and delirium and a complete divorce from reality.

When the two worlds converge violently in the last act, all the characters stand exposed, the sham and facade ripped apart. There are pointing fingers everywhere, the past and the future collapse into the present and the space of the stage is suddenly constricted and unable to accommodate the burden of the suddenly unloaded baggage. Dolly somehow emerges here as the strongest character, supporting a drunken Alka and roundly revealing the torturous truth about Daksha. Jiten, the aggressive oaf, is driven to guilty tears and he implicates Baa in his abuse of a pregnant wife before he finally drives off, crushing the old ragpicker in the driveway, to death. Sridhar, who has already revealed himself to be every bit as egotistical as Jiten seems now to don the mantle of the stereotypes as he prepares to leave with Lalitha. The play ends with Nitin finally revealing his 'gay' relationship with Praful, and the closing spotlight falls on the pitifully huddled figure of Alka in her drunken slumber before darkness envelopes the stage.

The play zeroes in on an Indian joint family, with the eldest male as the undisputable head, raising a gamut of questions on the nature of the relationships between the brothers and their wives (also sisters) and the manner in which identities form and firmly entrench themselves within these structures. Following some of the discussion on the family in the preceding chapters, we have noted the location to which the women are tied down, following the diktat of their men folk—they remain at home most of the time, with their chief duty being to care for the men's ageing mother Baa. As the enclosed, cloistered female world of Act I clashes with the male world of wheeling and dealing, corruption and adultery of Act II, it becomes obvious that both the men and the women have assumed roles that ill-suit them, and hence all the characters have to seek solace in fantasy and the unreal. The veneer is ripped apart and the revelation is made as to the nature of their true selves in the confrontation of Act III, and the realities of their lives emerge. The braggart and wife-beater, Jiten is revealed to be another pathetic escapist and a weakling who literally runs away from the scene of confrontation in tears; Nitin homosexuality becomes apparent in his revelations about Praful, the absent manipulator of the entire situation, an even the apparently 'correct' and 'sensitive' Sridhar show himself to be one of the many male chauvinists in the play in his game of one-upmanship with Jiten.

Sridhar's wife, Lalitha fills her vacant existence with her husband's work, writing poetry, making small talk and neurotically fussing over her bonsai. These bonsai are strategically introduced into the play, and become the dominant metaphor for Dattani, in his exploration of the self and identity in the play. The grotesque looking tree is deliberately acclimatized to its environment and adapts its growth accordingly, even bearing fruit (that are, however inedible) and turns into a dwarf, stunted in everyway and yet surviving. All the characters in the play are introduced to the bonsai, in a deliberate attempt at drawing parallels. Lalitha explains, "...you stunt their growth. You keep trimming the roots and bind their branches with wire and... stunt them" (Dattani, 244); and again, "I guess you can't call them fully grown—but when they've reached their dwarfed maturity, they really look bizarre.... Anyway, you plant the sapling in a shallow tray—you've got to make sure the roots don't have enough space to spread. You still have to keep trimming them as they grow" (Dattani, 246).

Alka is presented as a confirmed alcoholic and hence an utter misfit in the family, her case gains a certain kind of poignance in the fact that she has been used by her own brother as a veil behind which surreptitious homosexual relationships may continue. While Dattani is never judgmental in terms of sexual choices, we are able to trace an indictment of the subterfuge that results in the victimization of the unwitting Alka. It is the refusal to acknowledge one's true identity that comes under the scanner. Dolly is the only character that emerges unscathed and strong in the play, even as she willingly lets go of her brutalized reality to enter the life-generating fantasy that offers some comfort. Mother to the spastic Daksha, and nearly a mother to Alka, Dolly, however does not need an exterior support system to prop up her own sense of selfhood. Even in fantasy, she is aware of her own truths.

Meanwhile, all these identities seem somehow merged at the locus that is Baa, whose continued assertion of her presence by ringing the bell, acts as a reminder of the echoing patterns of behaviour and the perpetuation of stereotypes in the uneasy world that the characters inhabit. The play tries to establish the rapidly shifting values and structuring of the self in a locale where the traditional and the contemporary clash, but do not fuse to create new social landscapes. In such environments, only bonsai may thrive, at great cost to itself. Thus Dattani has recurrently used subjects that touch-upon the zones of experience that the 'normal' middle class society would sweep under the carpet and happily imagine did not exist. This is how Dattani would penetrate below the surface and makes visible the invisible issues that haunt so many of his plays.

In terms of pedagogy there has hardly been much interest in the work of Indians who write drama in English, and few universities that include a paper on Indian writing in English in mainstream 'English literature' courses would also include in its ambit, 'Indian English drama' as they would the genres of poetry and fiction. Although things are changing, as they stand, there is a lot of room for change and indeed, universities must open up to the idea of an English theatre based in India as a *bona fide* literary genre. This is an imperfect world for these purposes, and to quote Dattani again, a world:

> where if I wrote about the working classes, I am told, I would gain international recognition (but if I were, in fact a working class person, no middle-class critic or theatre practitioner would give me the time of day.]...where there is no real professional theatre... Where I am met with open hostility in parochial Universities. Where in literary circles, I am seen as inferior because I am a playwright.... (Dattani, xiv-xv).

It is against such a backdrop that one is to evaluate the achievements of Mahesh Dattani. Man of multiple roles, he has always managed to make his audiences sit up and listen, and listen with such involvement that they even begin to forget that they are in fact, watching a play in an 'alien' tongue.. He could, in a sense be seen as one of the strands that carry forward the traditions of Indian theatre through the necessary dynamic of change and innovation. Not having to repeatedly revisit his roots, he works instinctively and meticulously, anchored to the contemporaneous urban realities, collaborating with artists to put up his shows, pushing the frontiers of his art, and nudging his audiences into acknowledging it.

At 45, Mahesh Dattani is at the peak of his creative powers, continuously experimenting with new forms manners of expression. As a playwright he will never be stereotypical. The varied content of his plays seldom have his characters mouthing quotable lines, nor does thematic material rise to extraordinary heights. But what makes Mahesh Dattani one of India's finest playwrights is perhaps his manner of speaking to the audience with complete honesty. For the moment, he seems to have found the right combination where his art is not compromised upon and yet makes commercial sense. His expectations of his audience are high, and he does not provide quick or expedient endings, only perhaps a kind of insight into their own lives.

Works Cited

Dattani, Mahesh. *Collected Plays*, New Delhi: Penguin Books, 2000. p. xiv.

Vardhan, Manisha. 'I'm No Crusader: I'm a Theatre Person: Mahesh Dattani'. June 2004. http://www.3to6.com.

5

The Inconsistent World of Gays: A Psychoanalytical Approach to *On a Muggy Night in Mumbai / Mango Soufflé*

Kaustav Chakraborty

If you had told us
just one word,
On what was killing you inside…
and we would have screamed,
some more like we always do…
Your breath is gone,
But your voice remains,
We'll use it well to scream some more.
Scream…till our voices…
yours, mine, and all ours,
Will be heard.

(*Because I Have a Voice*)

The "world of invisible India" has almost become a cliché, being branded with all the works of Mahesh Dattani. This trademark might have had significance in the initial stage of the queer movement, yet in the present context is has become a kind of repressive tool, i.e., the logo is often used as a justification to retain the issues as invisible or camouflage the reality as projected truth, despite the increasing visibility of the LGBT Indians. Hence it is high time to undertake schemes in scrutinizing the reality of these gay Indians, a task itself that would ascertain the homoerotic situation as actual and therefore a locale essential to examine and interpret.

The problem of this paper is the homosexual bond between the gay characters that seem to be fraudulent, as revealed through Dattani's play *On a Muggy Night in Mumbai.* In the very beginning of the play, we find that Kamlesh, a well-off fashion designer who stays in a flat in Mumbai, has invited his friends for he needs their help to forget his former love Prakash, a man who seems to have moved on, gone 'straight'. In the party we have a gamut of homosexual males. There arrives Sharad, the liberated gay, who having come out of the closet hardly cares for the reaction of his surrounding 'straight' world. He has been living together with Kamlesh but after discovering himself as being utilized by Kamlesh as a way out to rise above his feelings for Prakash (Kamlesh still loves Prakash and has preserved their photograph, "...cheek to cheek, pelvis to pelvis. Naked"), he has left the flat and they are no more together. Apart from Sharad none of the male homosexuals are convinced and comfortable with their orientation. In the party we have Bunny, the surreptitious homosexual who plays a happily married father on a television sitcom as well as in real life. He, however, is conscious of his mask and tries to justify it:

> Camouflage! Even animals do it. Blend with the surroundings. They can't find you. You politically correct gays deny yourself the basic animal instinct of camouflage. (*Collected Plays*, Volume I, 70)

Ranjit, another invitee to the party, also leads a secretive life for; he boasts of maintaining a steady relationship with a man abroad where his sexual identity is no longer otherised, and for this dual stance Sharad calls Ranjit a 'coconut'—"you brown on the outside and white on the inside"(71). Only Sharad is the most outspoken of his identity: "If anyone of us can be straight, I am Madhubala" (85). The play reaches its climax when it is revealed that Ed, the man with whom Kamlesh's sister Kiran is going to get married, is none but Prakash himself. Prakash, is saved by Kamlesh, having lost his job on that very morning. He visited the community park looking for someone who might listen to his problems, and also planned to commit suicide. Luckily he found Kamlesh who was generous enough to listen to his stories and share his problems. Prakash and Kamlesh have long stayed together as couple but Prakash eventually begins to doubt his own reality and thereby starts visiting a 'straight homophobic psychiatrist' to rid himself of depression. He finally abandons Kamlesh with the feeling that he would never be happy as a gay man: " It is impossible to change the society, he said, but it may be possible for you to reorient yourself..." (69). However, despite his pose to act as a heterosexual male by marrying Kiran, he gets exposed in his attempt to reunite back with Kamlesh, under the shelter of institutionalized matrimonial relationship. In *Mango Soufflé*, the cinematic version of the play the entire episode has been vividly enacted:

> ED: Tell me, is it true?
>
> KAMLESH: What?
>
> ED: That you love Sharad.
>
> *Cut to*: Interior. Day. Bedroom.
>
> KAMLESH: What's more—he loves me...I want to be loved.
>
> *Cut to:* Interior. Day. Bedroom.
>
> *Ed moves closer to Kamlesh.*
>
> ED: You don't really love Sharad. You love me.
>
> *Cut to:*
>
> ED: You don't love Sharad. ...Nobody would know. Nobody would care. Kamlesh is frozen. I'll take care of Kiran. And you.

> *Ed begins to caress Kamlesh…*
> ED: No one will ever know. Not even Kiran.
> *…Kamlesh grabs Ed by the throat.*
> KAMLESH: Liar!
>
> (*Collected Plays*, Volume II, 219-221)

Hence except for Sharad, all the gay characters seem to have a very oblique and inconsistent relationships that might be called almost a saga of betrayal, a scenario where sex dominates love. Even a hint has been made that Kamlesh, immediately being separated from Sharad, has even taken the caretaker as his partner. Even in *Do the Needful*, the readers get surprised when the gay man Alpesh, who is forced to come and negotiate his marriage with Lata, is seen to be making love with the stranger, the Mali of Gowda's household, in the very cowshed in such less time of acquaintance. In Vikram Seth's fiction *The Golden Gate*, a homosexual man named Ed illustrates his similar experience of gay-interactions:

> I've been around gay bars—that scene
> Where if you are handsome, people paw you
> —I guess you've never had them claw you
> As if you were a chunk of meat…
>
> (*The Golden Gate* 109)

This problem finds echo in the letter written by the father of a gay man who is confused about what it means for his son to be gay, to the gay right activist Pawan Dhall:

> My son always complains to me that he is being changed by his partners time to time, and when he asks his partners why they can't remain fixed with one person, they laugh at him and say that in the gay world everyone is for everybody and there is no fixed thing as it's not a world of straight people. If this is true then comes the question, whether all this coming out and rainbow walks is to get affection or right to have multiple sex

> partners only? Is the gay movement concerned only with safe physical pleasure? I have asked my son to settle down with the guy he likes, but in return he said that papa, I am ready but they are not. I think that now is the time that we must come forward to see what is our real objective, is it a healthy society where everyone can live as a human being with the human qualities, or just a world of animals ruled by the natural instincts resulting in to a great chaos! (*Because I Have a Voice: Queer Politics in India* 259)

Contradicting the picture of this promiscuous gay world, we have a very well-knit committed world of the lesbian couple, represented by Dipali in the play *On a Muggy Night in Mumbai* as well as in the filmy version, *Mango Soufflé*. Dipali enters the party declaring that her 'significant other'—Tinu, her lesbian partner—is baby-sitting Dipali's niece, an act which itself shows the bond that exists between the two, and how both have been exposed to and accepted by Dipali's family members as couples. Even in between the play/film Dipali gets a call from her and the manner in she converses, reveals again the genuineness of their attachment:

> DIPALI: Ya, sweetheart...
> Sugar, have you checked her diaper?...
> Sweetheart, I'll talk to you later...But hey, don't be afraid to call if you need more help. Bye.
> (*Collected Plays*, Volume II, 182-183)

Dipali's involvement regarding her relationship and her honest understanding of her orientation gets again open when she says: "I'm all for the gay man's cause. Men deserve only men!" (60) In this connection one might recall the folk rhyme:

> Higamous hogamous, woman's monogamous.
> Hogamous higamous, man is polygamous.
> (*Sexuality and Gender* 5)

The question that arises at this juncture is then, why is it that the women involved in a lesbian relationship can be at ease with her orientation and remain settled with the partner while the men, engaged in homosexual affairs seem to struggle hard to copeup with their difference and hardly seem to get along with a consistent partner? The answer has already been provided by Freud who has observed this variation in attitude/ response. According to him the mother is, for the girl as for the boy, the parent around whom bodily based tender passion gets first organized. Since a man right from birth, initially gets exposed to a heterosexual world with his first 'love' (emotional and survival dependence) cum 'desire' (animal allure) mother, for him it is more difficult to re-adjust with the homosexual world. This is unlike a woman, whose case becomes easy for her very first contact with her mother, that makes the mother again her first 'admire' cum 'reliance', and thereby her very natural world of primary experience becomes the world of homosexuality. Dorothy Dinnerstein has elaborated this in the following terms:

> This means that in the mother—father—child triangle the heteroerotic side of the child's feeling has more primitive weight for the boy than for the girl, while the homoerotic side has more primitive weight for the girl than for the boy. The adult consequence of this difference is that a woman's heterosexual jealousy is apt to be more deeply complicated than a man's by homoerotic excitement, her rage more blurred,...not only is the homoerotic side of the boy's feeling in this early triangle later born and less primitive than the girl's; it is also more disgraceful. The adult consequence is that even where the homoerotic excitement is strong enough to complicate a man's heterosexual jealousy, this excitement is likelier to be suppressed, since it is too shameful to be admitted into awareness. (*Sexuality and Gender* 8-9)

Dorothy Dinnerstein thus explains the psychological reason behind the boy's awkwardness with his homosexual orientation on the basis of the guilt that he suffers for being disloyal to his first love, i.e. a female 'mother', and also from a sense of shame for trespassing his original world of heterosexual acquaintance. While in the girl's case, even though the father's animal allure is likely to be more powerful than it is for the boy, even then the mother becomes the centre of her 'sensual existence' with most of the bodily contact for comfort and sustenance. This means that for her, love of this kind is more evenly directed towards both the parents than it is for the boy, and the rivalry with the mother for the father's love is more evenly balanced against rivalry with the father for the mother's. In a woman's case, as observes Dinnerstein:

> The growing insight that this balance is scheduled to tip mainly in the father's direction is on some level wounding. To realize that one is a female, destined to compete with females for the erotic resources of males, is to discover that one is doomed to renounce one's first love. (*Sexuality and Gender* 8)

Hence, in the case of a woman like Dipali, who enters into a lesbian relationship, the bond is bound to be strong, for it provides her with a sense of relief of performing atonement for ditching the first love—the female 'mother'. On the other hand, she resists the men like Ed/Prakash, Bunny or Kamlesh to be secured with her homoerotic steady life.

Asha Kuthari Chaudhuri, while discussing this play, wonders:

> ...gay literature seems to have been beleaguered by unhappy endings. Homosexuals invariably move towards death, isolation, or a sham heterosexual marriage of the kind Ed and Kiran are heading towards. (*Mahesh Dattani* 50)

The reason of this apparent 'love, sex and dhoka' formula that seems to dominate the lives of these gay boys is what this psychological analysis has intended to underline. Even in Dattani's

Bravely Fought the Queen, the ending discloses the gay relationship that exists between Alka's husband Nitin and her brother Praful—her marriage itself has been a strategy designed to conceal their gay relationship. The plays written by Dattani highlight the homoerotic association as a reality and hence like any other actuality this has been depicted in all its factuality, including the limitations that need to be revealed, scrutinized for better understanding, for it is the compulsion of a civilized society to comprehend before complaining. Dattani himself has stated that being gay is not "right or wrong, it is a reality and we have to learn to accept alternative relationships and live with them" (Menon). The plays like *On a Muggy Night in Mumbai* or the films like *Mango Soufflé* authentically look at the fabric of alternative sexuality. The scenes where male lovers fight and unite, kiss as well as curse, make up but often do break may be shocking for the straight spectator but this shock is inevitably required to acquaint them with this gay world, which is not unnatural/abnormal despite being unique and different. Finally regarding the unpredictability of the gay boys, the reply given by Pawan Dhall is relevant:

> ...but what is perhaps problematic is the right to sexual autonomy. Please for a moment ignore what the rest of the gay world is telling your son (that your son can't have a committed relationship with another man because gay people can't/don't believe in being committed).
>
> Please also try to ignore what social customs say—that a person can be happy and responsible only if he or she is in one-to-one relationship. In my experience, both sides are wrong, because what they are saying does not reflect the lived realities of a whole lot of people. There are several gay and lesbian couples who even if not living together have been far more committed to each other than many heterosexual couples...
>
> On the other hand, there are several individuals who have multiple sexual partners, but seem to be more honest, hard

working, brave and considerate than many people in committed relationships. Do you think it would be fair to look down upon them just because they have several sexual partners? What is it that qualifies a person as good and responsible towards society? To my mind other qualities are more important in a person than monogamy.

(*Because I Have a Voice: Queer Politics in India* 260)

Hence if at all we stigmatize the gay characters in Mahesh Dattani's plays/movies with polygamous infidelity, we must do it keeping their psychological struggle in mind as well as should not exclusively evaluate their appeal on the sole basis of their sexual behaviour. In *Mango Soufflé* we see Kamlesh's helplessness in neither being able to forget his former love Prakash, nor could he persuade himself fully with the present one, Sharad:

Kamlesh: Help Me, Sharad.

Sharad: Why Should I?

Kamlesh: You very well know…It-it might work out between us, or maybe not…(*Backing away, louder*) Or maybe it's better I just go away for good. (*Collected Plays*, Volume II, 190)

"From childhood men have an instinct for representation," Aristotle wrote in *Poetics*, "and in this respect man differs from the other animals in that he is more imitative and learns his first lessons by representing things". Although Aristotle is using man in a generic sense, it is also true that our first lessons about gay and straight are conveyed through representations, which model for us the desired goals and limits of gender identification. It is particularly important to address the role of representations in creating and sustaining changing cultural ideas about gay people; the non-fantasized gay characters in *On a Muggy Night in Mumbai/ Mango Soufflé* should have obviously convinced us as men with real problems, and as a corollary, real men with a real world of their own that needs to be represented—by relocating the gay world, what used to be referred to as fringe issue to be maintained on the margin of the society, to the centrestage — for critical acclaim.

Works Cited

Chaudhuri, Asha Kuthari. *Mahesh Dattani*, Foundation Books, 2005.

Dattani, Mahesh. *Collected Plays*, Volume I and II, Penguin Books, 2005.

Menon, Sudha. 'A Scoop of *Mango Soufflé*. *Business Line*. 10 March 2003. http://www.blonnet.com

Narrain, Arvind and Bhan, Gautam. ed *Because I Have a Voice: Queer Politics in India*, Yoda Press: New Delhi, 2005.

Seth, Vikram. *The Golden Gate*, Penguin Books in association with Faber and Faber, 1986.

Williams, Christine L. and Stein, Arlene. ed *Sexuality and Gender*, Blackwell Publishers, 2002.

6

Mahesh Dattani's Plays: A Mirror of Contemporary Society

Dipanita Gargava

Mahesh Dattani, a director, actor, dancer, teacher and writer, is gifted with a versatile personality and has been awarded with the prestigious Sahitya Akademi Award for his contribution to Indian Drama in 1998. His plays have vividness and the themes are of contemporary interest. He manages to delve deep into the hearts to recreate characters with authenticity and a sense of liveliness. To read his plays is to imagine the plight of the individuals pining for same sex love and pleading for legal sanction for marriage.

Dattani not only deals with common and ordinary people but the common problems of these people in realistic terms. In many of his plays, he deals with various issues like homosexuality, gender discrimination, communalism and child sexual abuse. His most distinguishing quality is wide range of themes that he deals with in his writings.

Dattani's plays are written for the stage. It is the visual quality and dramatic effect which are of paramount importance. His plays have a universal appeal dealing with the contemporary issues. These plays embody many of the classical concerns of the world drama and can be staged anywhere in the world. He moulds his subject plays in such a way that it is both topical and appealing. There are no restrictions of language or culture and his plays speak across cultural and linguistic barriers.

The earlier drama which later on became the modern theatre in India began in the colonial cities which had been set up by the Britishers as commercial ports, Calcutta, Madras and Bombay. The urban middle class audience had an English taste and style. They formed the major part of the audience and much of the theater copied the British drama imbibing the aesthetics and even the architecture of the western Influence. This influence can be seen in the playwrights of Sri Aurobindo, T.P. Kailasam and others who were influenced by the Elizabethan style.

Until the development of modern theatre, the theatre remained a commodity for the wealthier group of people. But after India gained Independence in 1947, many playwrights felt the need to evolve and develop a theatre which was apart from the British model that is somewhat Indian. There emerged Pannikar along with Habib Tanvir, Vijay Tendulkar and Girish Karnad, members of what is often referred to as the "Theatre of Roots" movement, who began to study and analyze traditional Indian performance forms to see what could be included in the modern Indian drama.

The post-Independence Indian English drama was benefitted by the increasing interest of the foreign countries in Indian English literature in general and Indian English drama in particular. A good number of plays by Indian playwrights Asif Currimbhoy, Pratap Sharma, Gurucharan Das was successfully staged in England and USA. But the plight of Indian English drama is that no regular school of Indian English drama was established in our country. This was mainly because the encouragement drama received from several quarters immediately after India got freedom but it was monopolised by the theatre in the Indian regional languages while Indian English drama lagged behind.

However contemporary Indian drama, deviating from classical and European models, is experimental and innovative in terms of thematic and technical qualities. It is not an off spring of any specific tradition and it has laid the foundation of a distinctive tradition in the history of world drama by reinvestigating history, legend, myth, religion and folklore with context to contemporary socio-political issues. A cumulative theatrical tradition evolved by Mohan Rakesh, Badal Sirkar, Vijay Tendulkar and Girish Karnad, prepared the background of contemporary Indian English theatre. An attempt has been made here to study the plays of Dattani as a mirror of contemporary society as well as Dattani as a versatile playwright of the Indian English Drama.

Mahesh Dattani, a director, actor, dancer, teacher and writer, is gifted with a versatile personality and is the first playwright to be awarded with the prestigious Sahitya Akademi Award for his contribution to Indian Drama in 1998. The International Herald Tribune while praising Mahesh Dattani, praised him as "One of Indian's best and most serious contemporary play wrights writing in English." Alyque Padamsee calls him one of the most serious contemporary playwrights. There are two published texts of Dattani's plays, one a collection of plays while the other one is in parts. Recently his plays have been collected in a single volume called *Collected Plays* published by Penguin. He has successfully launched the Indian theatre in English.

Dattani's plays have vividness and the themes are of contemporary interest. He manages to delve deep into the hearts to recreate characters with authenticity and a sense of liveliness. To read his plays is to imagine the plight of the individuals pining for same sex love and pleading for legal sanction for marriage.

Dattani not only deals with common and ordinary people but the common problems of these people in realistic terms. In many of his plays, he deals with various issues like homosexuality, gender discrimination, communalism and child sexual abuse.' His most distinguishing quality is his wide range of themes that he deals with in his writings. His plays are written for the stage. It is the visual quality and dramatic effect which are of paramount importance. His plays have a universal appeal dealing with the contemporary issues. These plays embody many of the classical concerns of the world drama and can be staged anywhere in the world. He moulds his plays in such a way that they are both topical and appealing. There are no restrictions of language or culture, and his plays speak across cultural and linguistic barriers. Dattani makes an abundant use of Indian mythology, rituals and traditions and contemporary problems that, India is beset with but he elevates these themes to a higher level, touching the human chords that emanate love, happiness, sexual fulfilment and problem of identity. His plays have contemporary values and his plays can be said to have been impaired by Ibsen the Father of Realism. He handles every problem from gender issues to sexuality very successfully. His achievement as a playwright depends on the fact that his plays are a slice of life. They present reality as it exists. His plays have purely performance–oriented scripts that elicit from the audience and emotional as well as strongly intellectual response. His plays address the middle class and only the middle class. The reason is not far to seek—it is this class that constitutes his audience. He has created a vibrant, new theatrical form which is a marked development on the hither to stagnant Indian drama in English.

Seven Steps Around the Fire, the most popular play, dwells on the theme of eunuchs, their identity, their constitution and their connotation. Uma Rao, the sociology scholar, emerges as the most powerful character of the play, the mouthpiece of the playwright, who fights to establish the identity of a eunuch. Mammal, during her research on the class and gender–related violence and crime, meets justice in the nemesis of the play. A eunuch, a beautiful one, invited for marriage, and the final tragic death—all seem to be a misconstruct. This is all about marriage of a beautiful hijra Kamla to a son of a wealthy government minister named Subbu. Dattani has the courage of conviction to depict the lives of such people who are looked down upon by the society. He highlights the homosexual relation and questions why there can't be natural heterosexual relation and why can't there be marriage between homosexuals. The hijras are subaltern. They can't speak for themselves, so they must be spoken for. This is what Dattani tries to bring forth through his plays.

Issue of communalism has been subtly dealt with in the play *Final Solutions* which was first performed in 1993. This play foregrounds the Hindu-Muslim problems. It also tackles the theme of transferred resentments in the context of family relations. The characters in the play motivate us to think that angry outbursts lead to chain reactions. The play is a fine example of transferred resentments. The play mocks at the politicians who use people as their puppets. These puppeteers are the culprits. The playwright at the end of the play wishes to stop this game of hatred and communal tension through the character of Ramnik. Ramnik accepts that his father has done the black deed. We should forgive the offenders and forget the past. This can be the final solution.

Born in Bangalore on August 7, 1958, Dattani is a famous Indian English dramatist. He took admission in Baldwin's High School and St. Joseph's College of Arts and Science, Bangalore. He is a graduate in History, Economics and Political Science and a Postgraduate in Marketing and Advertising Management. He worked as a copywriter in an advertising firm and later on with his father in the family business. His theatre group, Playpen, was formed in 1984. He made his directional debut with *Mango Souffle*. The plays directed by him range from classical Greek to contemporary works.

Dattani's work probes tangled attitudes in contemporary India towards communal differences and consumerism. He had made brilliant contribution to Indian drama in English. His plays deal with religious tension, sexuality and gender issue. He takes issues that afflict societies the world over. He has chronicled the social victim and the follies, foibles and prejudices of Indian society. He shows us the hollowness of middle class lives. His plays explore what lies below the facades of characters and families to fool the world. The family in Dattani stands for society at large. Dattani's characters search for security and acceptance, to be true to themselves. In his world the socialization process initiated in the family unit has as its aim the stunted growth of a bousaitres. Dattani raises these and a number of other questions regarding gender and social stratification and hierarchy and sexuality. The most significant feature of Dattani is perhaps his use of language.

Dattani's stage techniques are aimed at making the audience intimate with the life of a family, its trials and debilitating secrets. He exercises great care in ensuring through his detailed stage direction that reader and potential directors understand all this. His characters speak the kind of English that most middle class Indians do. He also uses Indian English with great confidence and captures the rhythms of the spoken English.

Mahesh Dattani is a contemporary writer who writes specifically in English. His plays question some of the norms and conventions of society. In the process, interesting questions arise regarding gender and other issues like homosexuality, lesbianism, child sexual abuse. He tackles issues that afflict societies the world over. Dealing with issues like male-female ascendance divide, the patriarchal tradition, consumerism, communalism, he holds back nothing. Alyque Padamsee considers him as one of the most serious playwrights. Issues of gender discrimination are beautifully and aptly portrayed in the play *Tara*, a riveting play that questions the role of a society that treats the children of the same womb in two different ways. On the surface *Tara* is a story about conjoined twins—Tara and Chandan—who are surgically separated and yet remain entwined. However, the play deals with many issues on an emotional, psychological and social level. As the story unravels, one finds that the play is not so much about the twins' being conjoined but more so about people and personalities.

Dattani's characters are a personification of his perception. In his plays, the traditional woman as the mother is portrayed with some contempt, be it Sonal of *Where there is a Will*, Prema Gowda in *Do the Needful* Baa in *Bravely Fought the Queen*, Aruna in *Final Solutions*, while the younger woman is depicted as a scheming problem solver; Lata in *Do the Needful*, Ratna in *Dance Like a Man*, and Bharati in *Tara*. In contrast, men are not treated with such disdain and are often shown to be as victims suffering from a woman's machinations—Jairaj and Ratna, Patel and Bharati, Preeti and Hasmukh. Another striking feature of the plays is that at the end a question remains in the minds of the audience as to what is going to happen next? This makes each in the audience to question his own personality, thoughts, perceptions etc.

But more than the theme of the play itself, what makes Dattani's plays highly enjoyable is the characterization. He knows the world he is talking about and portrays an apt picture just the way it is—the hypocrisy, the prejudices, the dilemmas, nothing is spared. And yet, if there is a point where he stumbles, then some of the characters, though not the principal ones, end up showing much more understanding. Sharad from *On a Muggy Night in Mumbai*, Anarkali from *Seven Steps Around the Fire*, Alpesh from *Do the Needful* are some of them.

Dattani's plays deal with real scenarios that are tough to turn away from. They are couched in Indian urban speak. They shy away from myth and make-believe to tackle reality head-on, no matter what the impact of the collision. He does not seek to cut a path through the difficulties his characters encounter in his plays; instead he leads his audience to see just how caught up people are in the complications and contradictions of their values and assumptions. And by revealing the complexity, he makes the world a richer place for all of us.

Dattani has proved to be a good playwright, a successful observer who absorbs from everyday life and experiences, and responds to the sensitive issues that surround him. He sees, feels and experiences and from the depth of the heart pens down.

For Dattani, who writes plays for the sheer pleasure of communicating through this dynamic medium, whether it is in a stage play or a radio play, the characters speak his words. But he maintains the position of an outsider and never allows himself room in the plays he writes. In many ways it is a reflection of the non-judgmental person he is, and hence the stance of an observer. He neither advocates any change nor conveys a message but remains a passive observer. It is a discussion that gently pokes and provokes the audience.

He often tackles taboo subjects that are still under wraps in the South Asian society, but does not aim at changing society, only to offer scope for reflection that will give the audience some kind of insight into their own lives. It seems that the aim of Dattani is to bring out the complexities of any conflict and discuss the issues surrounding it. He wants to evoke a spirit of self-analysis among the audience through his plays.

His play *Final Solutions* stirred a hornet's nest of the issue of communal riots and disharmony. It is about being pushed into corners and the effect this has on people and society in general. He wants to reveal and bring to light socially relevant subjects out in the open and place areguments around the issue.

His recent play, *Thirty Days in September*, is close to his heart and brings back some vivid memories. Directed by Lilette Dubey and written by Dattani, the play treats the sensitive, and generally taboo issue of child sexual abuse, and most importantly, the wrapped up subject of incest. The play about love and betrayal, endeavours to lift the veil of silence, which surrounds child sexual abuse and addresses the issue unflinchingly. It builds on the trauma of Mala Khound, who lives with the haunting memories of her abused past. Her abuser—her uncle—subconsciously lives with her all the time, as a part of her dirty reflections. He damages her natural growth, deters her from pursuing her love interests beyond the ominous 30-day period, scars her soul, which finally transforms her into a woman who enjoys being taken advantage of. By marking a daring departure from the norm, the play ensures that we, as a society, no longer take comfort in the routine of uttering the word 'incest' in gutless undertones. The play also brings us closer to the reality of abused children—pleasure does form a part of their pain. The consequence of dangerous games can only be dangerous.

It is for his sensitive and insightful portrayal of forbidden subjects that his plays find a stately position in Indian drama but more enjoyable is his characterization that makes his plays enjoyable to his readers. He knows what the world he is talking about, and shows it just the way it is, with all the hypocrisy, the prejudices, the dilemmas. Nothing is spared.

Women play a pivotal role in all of Dattani's plays. According to him women form the largest minority in the world and perhaps the writer finds it interesting to illustrate their personal expressions, their dilemmas, their interpretations. What sets him apart from other contemporary Indian playwrights in English today is his perfect cuing into burning issues of social relevance like Issues pertaining to sexual identity, including the hijra community, or child sexual abuse (CSA) or hypocrisy about HIV-positive people, or religious intolerance, or gender inequalities, or social stereotyping, or even what constitutes the contemporary Indian family.

Ever since he first penned *Where There's a Will* in 1986, Dattani has treated each subject with a deep-seated identification rooted in everyday angst. Such charged emotions spare no one—neither the players and the director, nor the audience. Deep within platitude-ridden Indian society, his characters seethe and reveal, probe and discern, scathing their families and neighbours, leaving each reader or watcher with a storm within as the aftermath.

Dattani has repeatedly used what may be called the split-stage technique, which involves dividing the stage into two halves or two levels, one beside or above the other. Then he gives lines to characters in the two spaces in such a way that there is constant intercepting between the two actions. This not only makes for a tighter narrative but also a richer visual effect.

The technique can also be interpreted as Dattani's way of signalling that in India, as elsewhere in the world, multiple realities co-exist, resolutely, but that often only one reality–the heteronormative and patriarchal–is visible. His plays are a sustained effort at highlighting the otherwise invisible by situating it where it belongs along with the visible normative reality.

Mahesh Dattani as a playwright will never be a brand as his plays have varied content and varied appeal. His characters seldom mouth lines, which will be quoted by just about everyone, nor does his thematic content rise to extraordinary heights. But what makes him one of India's finest playwrights is in the manner in which he speaks to the audience straight from the depth of the heart. Much as his plays make commercial sense, his expectations of his audience is high and therein lies the difference between art and commerce. He does not provide ready-made solutions or fully resolved endings.

He aims not at changing society but only seeks to offer some scope for reflection in the hope that his plays will give the audience some kind of insight into their own lives. The social issues delved into in his plays are said to be both from his own life and his imagination, and what he calls "a marriage of both", but his confidence lies in reality itself as a resource.

Works Cited

Dattani, Mahesh. *Tara: In Collected Plays*, New Delhi: Penguin, 2000.

______, *Bravely Fought the Queen in Collected Plays*, New Delhi: Penguin, 2000.

______, *Final Solutions: In Collected Plays*, New Delhi: Penguin, 2000.

______, *Seven Steps Around the Fire*, New Delhi: Penguin, 2000.

______, *On a Muggy Night in Mumbai*, New Delhi: Penguin, 2000.

______, *Collected Plays*. New Delhi: Penguin Books India, 2000.

Iyengar, K.R.S. *Indian Writing in English*. Bombay, Asia, 1977.

______. *Drama in Modern India*, Bombary: The P.E.N. All India Centre, 1961.

Merchant, Hoshang, ed. *Yaraana: Gay Writing from India*. New Delhi: Penguin Books, 1999.

Narrain, Arvind and Gautam Bhan, eds. *Because I Have a Voice: Queer Politics in India*. New Delhi: Yoda Press, 2005.

Naik, M.K. *Dimension of Indian English Literature*. New Delhi, Sterling, 1984).

Pathank, R.S. *Indian English Literature; Marginalized Voices*. New Delhi: Creative Books, 2003.

7

The Theme of Gender Discrimination in Dattani's *Tara*

Anisha Rajan

Gender discrimination is prevalent almost everywhere in the world. Discrimination against girls and women in the developing world is a devastating reality. It results in millions of individual tragedies, which add up to lost potential for entire countries. Studies show there is a direct link between a country's attitude toward women and its progress socially and economically. Tragically, female children are most defenceless against the trauma of gender discrimination. In India the condition of women is far worse than what statistics say. The middle class women strive hard to maintain their family as well as work. In this twenty-first century too, women are discriminated on the basis of gender. Society has always tried to define her role, confined to the four walls of her home. Despite a long standing and vigorous women's movement with many achievements, patriarchy remains strong rooted in India. But the good news is that new generations of girls represent the most promising source of change for women and men in the developing world today.

Sociologically the word gender refers to the socio-cultural definition of man and woman, the way societies distinguish men and women and assign them social roles. The distinction between sex and gender was introduced to deal with the general tendency to attribute women's subordination to their anatomy. For ages it was believed that the different characteristics, roles and status accorded to women and men in society are determined by sex, that they are natural and therefore not changeable. Gender is seen closely related to the roles and behaviour assigned to women and men based on their sexual differences. As soon as a child is born families and society begin the process of gendering. The birth of the son is celebrated, the birth of a daughter filled with pain; sons are showered with love, respect, better food and proper health care. Boys are encouraged to be tough and outgoing; girls are encouraged to be homebound and shy. All these differences are gender differences and they are created by society.

Gender inequality is therefore a form of inequality which is distinct from other forms of economic and social inequalities. It dwells not only outside the household but also centrally within it. It stems not only from pre-existing differences in economic endowments between women and men but also from pre-existing gendered social norms and social perceptions. Gender inequality has adverse impact on development goals as it reduces economic growth. It hampers the overall well being because blocking women from participation in social, political and economic activities can adversely affect the whole society. Many developing countries including India have displayed gender inequality in education, employment and health. It is common to find girls and women suffering from high mortality rates. There are vast differences in education level of two sexes. India has witnessed gender inequality from its early history due to its socioeconomic and religious practices that resulted in a wide gap between the position of men and women in the society.

Mahesh Dattani's plays are noted for their innate freshness and candour. His plays discuss the social issues which entangle our lives. He appeared on the literary scene as the most potent force to mould and modify the established conventions of dramatic art. He set the direction of New Drama. The dramatic canvas of Dattani is coloured with real life conditions. In the play *Tara*, he shares the anguish of gender discrimination in society. The play *Tara* was performed as *Twinkle Tara* at Chidian Memorial Hall, Bangalore on 23 October 1990 by Playpen Performing Arts Group. The plot of the play revolves round the family of Mr. Patel. It is related with the life of congenial twins, one girl and one boy who are joined together at the hip. Chandan and Tara are to be separated through a surgical operation which will cause danger to one of them. Their mother Bharati insists on giving the third leg which was common to them, to Chandan so that he may lead a healthy life. Bharati and her father bribes the doctor and make him save Chandan, although they know that the leg suited Tara well. Mr. Patel remains a mute witness to the injustice imparted to their daughter. But the operation leaves Chandan with a slight limp and Tara crippled. Thus it turns out to be futile for both children. Bharati is shocked and goes out of her senses, and tries to repay Tara with all her love and affection.

The plot of *Tara* is arranged around familial relationship where each individual in his own way has to bear the burden of social values and their efforts to go beyond them, bring helplessness in their lives. In *Tara*, after the marriage of Mr. Patel and Bharati, Mr. Patel was forced to leave his parental home because this relationship was not accepted by his parents. The shadows of insecurity loom large around him. He had a painful realization. The insecurity of the separation from parents, subsequently the birth of Siamese twins, makes Mr. Patel isolated. He is forced to decide for the surgery of kids for their separation. In this surgery, the tragedy was imminent. The surgery was conducted, Tara becomes a cripple, Bharati goes insane and Mr.

Patel becomes violent and aggressive. He ignores the identity of Tara and doesn't care for the consequences involving the risk of life of Tara. It directly indicates the gender prejudices prevalent in society.

In *Tara*, Dattani concentrates on emotional crisis of Chandan; hence the action is almost internalized. All the major characters in *Tara*, Bharati, Mr. Patel and Chandan suffer with uncompromising sense of guilt and everyone seeks an outlet for guilt, sharing the suffering of Tara. More than social dilemma, the psychological tension of each character is more prominent. With a view to compensate for his loss, Chandan alienates from his social environment. Mr. Patel's sadistic approach to Bharati is a desperate attempt to escape the pain of the deprivation of the parental authority. The collective impressions of the pattern of behaviour including their inner psyche and external action, extends the impression that man has ultimately to bear the pain of guilt for his own wrongdoings. Here we see the self-reflective method in *Tara* has created the possibility of objective assessment of each character along with reflections on their interpersonal relationship. Dattani tries to establish that in the scheme of nature, there are predetermined roles and meddling of human intellect in them brings chaos and disaster. As Gajendra Kumar states, "*Tara* is not simply an exposition of dramatic contour and finesse but a critique of the complexity of human relationship in a society where life becomes chaotic and neurotic" (123).

The most striking part in the play is that Tara is discriminated by her mother who herself is a woman. Dattani brings out the root of gender discrimination by making the woman, the destroyer of another woman's life. Though Bharati's father also plays a part in this crime, it is Bharati who has to bear the brunt of blame ultimately. She might have done it also because of the huge fortune of her father, which he wanted to be inherited by Chandan, his only grandson. We see the motive of crime lying hidden in the patriarchal system in our society, where women are considered inferior to men.

Tara, who is the innocent victim of the society's injustice, has to carry the burden of being physically disabled all through her life. She secretly longs for two legs, when she says:

> *Tara*: I would wish for both…I would wish for two of them.
> *Chandan*: Two Jaipur Legs?
> *Tara*: No, silly, the real ones. (*Tara* 266)

She thinks that it is only her mother who strongly loves her. Somehow, Tara begins to assume that her father hates her. But she appears to be a bold girl, who cheerfully faces her critics and opponents. Her brother Chandan remains a strong support for her throughout.

A patriarchal society is perfectly presented in *Tara* where the major decisions are made by the male members. In such a society, a woman's identity is defined by others in terms of her relationship with men. Patel, the head of the family is very concerned about the future of their son, Chandan. He has great plans for Chandan and wants him to join college, whereas he does not speak about any plans for Tara. Patel wants Chandan to accompany him to his office. He wants Chandan to be bold and outgoing. He gets furious when he finds Chandan helping his mother with her knitting. He shouts at Bharati for making his sin do something considered to be feminine.

> *Patel*: Chandan, leave that damn thing alone!
> *Bharati*: (Frantic.) Go! Chandan, just go!
> *Patel*: (To Bharati.) How dare you do this to him? (256)

Patel feels disappointed at the growth of his son without any responsibility in life. He says, "I am disappointed in you. From now on you are coming to the office with me. I can't see you rotting at home!" (256).

The relationship of Bhararti and Tara, mother and daughter, need specific mention. Bharati's inner self is divided for her different commitments as a mother and a woman. The fractured images of her inner self cast it shadows in her love for Tara. Her guilty conscience makes her shower love on Tara. She is always very concerned and worried about Tara and her future. The play begins with the scene where Bharati is admonishing Tara for not taking her milk. In another context, she remarks to Chandan about Tara, "The world will accept you—but not her! Oh, the pain she is going to feel when she sees herself at eighteen or twenty. Thirty is unthinkable. And what about forty and fifty!" (254). It is only Bharati who has plans for Tara. It might be her guilty conscience which causes her to make safe her daughter's life. She says, "I plan for her happiness. I mean to give her all the love and affection which I can give. It's what she—deserves" (255). Patel does not seem happy about the way Bharati treats her daughter. According to him she treats Tara "as if she is made of glass" (DCI 257). Bharati's mental trauma makes her go out of her senses and she breaks down finally. Tara, when returns home after her kidney transplant, is depressed to hear about her mother's illness. She feels that only her mother loves her and she has lost it forever.

Chandan's response to Tara and her needs is very positive. Although he lives in a patriarchal society, he remains untainted by the poison of gender discrimination. He loves his twin sister very much and believes in her talent. When Bharati comments about the uncertainty of Tara's future, Chandan comforts her, "There's nothing aimless about Tara's life" (254). He assures that everything is going to be fine with Tara. The way they enjoy each other's company shows their strong bonding and relation.

Chandan does not find any difference between him and Tara unlike the society they live in. He despises attending college without Tara. He is disappointed when he learns about his grandfather's decision to leave the money all to himself, without anything to Tara. Chandan almost rejects the fortune left by his grandfather. He is shocked when his father reveals the secret of the past surgery on them. He feels guilty of having been a part of the disaster that occurred to Tara. Unable to see Tara suffering, he flees to London and there leads a new life. It is through the memory of Dan (the older Chandan) that the story gets unfolded. Dan comments," Locking myself in a bedsitter in a seedy suburb of London, thousands of miles from home hasn't put enough distance between us." (232). The bitter experiences that his sister had to undergo makes him resent the whole world, especially his home. He is tormented by the fact that his sister did not get a fair deal from Nature or society.

The attitude of the society towards girl child is depicted through the words of Roopa, who says, "The Patels in the old days were unhappy with getting girl babies— you know dowry and things like that—so they used to drown them in milk" (254). The grandfather's act of leaving his property and money to his male grandchild Chandan shows the prominence of men and submission of women. Roopa mocks Tara and calls her the silly one-legged, when things get worse between them. A woman becomes the tormentor of another woman. Dattani talks about the maturity of women twice in the play. They are intelligent and talented by birth, but it is not developed in the proper way. Bharati is guided by her prejudice rather than intelligence in her decision to give the third leg to the boy. This leads her to a sense of guilt and fear of losing her daughter's love. She tries to strengthen Tara by lavishing love and affection on her. Tara is intelligent too, but she does not get a chance to develop her talent fully. Her life is cut short by the negligence and cruelty of the patriarchal society. Bharati's concern for the future of Tara reflects her own insecurity. This anxiety emerges out of three main reasons—the unreasonable traditions of patriarchal society, Tara's handicapped condition after separation and the agony born out of the apathy of society. She has a realization that life is different for a girl and it is particularly intolerable for an unmarried girl.

Tara is considered to be an ideal character of Dattani. She has been widely applauded and variedly interpreted. In a male dominated world, preference is always given to male when the question of survival comes forward. All the propaganda of equality between male and female vanishes and equal opportunities to women in all the fields are defiled. Tara is sacrificed because she was a girl and had no right to have a better life than her brother. The idea of a complete girl child and an incomplete male child is so shocking that the sacrifice of the girl child is acceptable than a handicapped male child. The play shows injustice done to women.

Tara, although believes in her mother's love for her in the beginning, realizes the truth towards the end of the play. She is stunned to know about the motive behind her mother's love and affection for her. She is shaken to learn from Mr. Patel that she was deprived of her leg due to her mother's interference. Tara was denied the opportunity to live like a complete human being because she was a girl. As G.J.V. Prasad says, "This is a play about the injustices done in the name of construction of gender identities.—this hierarchisation and demarcation of roles does as much harm to men as to women"(141). Dan is the recipient of an unwanted tragic gift and will carry the burden of having wasted Tara's leg and contributing to blighting her life—and this role being assigned to him simply because of his being born a male.

He has to pay for the sins committed by his parents and grandfather. He has to apologize to Tara for being a part of the tragedy that befell her, though unknowingly.

The pathetic confession of Dan by the end of the play is the manifestation of Dattani's own anguish at the exploitation of an innocent girl. He deals with a wide variety of relations with distinctive aims and motives to come to final solutions. Dattani's portraiture of Dan (the older Chandan) and Chandan show the two stages of a man. We witness how a tragedy can alienate men and transform them. The delineation of Bharati and Patel's relationship and subsequently Chandan and Tara's relationship is to establish the fact that the evaluation of different relations with the canons of male and female binary cannot be absolute and ultimate. Beena Agarwal states, "The different relations projected in the texture of the play *Tara* justifies the fact that the relations are associated with the question of identity and self existence and the proper realization of them in human life is not arbitrary but an inevitable obligation and any effort to escape them only proves a preface to inadequacy and incompleteness in human life" (93). Patel is hostile towards Bharati, apathetic to Tara and possessive to Chandan and all these three impulses seems to be under the control of some invisible forces, specific to the experiences of Patel. His efforts to keep Chandan away from Tara, is inspired by the motive to separate Chandan from the hold of Tara, so that he might be able to tolerate separation. Bharati's possessiveness for Tara leads to a breach in father and daughter relationship.

Dattani focuses on the prevalent attitude of people almost everywhere to promote boys and discard girls. He brings out the particular situation in an Indian home in *Tara*. Women should be given equal opportunities to develop their potential. He shows how women are responsible for the degradation of their own group. It is high time men and women realize that they ought to complement each other in their lives. A complete life is possible to us only when we learn to value our both aspects, masculine and feminine. Then we will be able to realize a world full of possibilities.

> In a woman man is conceived,
> From a woman man is born,
> With a woman he is betrothed and married,
> With a woman he contracts friendship.
> Why denounce her, the one from whom even kings are born?
> From a woman a woman is born.
> None may exist without a woman. (*Guru Granth Sahib* 75)

Works Cited

Agarwal, Beena. *Mahesh Dattani's Plays: A New Horizon in Indian Theatre.* Jaipur: Book Enclave, 2008.

Dattani, Mahesh. *Tara. Drama Contemporary India.* Ed. Erin B. Mee. New Delhi: Oxford UP, 2002.

Kumar, Gajendra. "The Elements of Alienation and Death in *Tara*: A Psychoanalytic Study". *The Dramatic World of Mahesh Dattani: A Critical* Exploration. Ed. Amar Nath Prasad. New Delhi: Sarup, 2009.

Prasad, G.J.V. "Terrifying *Tara*: The angst of the Family". *Mahesh Dattani's Plays: Critical Perspectives.* Ed. Angelie Multani. New Delhi: Pencraft International, 2007.

8

Child Abuse and Its Psychological Repercussion in Mahesh Dattani's *Thirty Days in September*

Shiv Kumar

In the play *Thirty Days in September* Dattani portrays the psychological drama of a character who suffers from sexual abuse which happened when she was young. The entire play revolves around the central character Mala, who was sexually abused by her uncle when she was nine years old. Dattani lays bare her psychological trauma and portrays the consequences of that act. Apart from Mala, her mother Shanta is also depicted as a psychologically disturbed character who also suffers as the was raped when she was younger. The play unfolds the pattern of suffering where the objectified image is represented through a physical object on the stage which constantly reminds that Mala still leaves in the past. The memory of the childhood incident haunts her constantly which gradually leads her toward hysterical condition. As a result she always accuses her mother for not resisting her brother when he raped her and always contemplating and worshipping God.

But before she reaches that stage of madness, her boyfriend Deepak, performs a Freudian role by first advising her to consult a psychologist and secondly by creating situations where she can confront her past. This is the only means, he thinks, through which she can defy the domination of the past which has restricted her mental growth as the past memories in the figure of man always pursue her. When once Mala agrees to marry Deepak, and Vinay, her uncle, arrives on the scene Deepak attempts to utilize the moment by inciting Vinay to expose his past deeds. But the attempt does not help but rather sets the mood. Later when they reach home and the issue of Mala's marriage is again raised Mala confronts her uncle and exposes his reality and removes his false mask. She accuses her mother as well for her neglect and indifferent attitude towards her. But paradoxically her mother also reveals that she too was a victim of child abuse as he had sexually molested her when she was younger. This entire episode clears all misconceptions of Mala and she acknowledges her fault in accusing her mother. This entire confrontation not only empowers her to reject the infiltration of the hallucinating image of man but also helps both mother and daughter to come together to create a healthy relationship.

Mahesh Dattani is a well-known personality in contemporary urban theatre. His plays are situated around contemporary urban environment and he draws ideas and material from its milieu to represent them for urban audience. He brings issues and concerns, which normally do not belong to mainstream traditional theatre. He brings everyday life's complex and multiple issues onto the stage and presents them realistically without any value judgement over the concerns. He does not believe in the idea of aesthetic distance but rather prefers active audience participation so they could participate and reflect on the play and its issues. He mostly concentrates on the problems related to family, which are relevant to the immediate social context. His chooses issues from contemporary everyday urban life is and realistically portrays by penetrating deep into the problem to bring out its complex aspect. This is only possible by that person who has the access into the socio-cultural aspect of the society. In this context I am tempted to quote few lines from Mahesh Dattani's interview with Evin B. Mee:

> I think one has to be true to one's own environment. Even if I attempted writing a play about the angst of rural Indian society, it wouldn't ring true it, would be outsider's view—I could only hope to evoke sympathy, but never really be a part of that unless I spend a lot of time there. I think there are enough issues and challenges in urban Indian society (the milieu I am part of) and these automatically [form] the content of my work (157).

These lines express his dedication and desire to depict the complex problems of urban society which he has beautifully reflected in his writings. In his *Play Dance Like a Man,* Dattani brings the issue of prejudice and gender-based bias in contemporary Indian society on the other hand *Tara* raises the concern of parents fixation to male child, female infanticide and discrimination on gender ground. *Bravely Fought the Queen* raises homosexual theme and *Seven Steps Around the Fire* deals with the hijra community and exposes the exploitation prevalent in the society against them. *Final Solution* is widely acclaimed play and various critics have analysed it differently from partition allegory to communal violence. Even *Thirty Days in September* resonates contemporary issues, which are at heart of contemporary Indian society but here he goes beyond the traditional issues and deals with a very sensitive child abuse issue.

Mahesh Dattani's *Thirty Days in September,* published in 2001, depicts the story of a female character who was sexually molested by her uncle when she was nine year old, which continues for four consecutive years. This very sensitive issue of child molestation is brought onto the stage through this play. The setting of this play is around a modern urban Indian family of two. In this play he analyses how the world has been turning into a moral-less world where sexually blind people, just to satisfy their momentary thirst, destroy the entire life of a child. He also explores psychological consequences of these kinds of incidents on people and presents a micro picture of internally fractured structure of a family. In this family Shanta and Mala are depicted as psychologically traumatized individuals who are suffering the deeds of one person, i.e. Vinay. This play is the dramatic representation of physical and psychological struggle, from which the sufferers are struggling to come out. He depicts how one past incident can alter the trajectory of one's life completely.

This paper will mainly concentrate on the figure of the protagonist of the play Mala, around whom the entire play revolves and who occupies the major space in the play. This paper will attempt to examine the consequences of child abuse and how the solution is provided within the world of the play. The roles played by other characters, who help her to overcome the burden of past to normalize and mobilize her life, will also be analysed.

Instead of directly jumping into the narrative world to expose the reality Dattani presents two fundamentally different versions of interviews. These two interviews are self-explanatory in nature and provide a contrast between two as one is recorded in past and the other is in the process of recording. The playwright places two opposite versions of Mala's interviews to compare and contrast each with other to provide a comprehensive picture to the audience.

In the first interview, which takes place in February 2004 after the death of her maternal uncle and continues till the end when Mala finally rejects the authority of Man figure, she is depicted as a fully conscious and grown personality. Here she has come out from her psychological struggle with the help of Deepak and is confident enough to face the world. This interview also reflects that she is conscious about her subjective individual identity and ready to condemn the culprit, as it was not her or her mother's fault.

The second interview was recorded in the past, on 30 September 2001, when she first goes to consult the counsellor after Deepak's insistence. This interview reflects a mentally unstable person, who has lost the guarantee about future and is not ready to face the world due to a childhood experience, which has consequently objectified her mental growth. She is depicted as a person who has lost her subjective identity and accepts everything as her own fault, as she acknowledges, "I know it is all my fault really... it is not anybody's fault except my own" (9).

Throughout the play Dattani exposes this self-accusation pattern so the reality beneath the accusation could be exposed to the audience. This feeling gradually destroys the sanctity of home and relationship as Mala feels that not only she, but her mother as well, has played a part in destroying her life.

The play begins with a fully conscious and confident Mala who "has taken a journey and has arrived somewhere psychologically" (8). This opening comment sets the tone of the play and foregrounds the issue of psychological dilemma of the character. For her this entire experience proves to be a therapeutic process and how she has woken up after a long sleep "after many years, as if from a comma" (33). This is achieved by facing the dark secrets of her life, which finally normalizes her life. So this entire drama is unfolding of her mental as well as physical struggle to come out from static past and how this is achieved with the assistance of Deepak to whom later she marries.

Mala occupies the central space in the drama and the entire play revolves around her. She suffers from psychological trauma due to her childhood incident when she was beguiled by her maternal uncle, who rapes her, which changes her life's trajectory. She becomes a victim of serious psychological repression. This incident proves to be a fatal setback of her life which virtually obstructs her growth into maturity as she constantly identifies herself with her childhood image. This objectification into time and space is represented on the stage by the doll, which becomes an 'objective correlative' to her unspoken feelings. This objectification also severely affects her mental growth. The doll represents the loss of subjectivity as the 'I' loses its essential identity and the physically grown body becomes an extension of childhood's fixed and static picture. The history of Mala overcomes her present, which obstructs her entry into the progressive future. This stimulates her sense of alienation and she remains confined within her childhood world.

This stationary effect adversely affects her mental growth and natural development as a result she becomes incapable to create or make my kind of humane relationship with other men. The constant recurrence of past memories makes her incapable of loving anyone. For Mala to maintain a healthy and normal heterosexual relationship with Deepak becomes unbearable because she feels she cannot love anyone except her uncle, as she burst out, "I see this man everywhere. I can never be free of him. I am not sure I want to be free of him" (54). Her many sexual relationships could be seen as an attempt to replicate the same frozen moment of history which has changed her life when she was nine year old. But the supplement theory to which she takes recourse does not culminate in fulfilling her desires and the explorations finally ends in alienation from body, self and society.

Apart from Doll her childhood fixation is depicted in her reaction when she tries to seduce a man who comes with her fiancé

Radhika. When Radhika leads him away from the seductive clutches of Mala, people around starts staring at her and her reaction to the situation again reminds the audience that she is yet not able to come out from her childhood memories. Her mimicry like a child to this situation reflects that she still lives a life of an eleven-year-old girl as "Mala follows head held down like a schoolgirl caught in a net" (22).

The home is considered as an intensely private space and the atmosphere of their house is not that of love but rather it is a claustrophobically fragmented house which has turned into a living hell as "this hell is where [both] belong" (54). It is the same house where Mala was sexually abused despite the presence of her mother in other room. This creates fissures in her mind, which leads towards a condition of personality disorder. She represents a divided self, as once she enters into the house she becomes hysterical and vents out her frustrated rage on her mother. Throughout the play she accuses her mother for her life's tragedy and points out that just because of her unconcerned and neutral attitude everything has happened. She feels that she could have prevented the continuation of abusing by protesting against it but she always remained absorbed in her religious duties and worshiping god.

On the other hand, Shanta is depicted as an introvert figure who does not share her feelings with anyone, not even with her own daughter. The intense pain and bleak reality are hidden beneath her silence who always fears to confront the questions related to past. She represents the dilemma of facing truth and pretends to 'forget' everything so she could not face the truth. She escapes into the world of religion which seems to be the only possible means of shelter as her husband has already deserted her because her life, like her daughter, is dominated by past. She actually does not exist in present but lives in past, which does not create a mutual atmosphere between husband and wife and results in separation. Both these women live in their past and are unable to liberate from it, as Vinay says to Shanta, "you always go into your own world" (45). This world of Shanta is a repressive world and to come out from it seems impossible for her. She passively bears the assault of past and litany of her daughter and remains silent so her past would not affect her daughter's life.

At this point of dramatic crisis, Deepak enters into the picture to rescue his beloved from fragmentation. He could be seen as a Freudian figure, who although not a psychologist, but helps Mala to mobilize herself to come out from the past. He attempts to cement Mala's determination to face the repressed truth so she could free herself from the clutches of history. He first asks her to consult psychologist and tries everything but nothing comes out. Finally he decides to go for the last option as "there is only one way to find out [the truth]" (45). Later by getting a 'hunch' from the counsellor, he actively tries to create a situation of confrontation between Mala and her uncle Vinay. During the dinner party Mala's uncle creates a façade of normality where everything seems to be normal. But still a sense of guilt pervasively exists in his mind, which is reflected in his conscious remarks, which brings the question of Mala on the table, which Deepak fully utilizes to penetrate into the matter. But he does not succeed, as nobody was ready to face and expose Vinay publicly. This beginning of arguments sets the tone, which later culminates when they reach at home. Here again the question related to Mala is raised which infuriates her and she finally outburst her deepest feelings about her uncle and mother. This confrontation lays bare the past truth and reveals truth, that he has not only molested Mala but his own sister as well when she was younger. This clarification helps them to recuperate into a normative function of life. This revisiting of past was important to destroy the stratified image of both the women as it clears the way to enter into future, as Michael Walling says, "The trauma associated with past need continually to be revisited and reinvented to allow us to reinvent and so empower ourselves in the present" (74).

Apart from rescuing motif he is deliberately placed opposite to uncle Vinay who wears the camouflage of ethical morality. To compare and contrast both the characters, Dattani merges two different scenes into one to give a comparative picture of both the characters to the audience. In the scene when Mala goes to Deepak's house to avoid staying at home after her uncle's arrival. Deepak instead of manipulating or taking advantage of the situation like her uncle did; treats her like a baby in a "non-sexual way" (44). This reference provides a comparative stance, as he is shown as a figure, who truly loves Mala and attempts to create a reciprocal relationship with her to help her. Here Dattani brings to life the image of Mala's mind, which haunts her constantly. Here again the hallucinatory image is portrayed which tries to lures her back into past. But true love and concern of Deepak wins the situation, who does not let her past to dominate her present when she is with him.

But still the audience or the reader is given the entire depiction of past incident which hauntingly dominates her life. Here Dattani employs theatrical strategies through which the entire childhood incident is re-enacted to give a comprehensive view to the audience about her past and through it to win the sympathies of the audience as well. The psychological effects of this incident are represented in the frozen figure of a Doll, who represents the static image of Mala's childhood figure where "we cannot see the doll's face, just its ragged limbs. The dress on the doll is lifted and pinned at the doll's forehead" (45). Dattani does not conceive his audiences to be mere spectators of the play who enjoy the aesthetic pleasure of the enactment, but rather forces them to actively participate in the play so they could provide their value judgments apart from creating meanings.

To achieve complete participation of audience he deploys the technique of representing the character according to certain stereotypical types. Mala's uncle Vinay is depicted as Hobbesian figure who believes in personal satisfaction and does not care about ethical, moral or familial relationships. He represents, what Michael Walling calls, the "life denying social structures", who consciously kills the soul of a child for his personal satisfaction (74). He manipulates the paternal authority by molesting his own younger sister for sexual gratification. Later he changes his sexual orientation towards his niece and satisfies his physical needs by sporadically rapping her also for four years whenever she comes on holiday. Through him Dattani exposes the self-centered mean ideology of people like him whose Hobbesian thirst does not acknowledge any social and ethical boundaries. His ubiquitous personality is exposed to bare minimum at the conclusion of the novel when his past deeds are laid bare in front of the audience.

The effect of child abuse drastically dominates her psyche that even till the of the play the figure of Man does not leave Mala and constantly tries to seduce her back into historical past. At the end of the interview, the apparition of Man again tries to influence Mala by reminding her past incident but she resists the infiltration of history in the figure of Man as "he as a person is not important to me anymore" (58). This self-assertion of Mala reduces the importance of the incident of the past, which is displayed when "the spotlight on the man fades out" (58). Here Dattani deploys dramatic technique and stagecraft as a medium to communicate the meaning of the scene rather than relying on narrative form. Instead of physically removing the Man from the stage the lights are removed from him and he is left in darkness. The same darkness which has until now dominated the psyche of both the female characters. This fading out of lights symbolizes the reducing importance of the bleak part of past from her life. This also signifies that now onward these females will live their lives fully without any negative or adverse dominating influence of past. With this incident the interview also finishes and she is depicted as an enlightened being, who is completely out of the influence of past memories and ready to acknowledge her mother's role.

With this diminishing of Man's status the domestic space also changes from a claustrophobic hell to a living space where human relationship can be built. It is in the same private space where through final confrontation the peace and freedom in restored and Shanti is seen as "praying with a sense of peace around her" (58). The relationship between mother and daughter is restored as both have gone through the same experience, which creates a mutual understanding between them. The experience of suffering brings them together in the end of the play where Mala apologizes to her mother as "it's no longer your fault, mother. Just as it wasn't my fault" (58). She recognizes that it was not either's fault but rather of a third person who has destroyed a major part of their lives.

Within this small world of four characters Dattani fully dramatizes the effects of child abuse and its repercussions. Instead of dealing with the social aspect of the incident he entirely concentrate on the psychological effects of this gruesome heinous act on a particular individual. Through the depiction of Mala's mental struggle to come out from frozen moments of past Dattani has not only provided an alternative solution but also placed the child issue at the center of the society. This entire dramatization on the stage could also be seen a psychological struggle which happens within the mind of Mala which Dattani beautifully captures on the stage. So I would conclude this paper with the words of Lillete Dubey, who says that through this play Dattani "manages to bring home the horror and pain within the framework of a very indefinable mother-daughter relationship" (4)..

Works Cited

Dattani, Mahesh. "Thirty Days in September". *Collected Plays Vol. 2. Screen, Stage and Radio Plays*. Penguin, Delhi. 2008, 1-58.

Mee, Erin B. "Invisible Issues: An Interview with Mahesh Dattani". *Mahesh Dattani's Plays: Critical Perspectives*. Ed. Angelie Multani. Pencraft International, New Delhi. 2007, 156-164.

Stevenson, David L. "Everyone will be in Costume! And will have Masks on! Gender and Performance in *Bravely Fought the Queen*". *Mahesh Dattani's Plays: Critical Perspectives*. Ed. Angelie Multani. Pencraft International, New Delhi. 2007, 67-75.

Walling, Michael. "An Objective Correlative for T.S. Eliot's Hamlet". *The Journal of Aesthetics and Art Criticism*. Vol. 13, No.1. Blackwell Publishing on behalf of The American Society for Aesthetics. 1954, 69-79. Stable URL: http://www.jstor.org/stable/427018. Accessed: 27/04/2011, 06:00.

9

The Noesis of Otherness in Indian Society: Mahesh Dattani's *Seven Steps Around the Fire* and *Dance Like a Man*

M. Preetha

India is one of the developing nations of the modern world. It has become an independent country, a republic, more than a half century ago. During this period the country has been engaged in efforts to attain development and growth in various areas such as building infrastructure, production of foodgrains, science and technology, and spread of education. The life expectancy has increased and many diseases have been controlled. However, there are many areas in which Indian society is experiencing a variety of problems. Some of these problems have their roots in our colonial past while others are related to demographic changes, socio-political conditions and cultural processes. The present paper throws light on the discourse of otherness in Indian society that is resulted as an outcome of the socio-psychological perceptions of the Indians.

India has the longest and the richest tradition in drama. During the age of the Vedic Aryans, drama was performed in a simple way. Different episodes from the *Ramayana*, the *Mahabbharata*, and the *Bhagavad Gita* were enacted in public. It was didactic in nature dramatising the struggles between good and evil. In 1920s a new form of drama came to the fore in almost all the Indian languages. It was a drama largely influenced by prevailing movements like marxism, psychoanalysis, symbolism, and surrealism. Badal Sarcar, Vijay Tendulkar, Girish Karnad and Mahesh Dattani have contributed to the modernization of the Indian theatre. These playwrights have made instaurations in terms of both thematic concerns and technical virtuosities.

The study of drama is both sociological and psychological. It reflects the life of the people, literate as well as illiterate, through stage production. In this modern world, there are numerous psychological conflicts arising out of the social problems. The playwrights who follow the tradition of social realism are A.S. Panchapeakesha Ayyar, A.C. Krishnaswami, V.V. Srinivasa Iyengar, S. Fyzee Rahamin and Mahesh Dattani. They ruminate on the contemporary social problems like intercaste marriage, untouchability, sex, power and wealth. Their plays are more panoptic in scope and add a new color to the Indian drama.

Mahesh Dattani is a playwright of world stature. He has steered the Indian English drama to a new direction. He does not adhere to any established dramatic tradition but customizes the Indian theatre to reverberate the real life experiences. He has developed the stage as a powerful medium to patent the cause of marginalized and capture the roots of the fractions of human psyche in the era of value crisis. Smita Lakhotia coercee that "He is a citizen of the modern world. He bares life to the bone and acts as a spokesman for all marginalized people. He does not write on conventional subjects but exposes the mean, ugly and unhappy things of life."

Dattani's firm conviction is that drama can successfully be used as a tool for creating social awareness. Hence the dramatic canvas of Dattani is coloured with real life conditions and for him man is an integral part of society and consciously or unconsciously the cowering influences of societal set-up, determine the fabric of relationship around him. He possesses an exceptional sensibility for the suffering in society born out of gender discrimination. He delves deep to examine the psychic reactions of those who are the victims of discrimination. He coerces the fact that self and 'society' are two distinctive entities, but he maintains the opinion that it is the harmony of the too that constitutes the balance of human life. His vision is that individual cannot survive in isolation and so he has to make perpetual struggle to coordinate his will with the scheme of nature and society.

The play *Seven Steps Around the Fire* was first broadcasted as *Seven Circles Around the Fire* by BBC Radio on 9 January 1999. The play represents the quandary of hijra community who are not acknowledged by the mainstream society in India. The hijras are isolated from the sexual majority. They form a community of their own and seek identity in their collective strength. They are not permitted to mingle with other human beings and are often prohibited to express their concern for human relationship. Dattani ventures to explore the misery of these marginalized 'other' of Indian society who struggle against the irresistible forces of social apathy. The play also discusses the sanctity of marriage and the social conventions behind every ceremony. Dattani breaks through the stereotypes in Indian society and ridicules the discrimination of the marginalized people.

Transgendered communities have existed in most parts of the world with their own local identities, customs and rituals. They are called *baklas* in the *Philippines*, *berdaches* among American Indian tribes, *serrers* in Africa and hijras, *jogappas*, jogtas in South Asia. The hijra community in India has a recorded history of more than 4,000 years. The term 'hijra' is derived from the Arabic word, 'ijara,' which refers to eunuchs. The common feature among the hijras is their mode of dressing: they adopt feminine costumes and apparel. They live in communes ranging from five to fifteen people and traditionally earn their living by collecting alms and by receiving payment for performances at weddings, births, and festivals. When individuals join a hijra community, they take female names and use female kinship terms, such as sister, aunt, or grandmother for each other. They engage in a deliberate parodic rendition of a culturally validated model of feminine behavior.

Hijras in India trace their origins to myths in the Ramayana and the *Mahabbharata*. Rama, while leaving for the forest upon being banished from the kingdom for 14 years, turns around to his followers and asks all the men and women to return to the city. Among his followers the hijras alone do not feel bound by this direction and decide to stay with him. Impressed with their devotion, Rama sanctions them the power to confer blessings on people on auspicious occasions like childbirth and marriage, and also at inaugural functions. This set the stage for the custom of badhai in which hijras sing, dance and confer blessings.

The legend in the *Mahabbharata* is that Aravan, the son of Arjuna and Nagakanya, offers to be sacrificed to Goddess Kali to ensure the victory of the Pandavas in the Kurukshetra war. The only condition that he made was to spend the last night of his life in matrimony. Since no woman was willing to marry one who was doomed to be killed, Krishna assumes the form of a beautiful woman called Mohini and marries him. The hijras of Tamil Nadu consider Aravan their progenitor and call themselves Aravanis.

The prejudice of the traditional binary divisions is translated into violence, often of a brutal nature, in public spaces, police stations, and prisons. The main factor behind the violence is that society is not able to come to terms with the fact that hijras do not conform to the accepted gender divisions. In addition to this, most hijras have a lower middle-class background, which makes them susceptible to harassment by the police. The discrimination based on their class and gender makes the hijra community one of the most disempowered 'other' in Indian society.

It is by taking advantage of this discomfort and embarrassment at their existence, that hijras in the twenty-first century India are making their living. Begging isn't their only source of income. It's an age-old custom in the country to have hijras bless childbirths, weddings, housewarmings and other auspicious occasions. They are believed to possess occult powers, and their blessings and curses are both considered potent.

The protagonist of the play, Uma, is the wife of Superintendent of police, Suresh, and, the daughter of the Vice-Chancellor of Bangalore Univeristy. She is a Ph D scholar in sociology. She investigates the real iife condition of hijra community in Indian society as a part of her research work. Uma comes to know about the murder of a hijra, Kamala and decides to unveil the mystery of the murder. Police has established that Anarkali, a person from the same community as responsible for the murder. Uma is not convinced by the apathy of Suresh and of the other police officers.

The mainstream society is apathetic to the hijras and there is no provision of separate cell for a hijra in prison. When Uma questions her husband, Suresh, the reason for putting her in male prison, he remarks: "they are as strong as horses" (*Seven Steps* 237). Moreover, he corrects Uma saying that "they are all liars" (*Seven Steps* 237). The discrimination towards these people is also reflected in their addressing. Uma uses the pronoun 'she' to address, Anarkali, whereas the police Constable, Munuswamy uses the pronoun 'it' and does not recognize her identity as a person. He asserts, "She! of course it will take you. We will beat it up, if it doesn't" (*Seven Steps* 233). They are the social victims and exist only in margins. Nobody wants to be accosted by one of them—be nudged with their elbows, stroked on the cheek, taunted, cursed and flashed.

Uma visits the central jail to interview Anarkali, the chief accused in the case. In the opinion of the constable, Munuswamy, the idea of investigating the case of a hijira is a futile process. However, Uma forgetting her pride and high social status, decides to proceed further. Her humanitarian insight enables her to develop sisterly affinity with them. Anarkali confesses that "I didn't kill her, she was my sister" (*Seven Steps* 236). She further states: "would you kill your sister" (*Seven Steps* 236). Swayed by human sympathy she gets emotionally involved in the whole affair and identifies herself with their suffering. She befriends Anarkali, and Champa, the chief of hijras to gain insight into the problems of hijra community away from the noesis of the public.

Uma tries her best to win their confidence in her to raise voice against the injustice done to them. She decides to visit Shivajinagar to meet Anarkali's friend Champa. Uma offers bail amount to Champa for the release of Anarkali. Uma initially suspects that the rivalary between Kamala and Anarkali as the reason for the murder but the intervention of Salim diverts her focus from Anarkali to Salim. She decides to visit Mr. Sharma's house so as to meet his body guard, Salim who was expected to marry Kamala. Mr. Sharma dissuades her from investigating Salim as his son may get mentally sick with Salim's absence. He requests her to suspend her investigations till the marriage of her son.

At the marriage ceremony of Subbu, the hijras begin to dance and sing in praise of the couple, but with the dancing of Anarkali, the memory of dead Kamala begin to haunt Subbu. Inspite of being born and brought up in luxury, he is very weak and nervous. He is unhappy with the arrangement of his marriage and yells out that "I hate weddings. I don't want all this! I don't wish to go ahead with this" (*Seven Steps* 267). In a state of frenzy, he snatches the gun of Suresh and aims at his father. He cries out, "You killed her?" (*Seven Steps* 280) and thereby brings reveals the murderer to light. Mr. Sharma has connived with Salim to kill Kamala when he realizes that his son, Subbu had secretly wedded Kamala. The minister has burned Kamala to death, and hastily arranges for his son to marry another girl. He cunningly gets her sister, Anarkali arrested as a convict. Mr. Sharma forces his son into marrying the girl of his choice which he justifies saying "My truth is in ensuring he is on the right path" (*Seven Steps* 276).

The brutal murder of Kamala raises the issue of an abandoned section of humanity without a legal system or a forum for redressal to protect the lives and dignity of hijra community. Anarkali and her community know who the murderer was, but no one dares to reveal the truth, as they feared persecution and annihilation. Champa exercises her absolute authority in her community but fears to reveal the truth in front of police officers: "We cannot speak... when we want to speak nobody listens. When we cannot speak..." (*Seven Steps* 259).

Subbu shoots himself amidst marriage festivities and chanting of mantras. The death of Subbu reveals the mystery surrounding the murder of Kamala. The revelation inturn does not bring about any change of state in the society:

> They have no voice. The case was hushed up and it was not even reported in the newspaper.... Subbu's suicide was written off as an accident. The photograph was destroyed. So were the lives of two young people... but Anarkali's blessing's remain with me... I did not want is what they want... to move on. To love, To live. (*Seven Steps* 282)

The society accepts a hizra for gracing the ceremonies of marriage and births but would not allow them to be portrayed of such ceremonies. She is murdered simply because she had fallen in love with subbu a young man having a status of importance in society. "Not for them the seven rounds witnessed by the Fire God, eternally binding man and woman in matrimony, or the blessings of 'May you be the mother of a hundred sons" (*Seven Steps* 240).

Nidhi Singh supposes that the play "questions the stance which rejects the possibility of love, loyalty and dedication in a relationship between a eunuch and a homosexual". Their love is not a conventional love but a realization of life beyond the hold of social rituals. Dipendu Das relates that "Hijras in India comprise of the most exploited and impoverished sections, who resort to begging in public spaces often with seemingly gestures and actions mainly because they are left with little option to earn a living through decent means". Dattani foregrounds the pigeon-holes in Indian society and calls for an emotional and psychological change in the society. He propounds the idea that the Indian society should be liberal in their approach to the fellow human beings and create a milieu of harmony and peace.

Dance Like a Man was first performed in Bangalore in 1989. The play conceptualizes the gender issues with an exceptional originality. The social myth that defines the role of male and female is preconceived in Indian society and the efforts to cross the boundaries pose threats to their individuality and identity. The confrontation between individual's choices and the noesis of society is the central motif in the play. Dance is an age-old tradition in India. The magical land of India has given birth to many forms of mesmerizing dances. Different periods and environments have helped in shaping varied forms of dance in

India. Indian dance is infact considered as an exceptionally convoluted art.

In dance forms like Kuchipudi, male dancers very often imitate their female counterparts in the areas of dress, ornamentation and presentation. When men take up dancing as their career, there is immense social and parental pressure on them to become doctors, entrepreneurs and engineers so that a lucrative career is assured. With all this psychological stigma, social approbation and economic sanctions, dance is becoming more and more marginalized. The male dancers who aim to excel in this field are considered as an alien 'other'. These misconceptions continue even today in different parts of India and Dattani throws light on this psychological condition in this play. The cumulative effect of these misconceptions is such that very few men take up dance as their profession.

Dattani explores through this play two key aspects; the general inhibitions to a man taking dance as a career and that too a dance which is usually and traditionally performed by women. He deals with the crisis of three generations in the family of Amritlal, a dictatorial householder, his son Jairaj and his granddaughter, Lata. The play focuses on the life of the life and ambitions of the couple, Ratna and Jairaj, classical dancers based in Bangalore. In their young age, they were exposed to the ire of Jairaj's father who does not understand their devotion to dance. As they reach their mid fifties, they reflect on their past and reneumerates how it moulds and modifies their identities in the present.

Jairaj and Ratna got married much against the wish of his father. The father, claiming to be a freedom fighter and social reformer, is a manipulator by nature. Amritlal has fought for the freedom of the country but he does not give freedom for his son to choose his own career. Jairaj has an innate passion for the classical dance Bharatanatyam but his father being disgusted with the effeminate nature of the art of dance, tries his best to dissuade his son from pursuing his career in dancing. Amritlal is entrenched in his own belief that Baratnatayam is a craft of prostitutes. He replicates an authoritative Indian father whose definition of manhood and employment is rooted in the age-old conventions of Indian society. He corroborates that men should not take up dancing as their profession.

Amritlal's bondages does not permit Jairaj to exercise his own will. He challenges his father, "Reform, Don't talk about return to our society, you would let them practice them their own art" (*Dance* 119). The gender defined roles are so strongly rooted in Indian society that Amritlal criticizes Guruji's long hair and his way of walking. Unlike Jairaj, Ratna protests to make her spaces, to defend her rights. She is very assertive and more competent to fight for her identity, "You can't stop me from learning an art" (*Dance* 132).

Amritlal contrives a conspiracy with Ratna to disempower the passion of Jairaj. He convinces his daughter-in-law that her husband is merely a drag on her. He assures Ratna that he will help her to flourish in her carrier if she agrees to bring down Jairaj's obsession and thereby make him take up masculine jobs. He grants his permission to Ratna to dance with the condition that she should restrain Jairaj: "A woman in a man's world may be considered as being progressive. But a man in a woman's world is pathetic" (*Dance* 140).

Ratna carves her own method to give shape to the manhood of Jairaj and Amritlal moulds him to his own convictions of what a man should be. His father has curved down all his passions, warning him against the art of dancing that was socially neglected art and only permissible for the women like Devadasis. Jairaj is discouraged by desperate comments: "Where will you go being a dancer? No where! What will you get being a dancer? Nothing! People will point at you on the streets and laugh and ask" (*Dance* 118).

Jairaj being dominated by his father, fail to realize his perfect stature as an individual and above that fails to achieve perfection as a dancer. This conspiracy adversely affects the personal relationship of Ratna and Jairaj. The impression of suppressed desires echoes in his resentment. He complains:

> Bit by Bit. You took it when you insisted on top billing in all your programmes. You took it when you made me dance my weakest items. You took it when you arranged the lighting so that I was literally dancing in your shadow. And when you called me names in front of their people. Names I feel ashamed to repeat in private. (*Dance* 161)

Ratna humiliates him by calling him a spineless boy who couldn't leave his father's house for more than forty eight hours. This creates disharmony between the two that ends up in extreme bitterness. The feeling of being inadequate overpowers Jairaj that he takes to drinking, all the time hoping that his infant son, fondly named by him as Shankar, will become a consummate dancer, like a man to dance Tandav, Lord Shiva's dance : "The Lord of dance, beating his drum and trampling on the demon" (*Dance* 159). Luck does not permit him to fulfil his dreams through his son as he dies in infancy when the nurse, in the absence of the mother drugs him with opium so as to keep him asleep. This scotches the ambitions of Ratna and Jairaj. Their discontent subsequently casts its gloomy shadows on the life of Lata, their daughter. They trust their ambitions on her. They wish that she should become a world-renowned dancer. When they succeed in doing so, they realize that this is life all about: "We were only human. We lacked the brilliance. We lacked the magic to dance like Gods" (*Dance* 165).

Dance Like a Man is a powerful human drama that provides an insight into the contemporary Indian social scene, reflecting the aspirations of a middle class South Indian couple who fails to accomplish their goals of becoming a great dancer due to the adverse social conventions. Beena Agarwal signifies the idea that some believe: "Dance is a feminine art and man's attempt at being a dancer would be a prelude to the tragedy of a man (society). The psycho-cultural conflict prepares an intense tragic tension mounting to the disastrous collapse of two gentle persons and consummate artists".

Jairaj is a victim of stereotypical Indian patriarchy and prejudice. He struggles to prove his manliness despite his choice as Bharatnatyam as a profession but the social conventions hamper his growth as an individual and disenable him to fulfil his dream. In this conflict, he loses his identity as an artist and most importantly as a man. The main focus of Dattani is to crticise the noesis of otherness in Indian society that is constructed on the basis of stereotypes in the society. It is a state of the elevation of human consciousness that wraps the distinction of male and female into a state of integrity, corresponding with the patterns of life. The idea of the play imparts a rare magnanimousness and solace to the rage of passion brocaded in the play.

In *Seven Steps around the Fire* and *Dance like a Man*, Dattani has certainly given a new and unconventional voice in Indian theatre. Gouri Nilakandan Mehta adduces that "his subject is from within the complicated dynamics of the modern urban family. His characters struggle for some kind of freedom and happiness under the weight of tradition, cultural constructions of gender and repressed desire". He ponders the position of the

Marginalised 'other' in both these plays. As a playwright, he is not stereotypical and calls for a change in the mentality of the citizens of India. The flexibility and ease of his expression, breaking the barriers of tight fisted dramaturgy initiate a penetrating insight into the psycho-philosophical spectrum of human behaviour affecting human relationship at personal and interpersonal level adds new dimensions to the theatrical canons. Mahesh Dattani is at the peak of his creative powers, continuously experimenting with new forms and manners of expression. In his dramatic world, drama instead of being an expression of art has become a realization of life and it is a prolusion to the tradition of unconventional popular, Indian theatre. The echo of his theatrical art both in terms of form and content counters his prominence in the theatrical world at the global level.

Works Cited

Agarwal, Beena. "Gender Issues in *Dance like a Man*: A Socio-Psychological Analysis." *Mahesh Dattani's Plays: A New Horizon in Indian Theater*. Jaipur: Book Enclave, 2008. p. 97.

Das, Dipendu. "Gender Hegemony and the Politics of Marginalisation of Sexual Minority: Mahesh Dattani's *Seven Steps around the Fire*." *Contemporary Indian Writing in English: Trends, Concepts and Techniques*. Ed. Nigamananda Das. New Delhi: Adhyanan, 2007. p. 84.

Dattani, Mahesh. *Collected Plays*. Vol. 2. New Delhi: Penguin, 2005.

Lakhotia, Smita. "The Thespian Art of Mahesh Dattani: A Critique." *Indian Literature in English: Critical Views*. Ed. Satish Barbuddhe. New Delhi: Sarup, 2007. p. 312.

Mehta, Gouri Nilakandan. "Dismembering Traditions within Postcolonial Contexts: A Retrospective Look into *Dance like a Man*." *Mahesh Dattani's Plays: Critical Perspectives*. Ed. Angelie Multani. New Delhi: Pencraft, 2007. p. 100.

Singh, Nidhi. "The Not-so-gay 'Gay' Plays of Mahesh Dattani." *Contemporary Indian Drama: Astride two Traditions*. Eds. Urmil Talwar, and Bandana Chakrabarty. Jaipur: Rawat, 2005. p. 159.

10

(Re)Framing the Present through the Past: Dattani's Synchronization of Discord in *Dance Like a Man*

Rashi Sharma

Mahesh Dattani has invariably been hailed as one of the leading dramatists contesting discord in society at various levels. The discord, usually springing from one's own self, sometimes from family and friends, and also originating because of societal forces, finds vivid and sombre depiction in his plays in myriad forms. His work probes tangled attitudes in contemporary India towards communal differences, consumerism and gender issues and attempts to dissect what largely remains under the carpet. Dattani takes up "the complicated dynamics of the modern society" and vividly displays their sweeping dimensions (A. Madhvi Latha 231).

Though, like an aware and trained artist, Dattani does not suggest any remedy for such issues, his presentation of problematic contemporary psyche and the discord that it sprouts on the earth of human mentality, however, reverberate in the readers' mind unsettling their otherwise poised sensitivity toward the dissensions. This translation of contention is accompanied by his astute and proficient use of past and present, novel and unusual themes, and more importantly, his experimentation with the use of spoken language. He makes use of "contemporary problem India is beset with, but elevates these themes to higher levels, touching the human chords that emanate love, happiness, sexual fulfillment and the problem of identity." (Dhawan 19)

This paper seeks to contextualize Dattani's endeavour to harmonize conflictual sensibility of the characters in *Dance Like a Man* where past seems to dominate the present and yet tends to shape it. In addition, the paper also attempts to map out and challenge how the play strives to synchronize multiple dissonances among the fissured characters. Dattani, with placid cadence and candid expression, "unravels the complicated dynamics of human relationships as his characters struggle for some kind of freedom and happiness under the weight of tradition, cultural constrains of gender and repressed desire." (Kanakaraj, et al 209)

Dattani staunchly experiments with techniques of presentation and in his play *Dance Like a Man* he makes use of the flash-back technique and the split scene device. With the help of these devices he shows the discord among various characters which appears at various levels in the play. The dissonance between Jairaj and his wife Ratna Parekh reveals a chasm between the two that has many facets to it. Similarly, the abyss between Jairaj and his father Amritlal is too conspicuous to be ignored. It is Jairaj who is affescted not only by his father but also by his wife. He is a sufferer who struggles hard to sustain his individuality but fails miserably because of the pressures he receives from his life partner and his father.

The play opens with the conversation of Lata Parekh and Viswas who are chatting light-heartedly regarding their future. Viswas is there to get the approval of Lata's parents for their wedding. Lata is a classical dancer whose career is about to commence with her maiden performance before the President of India. Unfortunately, however, her *mridangam* artist Mr. Sriniwas trips over his *dhoti* and is injured badly. Lata's parents are in the hospital to see Mr. Sriniwas.

Lata tells Viswas about her ancestral house, her grandfather and parents. Later, when she is busy making coffee for him, he opens a cupboard and removes a splendid brocade shawl. He wears it and struts around without being noticed by Lata. He imitates the old man in a mock fatherly voice. It is exactly at this moment when Ratna and Jairaj enter and stare at Viswas's frolics. Viswas gets embarrassed and offers some explanation but Ratna and Jairaj are too engrossed in their problems to pay any attention to Viswas's attempts to explain his situation.

Ratna is extremely worried about her daughter's performance in absence of her *mridangam* artist. She flares up abruptly when Jairaj tries to calm her down. She accuses her husband and his father Amritlal for their present lot. She says, "Yes, your father was right. Dance has brought us nowhere. It's his curse on us. Nothing seems worth anymore" (*Dance Like a Man* 21). She insults him out of sheer desperation and calls him "a spineless boy who could not leave his father's house for more than forty-eight hours."(21)

Dattani successfully renders a realistic description of the frustrations and failures of the last forty years of Ratna's life and shows how these failures cast their shadow on their present life. Such failures, we come to know later, have economic and social extensions which are further associated with one's individual demands and gratifications. The clash of interests that the playwright has invested in the characters remarkably exposes the vacuity and emptiness that surrounds their relationship. The volcanic eruption of the suppressed feelings of Ratna, for instance, makes Jairaj bitter and sarcastic. Her remark that he "stopped being a man for [her] the day [he] came back to [his] house" unhinges Jairaj (21). When he retaliates by saying, "For forty years you've been holding that against," Ratna strikes back, "You're right, I'm worrying about nothing, because nothing is what we are!"(21)

The blame game starts and the readers get a sumptuous feast of contemporary relationship where the sweetness of love and care has been replaced with spicy and abusive accusations. Gifted with the sensibility to see beyond the stereotype representations of men and women in society, Dattani attempts to penetrate into the abstruse world of emotions and inner discord of his characters. This becomes the axis around which his characters move in order to realize their strength and prove their dignity. B. Yadava Raju rightly remarks that "human relationships and family unit have always been at the heart of his dramatic representation." (*The Plays of Mahesh Dattani* 69)

Jairaj is taken aback when he gets the taste of genuine feelings of his wife toward him. Their interaction and accusations expose the hollowness and meaninglessness of their relationship and the discord they are bound with. The fissures in the relationship between Ratna and Jairaj become too staid to allow their relationship run in a smooth manner. It is true that they could not become successful professional dancers as they had anticipated. The frustration and depression of 40 years of their past life leaves an ineffaceable imprint upon their psyche and keeps on tormenting Ratna for her supposedly failure in life. She dreams of touching the apex of her art but her middling career makes her position doleful. Dattani skilfully shows, Aditi De asserts, how "within platitude-ridden Indian society his characters seethe and reveal, probe and discern, scathing their families and neighbours, leaving each reader or watcher with a storm within as the aftermath." (www.hindu.com)

The volcano of discord keeps on simmering in her heart and she is no longer in a position to control her feelings, as a result, a natural eruption of her suppressed emotions takes place. The past of this couple leaves them down in the dumps and scratches the very placidity of their life. Where Ratna suffers for her over—ambitious nature, Jairaj undergoes excruciating experience both at the hands of his father and his wife.

In the nineteen forties, people could hardly wish their children, especially boys, to go for a classical dance form like Bharatnatyam due to the social stigma attached to it. Moreover, the association of this dance form with Devdasis, too, blemished its image. Dattani, in an interview with Ranu Uniyal, says:

> [I]t is a dance form of the Devdasis, it's a prostitutes dance and people from respectable families did not perform or practice that dance form. It is doubly difficult for the man, you know, what business does a man have learning a prostitute's dance. So it brings about gender roles, what is expected of genders as well. And also the tensions between the couple and how they solve, how they felt they used their relationship to develop their careers, dances and how they reconcile to the fact that the time wasn't right for them.(*The Plays of Mahesh Dattani* 182)

This was the reason why Amritlal could never reconcile himself to the hard fact that his only son has decided to be a classical dancer rather than opting for any other respectable way of living. It is pertinent to mention here that the patriarchal set-up has a deep impact upon the psyche of the people who consider it disparaging to do anything against the accepted social norms and customs of the society. Dattani talks about the gender roles through the characters of Ratna and Jairaj that man and woman are expected to play in most of the societies including Indian. Man in Indian society is considered as head of his family and, as per expectations and requirements, he is supposed to act in a particular characteristic way. He is not easily accepted in the roles usually played by women. This is the main cause of discord between the father and the son who are unable to cope with each other because of their dissonances regarding Bharatnatyam. Jereme Mortimer observes, "Mahesh Dattani does not seek to cut a path through the difficulties his characters encounter in his plays; instead he leads his audience to see how caught up all are in the complications and contradictions of our values and assumptions." (www.anitanair.net)

Amritlal is a freedom fighter as well as a social worker who is benevolent enough to donate money to his friends and relatives. But, at the same time, he is not ready to part with his money for the sake of upliftment of an art form. He regrets having allowed his son for continuing with his dance practice in his house. He says:

> I thought it was just a fancy of yours. I would have made a cricket pitch for you on our lawn if you were interested in cricket. Well, most boys are interested in cricket, my son is interested in dance, I thought, I didn't realize this interest of yours would turn into an... obsession. (36)

Amritlal is unable to gauge the depth of his son's passion for dance and disapproves of his reverence for his Guru and the art form itself. He considers his calling for nation's freedom superior and refiner than Jairaj's interest for dance. He is undoubtedly an opinionated old man for whom any diversion from set standards is deprecating and disgusting. The derision for something different is not a strange phenomenon. The human behavior has always been like this only. Any new idea or action has first to face severe criticism and disapproval at the hands of so-called sophisticated people. These people wring and squeeze the desire of any individual to experiment with new things and force them to adjust with their ideologies, however irrelevent and irrational they may be. The trouble of Amritlal commences from the negation of his will and order by Jairaj. He says to Jairaj that "there comes a time when you have to do what is expected of you. Why must you dance? It does not give you any income. Is it because of your wife? Is she forcing you to dance?" (37)

He further expresses his hatred for such practices and wishes to eradicate certain practices which are a shame to the society. He says, "I will not have our temples turned into brothels."(38) At this Jairaj remarks, "And I will not have my art run down by a handful of stubborn narrow-minded individuals with fancy pretentious ideals"(38). He further retaliates, "You should be pleased that people from respectable families like yours are interested in reviving this dance. You should be encouraging us instead of being a hindrance."(38)

An alert reader finds such episodes as representative instances of the dichotomy between past and present, between tradition and modernity, and between patriarchy and individuality. If Amritlal is a staunch follower of tradition and the values attached to it, Jairaj is a rebellious youth—a protestant against the set make-beliefs. He is an educated intellectual who does not fight shy to go against his father's stern instructions and choose a dance form his father disapproves. If Amritlal represents past and its heritage, Jairaj represents present which has the seeds of colorful and healthy future for the generations to come. His rejection of his only son, nevertheless, has another dimension that is deeply attached to patriarchy. He is not so much hurt by the occupation his son has chosen as he is hurt by his son's rebellion against him.

Jairaj calls his father prudish and conservative like the British who is unable to see the lusture of a great art. He does not want to get typecast as an emblematic man denying the beauties of life for the sake of petty money matters. His passion for dance is praiseworthy for he has to bear the brunt of his father's satirical remarks for keeping his fervour intact. His father is highly critical of his way of living and this becomes the key reason of their strife. When Ratna tells Amritlal about Jairaj's decision to learn *kuchipudi* in which a man has to dress up like a woman, Amritlal, no longer to control himself, forbids Jairaj to take any more lessons from his Guru. He asks Jairaj to 'grow up,' at this Jairaj remarks, "I don't want to grow up! You can't stop me from doing what I want."(45) Unable to withstand the pressure of society and his father, Jairaj decides to leave the house with his wife.

This is how the past in form of his father sows seeds of dissension in the present life of Jairaj. However, he is caught in the tortuous web of his life. The miasma of his complex problems does not let him remain stable and he comes back defeated and exhausted to his father's house. His efforts to sustain his dignity without his father's aid and support end in smoke. The devastating weight of hackneyed traditions and corny ideologies of his father is too much for him to bear.Within 48 hours he realizes that he lacks the grit and gumption to cross the labyrinth of life. He has to leave the house of Ratna's uncle as he was making advances towards his wife. Instead of testing his perseverance any more he chooses to live in his father's house. The economic factor also plays a major role. He could have lived on his own if he had been economically independent.

Amritlal allows him to stay there on his own terms and conditions. He forbids him to grow his hair. He declares, "Tell him that if he grows his hair even an inch longer, I will shave his head and throw him on the road"(40). Amritlal's list of conditions, which he imposes upon his son and daughter-in-law, is a telling truth how a wounded patriarch would force the defeated son to agree with his terms and conditions where any violation would mean expulsion from the house. He knows that Jairaj is not as good a dancer as Ratna is. He makes her confess that she has married Jairaj not because she forms any high opinion of him but for the simple reason that he would allow her to dance. Amritlal takes advantage of this weakness of Ratna and allows her to continue with her dance practice but with the condition that she will no longer be visiting that old Devdasi of Mysore school. Amritlal also persuades her to help Jairaj grow up as a man. He coaxes her by permitting her to dance and shape her career as she dreams. He makes it very clear to her that her dancing career depends entirely on his wishes: "A woman in a man's world may be considered as being progressive. But a man in a woman's world is pathetic"(50). He further explains his motive by saying, "Help me make him an adult. Help me to help him grow up"(51). When Ratna asks, "And once he stops dancing –what will you do with him then?"(51) Amritlal says, "Make him worthy of you"(51). Sangeeta Das points out this facet of Dattani's play when she says:

> The impact of patriarchal authority in a joint family and kowtowing of the rest of the family members before their decisions has been successfully spotlighted in this play... the result of such high-handedness is quite natural... No sooner did Aamritlal close his eyes than Jairaj changed absolutely starting by alteration in the house. Too much of stringency leads to revolt which, though remains uncover, gushes forth whenever it finds an outlet. (*The Plays of Mahesh Dattani* 116-17)

This clearly proves his stance on the gender roles which become the main reason of discord between the two generations. After this argument he leaves the stage and is not seen in the forthcoming scenes but his presence is felt through his daughter-in-law who now dominates her husband. Ambition to become a successful dancer turns her into an egotistical being. B. Yadava Raju comments that she "buys her freedom to dance at the expense of Jairaj's desire to become a male Bharatnatyam dancer." (*The Plays of Mahesh Dattani* 71)

The complex web of relationships, which underplays ethics and morality, keeps a Dattani character entangled between his desire and duty, between what he can get and what he has to forgo, and between what he is and what he had been. This seemingly traumatic exercise leads the character into the cauldron of fuming acid where he suffocates, tends to loss himself, and gasps for fresh air for his whole being. His characters, an informed reader notes, tend to either ignore or escape what troubles them and plunder their assumed placidity. Tanu Pant rightly observes:

> [Dattni] deals with issues which are very much a part of the educated urban society but the people do not want to confront them and Dattani provides a platform for these issues, so that the people are aware of the fact that they are a reality and not just the fantasies of a playwright. (*The Plays of Mahesh Dattani* 46)

Reading a Dattani play, as a matter of fact, is like having a voyage deep into the sea of troubled water of relationships where the tempest of conflict intensifies its complexities. The discord in his plays, Rozario Ignatius maintains, "stem from the opposition between tradition and modernity in perception of matters relating to core human relationships like love, sex, marriage and even faith." (*The Plays of Mahesh Dattani* 107)

In the second flashback of Act two, the plan of destruction of Jairaj is executed by degrees. Ratna ceases to be a wife anymore. She makes him feel inferior in front of her acquaintances. She uses him as a prop, as a tool and as a choreographer for her dance items. She makes him dance on his weakest dance items. As a result his self-esteem is gone and he starts taking country liquor in order to overcome his frustration.

Dattani has exposed the trampled feelings of Jairaj with perfect artistic sensibility which, at the same time, reveals the hollowness and void of his inner self. He is nothing but a marionette in the hands of his father, wife and society. His will is not strong enough to enable him to face the trials and tribulations of life. He is deeply wounded to see his self-esteem mingled with dust. He says to his wife:

> "I want you to give me back my self-esteem!"
> Ratna says, "When did I ever take it?"
> Jairaj opens up, "Bit by bit. You took it when you insisted on top billing in all our programmes. You took it when you made me dance my weakest items. You took it when you arranged the lighting so that I was literally dancing in your shadow... And you call me disgusting."(69-70)

The scheme of Ratna to nullify her husband is an instance of self-centered humanity that stands on the platform of ruins of others and uses the debris for their upliftment. The relationship between Ratna and Jairaj is not based upon love and understanding. The foundation of their relation is the self-centred approach of Ratna who neither loves nor cares for her husband. The sanctity of their relation is always at stake as Ratna's foremost ambition in life is to be a successful dancer only. Had she loved her husband truly she would never have abiden by the desires of her father-in-law. Her stance is for the fulfilment for her earnest ambition and not for the softer delicacies of life. Her will is stronger than Jairaj and this becomes the reason of Jairaj's obliteration. Jairaj accuses Ratna to make entanglement with his father and destroying his career, "He knew he had us in his hands when we came back to him. We would have listened to anything he said"(70). Ratna reacts sharply and makes him realize of his inherent weakness and comments, "You would have listened. Not me. Yes! He realized he could not stop me. But he could stop you—through me."(70)

This blatant acceptance of Ratna proves how much she can stoop in order to translate her dreams. She has no concern with the well being of her husband. She survives only for her whimsical passions and visions. Jairaj becomes a decrepit wreck because his aspirations to become a Bharatanatyam dancer are reduced to ashes by the manipulation of his father and his wife. He bursts out and says:

> You destroy me first, then give the impression that there wasn't much to destroy in the first place, then blame it all on my father, then suggest I make myself useful by being your stage prop, then use the words 'regret' and expect me to shrug my shoulders, resign myself and believe that my calling in life is to serve you. (71)

Ratna reacts sharply at this and shows her husband his real worth by commenting, "[A]sk yourself your true worth and you will get your answer."(71)

Ratna is too engrossed in her dance that she ignores her duties as a mother and a wife as a result her son Shankar dies because of the overdose of opium given to him by the *aaya*. This instance, too, proves Ratna's failure as a sensitive human being. Later she focuses her attention on her daughter Lata and tries her level best to make her maiden performance a stupendous one. Lata gets rave reviews from the critics and her parents' dreams come true when they read about the scintillating presentation of her art form. When Lata is appreciated for her performance Ratna feels jealous of her own daughter and gets disturbed. She wants to paste the reviews of Ratna's performance in her own album. When Jairaj objects, "At least you have a daughter to be jealous of"(66). She breaks down and leaves for her bed-room.

Lata is married to Viswas and is blessed with a baby. Jairaj and Ratna die with the passage of time. When they meet in heaven Jairaj says, "We were only human. We lacked the grace. We lacked the brilliance. We lacked the magic to dance like God"(74). This uttering of Jairaj signifies the pettiness of human ambitions and aspirations to touch the apex of their dreams. Every human suffers from one fault or the other; as a result his quest for perfection in life only ends in discord and dissension. Ratna and Jairaj might have become successful dancers but they have failed terribly as a couple. The unison and harmony which is the prerequisite for a dance form is strangely missing from their own life. Art has the magic to transform the baser desires of human beings into the sublime ones. A true artist can reach the glory of God, provided, he leads a true and pure life without any manipulation to harm others. This is what remains missing in the life of Ratna and Amritlal. Both these characters lead a phony life utterly devoid from the basic human qualities of love and sympathy. The play ends on Jairaj's admission that they were only human and lacked the grace and magic to dance like God. Moreover, art can bloom only in the hands of those who are capable enough to rise above their individual interests and gains.

Dattani has brilliantly shown how the past of Ratna and Jairaj affects their present and dominates their overall mental makeup and thought process. The past of Jairaj's family continues to haunt his present and plays a vital role in framing his present though in a negative way. The past in the play becomes a living character that has its domination over the present that succumbs and becomes injured. The present attempts to revive itself but seems to fail. Dattani succeeds in reframing the present through past by attempting synchronization of discord among the characters at various levels.

Works Cited

Das, Sangeeta. "The Sensational Issues in the Plays of Mahesh Dattani." *The Plays of Mahesh Dattani.* Ed. R.K.Dhawan and Tanu Pant. New Delhi: Prestige Books, 2005.

Dattani, Mahesh. *Dance Like A Man.* New Delhi: Penguin, 2006. All references from the play have been included in the text.

De, Aditi. "Unmasking Our Worlds." http://www.hindu.com/lr/2005/08/07/stories

Dhawan, R.K. "The Plays of Mahesh Dattani: A Critical Response." *The Plays of Mahesh Dattani.* Ed. R.K.Dhawan and Tanu Pant. New Delhi: Prestige Books, 2005.

Ignatius, Rozario. "Contemporary Social Issues in the Plays of Mahesh Dattani", *The Plays of Mahesh Dattani,* ed. R.K.Dhawan and Tanu Pant, New Delhi: Prestige Books, 2005.

Kanakaraj, S. et al. "Psyche of Tempered Individuals in a World of Gender Politics: A Study of Mahesh Dattani's Select Plays." *Explorations in Indian English Drama.* Ed. T. Sai Chandra Mouli and M. Sarat Babu. Delhi: Authorpress, 2009.

Latha, A.Madhvi. "Unmasking the Realities of Dwarfed Maturity and Neutral Maturity." *Explorations in Indian English Drama.* Ed. T. Sai Chandra Mouli and M. Sarat Babu. Delhi: Authorpress, 2009.

Nair, Anita. "Mahesh Dattani-The Invisible Observer." May 2001 http:www.anitanair.net/profiles.

Pant, Tanu. "Mahesh Dattani: The Face of Indian Drama." *The Plays of Mahesh Dattani.* Ed. R.K.Dhawan and Tanu. New Delhi: Prestige Books, 2005.

Raju, B. Yadava. "Mahesh Dattni's *Dance Like a Man*: An Analysis in Technique and Theme." *The Plays of Mahesh Dattani.* Ed. R.K.Dhawan and Tanu. New Delhi: Prestige Books, 2005.

Uniyal, Ranu. "Conversing with Mahesh Dattani," *The Plays of Mahesh Dattani.* Ed. R.K.Dhawan and Tanu Pant. New Delhi: Prestige Books, 2005.

11

Mahesh Dattani's *Final Solutions*: A Brief Rereading

Pinaki Roy

Spectators watching Mahesh Dattani's *Final Solutions* (first performed in July 1993) or readers reading the 'Stage Play in Three Acts' cannot help comparing it outrightly with the Nazi-sponsored *Holocaust* and Anne Frank's *The Diary of a Young Girl* (1947), which was written in background of the militaristic-state-sponsored carnage that killed around 7.13 million Jews, Gypsies, Slavs, Pleas and Russians. The first-mentioned association comes with Dattani's usage of the title. While Adolf Hitler's cronies used the singular 'Endlösung' or 'Final Solution' as a codename for the extermination of particularly the Jewry, the Bengaluru-based Indo-Anglican dramatist's appendance of a 's' adds to the multifariousness of the communal clashes.

The second association is, however, more metaphorical. Dattani's play open as a diary entry that is being read out by Daksha, the early-life Hardika Gandhi. In the first volume of the *Penguin Original*-edition of *Mahesh Dattani: Collected Plays* (2000), Daksha's reading-out lasts for sixty-six lines and she continuously addresses her notebook as 'Dear Diary' (Dattani 165-7). By the time, her entry ends, it has described appalling religious carnages. Similarly, almost all the entries in Frank's

Diary, penned by a young girl initially delirious over the memoir's presentation amidst turbulent times, begins with endearing addresses to the diary. Importantly, both have suffered unbearably by the time readers have finished reading about them, and there comes their 'relationship'.

Alexandra Viets, in her "A Stark Look at Modern India", published in *The New York Times* of 27 July 1994, informs that *Final Solutions* was 'written early in 1991'. Whatever might have been the time of its conception, the play's second performance on 11 December 1993, and that too in India's financial capital, could not only have been more appropriate but also it required considerable courage on part of the dramatist and the director, Alyque Padamsee. On 6 December 1992, a 1,50,000-strong contingent of Hindu nationalists demolished the sixteenth century *Babri Mosque*, situated on the Ramkot Hills, Ayodhya, and communal riots broke out in many parts of India, particularly at Mumbai, Delhi, and Hyderabad, that killed off at least two thousand people and led to the 12 March 1993 *Mumbai Blasts*. In Mumbai alone, nine hundred and fifty people were butchered between December 1992 and January 1993. The integrated nation was facing the gravest threat since the early-post-independence English-sponsored communal hostilities. Enacted in this grim milieu, Dattani's *Final Solutions* won rave reviews as it exposed the futility of communal killings and underscored the fact that, as Padamsee writes, "[t]he demons of communal hatred are not out on the street...they are lurking inside ourselves. The mob in the play is symbolic of our own hatred and paranoia" (Dattani 161).

Mahesh Dattani has always been concerned with truthful depictions of the Indian society in his plays. In *Where There's a Will* (1988), the spirit of Hasmukh Mehta tries to retain control of his family by installing a former mistress in his house through a will. He comes to know how his greedy daughter-in-law has had hastened his death by substituting his blood pressure pills with vitamin tablets. *Dance Like a Man* (1989) focuses on the problematic relationship between the father, Amritlal, and his Bharatnatyam-dancing son, Jairaj. *Tara* (1990) deals with gender discrimination. *Bravely Fought the Queen* (1991) displays the boredom of suburbia and the emptiness of human lives reeling in capitalism. *On a Muggy Night in Bombay* (1998) is about the turmoil the homosexual Kamalesh faces when he learns that his sister is scheduled to marry his former lover. Cody and Springchorn outrightly identify *Final Solutions* as a play that deals exclusively with 'communal hatred' (328). Prasad and Subhashini add:

> In *Final Solutions*, Dattani gets to grips with the sectarian tension and mistrust between two major communities of India. The tense interface between the two communities of India in the aftermath of Partition provides the context for the basic situation. As the situation triggers action, the play unfolds palpable tension, which climaxes into a final confrontation between the frenzied bands of the two communities and then into a statement on tolerant togetherness. The initial situation depicts a communal riot, which has periodically tended to throw Hindus and Muslims into spontaneous combustion. The play establishes the initial situation in such a way as to foreshadow the tensions, which emerge in the action. The ideas, which are discussed, grow out of and illuminate the course of action embodied in characters.

Most of the *dramatis personae* of Dattani's 1993 play possess ironically-applied names or surnames. The split personality of 'Daksha' and 'Hardika' deserves first mention. Significantly, 'Daksha' is an archetypal name—an incarnation of the Hindu god, Vishnu, who changed himself into a beautiful woman and is still commemorated before different holy rites. On the other hand, Daksha, the son of Lord Brahma, became responsible for the death of his daughter, Parvati, when he was lambasting his son-in-law, Lord Shiva, and became symbolic of perpetrator of strife (Sarkar 207-08). Through her diary entries and subsequent appearance in the play, Daksha first appears as a beautiful and persecuted child-bride, who slowly sows within herself the seeds of communal prejudices and later changes herself into the discriminating 'Hardika'. Significantly, 'Hardika', like 'Daksha', is not a Gujrati name at all but a first name of the Marathi girls, and it means 'full of love', which obviously she is not.

Bijay Kumar Das underscores the importance of Hardika-Ramnik Gandhi relationship in conveying the massage of tolerance and peacefulness at the conclusion of *Final Solutions*. To quote him:

> Ramnik tells his mother [Hardika] that the owner of their shop was a Muslim and after an earlier riot, when he left, the shop was bought by Ramnik's father at half its price. That is why he wants to make amends for it by giving a job to Javed. Hardika tells her son why he kept it a secret from her. Ramnik answers, 'You have to live with this shame for a few years now'. The play ends with Hardika's regret for the past misunderstanding and change of heart (54).

Next in importance comes Ramnik Gandhi, the patriarch of the Amargaon family with which the hounded Babban (alias 'Bobby') and Javed find refuge. It is unnatural that any Indian would miss the connotation of Ramnik's famous surname, and while speaking on phone to Noor Ahmed of Jeevnagar regarding the 'safety' of his daughter Tasneem, he jokes, "No relation to the Father of the Nation, of course. It is a common surname" (Dattani 170). In the essay, "Critique of Violence: Mahesh Dattani's *Final Solutions*", Gill identifies Ramnik Gandhi to be as guilty as the perpetrators of communal violence, added to which he is a hypocrite[2]. In this context, readers of the Indian history can only recall how Mohandas Karamchand Gandhi had, during a conversation with Abul Kalam Azad on 3 March 1947, asserted that India would be divided over his dead body but failed to stop not only the partition but also the ensuing religious carnages. A critical coalescing of the Indian leader with Ramnik Gandhi would not be out of context.

In course of dialogues with Javed and Bobby, Ramnik Gandhi tries to make them wake up to the futility of violence and offers to employ Javed. Interestingly, he lips communal harmony but suspects Muslims to be behind every act of violence. When this is revealed during an altercation with Javed, Ramnik Gandhi slaps him:

> Why must I defend myself to you? You are the criminal...no matter how much you attack me, you cannot justify your being a riot-rouser. [...] You...you scum. If I had known what you were... (Dattani 198).

Aruna Gandhi, the wife of Ramnik and the mother of Smita, is presented in the play as a meek and religious woman intermittently shocked at the rudeness of her college-going daughter. Laxmi Sharma, in her article "Social Issues in the Plays of Mahesh Dattani", seems to accuse Aruna of obliviousness and complacence. Gill thus focuses on the role of Aruna Gandhi, whose first name ironically relates to the sun:

> Bobby [...] tries to convince Aruna [Gandhi] that God is not biased by picking up the idol and grasp it in his hands: 'you can not remove my smell with sandal paste and attars and fragrant flowers because it belongs to human being who believes, tolerates, and respects what other human beings believe that is the strongest fragrance in the world'. By doing so, [...] [he] at the same time hurts the sentiments of Aruna, a Hindu woman, when, in fact, Islam does not allow any women to ever

> enter their mosques, showing open disrespect towards women. However, hurting Aruna's feelings can be a small offence on Bobby's part when Aruna, perturbed over this action cries, 'Oh! Is there nothing left that is sacred in this world?' He tries to calm her by the logic of fraternity and forgiveness: 'The tragedy is that there is too much that is sacred. But if we understand and believe in one another nothing can be destroyed.... And if you are willing to forget. I'm willing to tolerate'. Later on Aruna herself admits to god's oneness. Through dialogues and reflections like these, Dattani makes a strong plea for humanism, love and understanding.

If Aruna Gandhi symbolises passionate religiosity which often results in the communal confrontations in India, Smita Gandhi has a more tolerant and liberated mindset. The name 'Smita' means 'ever-smiling' in Sanskrit, and she has the potency to bring smile to the strife-tired Indians by protesting against the narrow-minded religious views usually nursed by family seniors. She thus stands up to the implication of her name. Chaudhuri especially appreciates Ramnik's daughter for her direct way of speaking:

> The smug and often parsimonious Aruna is shaken out of her complacency though Smita's outburst against her rigid and restrictive practices that have for long chocked her. [...] The diminutive Smita suddenly gains stature and individual identity, unafraid to speak up for what she thinks is right, maintaining that she had kept her silence only to remain non-partisan, to both her parents (81).

Oommen has censured the character of Smita for betraying the trust her friend Tasneem has placed in her. She has publicised it that Javed is "a jihad-mercenary, hired to start riots" (Oommen 352).

Smita Gandhi also provides a romantic angle to the play which otherwise deals with the complexities and racialities lurking within human relationships. She falls in love with Babban who does not belong to her religion and repeated attempts to suppress her feelings take her almost to the realm of paranoia. Das writes about how Dattani makes it clear as the play advances that "Bobby and Smita knew each other" (Das 53). However, her past and rekindled attraction to Babban (also known as 'Bobby') becomes problematised when she learns that he is in love with Tasneem, and this forces her to intrôspect. She reviews the rituals she has had been following and begins to nurse animosity towards her own faith, oblivious to the fact that certain rituals are prevalent in Islam too. She feels like 'a rat in the hole' (Dattani 210) and is bent on showing that her religiously-minded mother has had been wrong in disallowing the two Muslim entrants – Javed and Babban – from filling water from pitcher or eating with them. When an indignant Aruna Gandhi inquires whether being a Hindu 'stifles her', she replies, "No living with one does [...] [b]ecause you know they don't believe in all the things that you feel are true. Doesn't that make your belief that much more weak? Do two young boys make you so insecure? Come on, mummy. This is a time for strength! I am so glad that these two dropped in. We have never spoken about what makes us too different from each other. We would have gone on living our lives with our petty similarities?" (ibid. 211).

The presences of the two characters, Bobby/Babban and Javed, who belong to the minority community, make Dattani's play both poignant and intriguing. During the play's first performance at *Guru Nanak Bhawan*, Bengaluru, on 10 July 1993, these two roles were played respectively by Preetam Koilpillai and Rahul Matthan. The name 'Babban', of Kurdish origin (usually given to females) signifies 'friendship', while the Persian name 'Javed' means 'exempth from death' or 'eternal'. They are actually young men hired by religiô-politically-motivated people to disrupt social harmony. Dattani implies that by participating in such disruptive activities, these unsuspecting young men not only aggravate interreligious tensions but also endanger their own lives because their hirers would not be ready to rescue them if they were in danger. Javed is exploited by politicians in name of 'jihad' or 'holy war', and true to his name, he becomes an 'eternal' enemy of the Hindus, allowing himself to be trained in acts of sabotaging. During a conversation with Ramnik Gandhi, he recalls, "It was different when I used to attend the meetings. I was swayed by what now appears to me as cheap sentiment. They always talked about motherland and fighting to save our faith and how we should get four of theirs for every one of ours" (ibid. 205).

Sent to a Hindu 'mohalla' to disrupt a 'ratha yatra', Javed remembers the basic (but erroneous) concept of 'jihad' and throws a stone to the carnivalesque procession, resulting in a spree of violence and stampede in which the head priest, 'poojari', is killed. Bobby – friendly to the core as his name suggests – saves him and finds him shelter in Ramnik Gandhi's house. It is where the two Islamic youths review their past actions and find themselves both sinners and sinned-against. Javed recalls his action of hitting the procession hard. He had been handed a stone and a knife by a politically-motivated criminal and he 'screamed with pleasure' as he came in sight of the 'poojari'. However, when the moment of killing the priest arrives, he humanely fails to act:

> The poojari backed away, his last words were his god's name. He looked up at the knife in my hand as I lifted it above the heads around me. He begged for mercy but I couldn't hear him at all! There were screams all around and I was screaming too, but no longer with joy as fear came faster and faster confusing me! I got nauseous and cried. Why am I here? What am I doing here? [...] I let go of the knife. [...] The knife fell to the ground. The joyride was over (ibid. 208).

However, Javed's self-desistment does not save the priest. He watches "someone pick up the knife and pierce the poojari" (ibid. 208).

Painting a conceivable 'terrorist' with sentiments and humanity, Dattani requests his readers who are religiously biased and tend to presume to be aware of the dangers of such presumptions. These only lead to mindless killings and make societies susceptible to external aggressions.

Gill writes how there is an identifiable similarity between Hardika Gandhi and Javed:

> Hardika and Javed both have the bitter tastes of the minority community. Hardika's father was murdered because they were member of the minority Hindu community in Pakistan during Partition and Javed has become a terrorist because he is from the minority Muslim community in India. Javed explains to Ramnik his reasons for involving himself in terrorism and acts of sabotage on the Hindu procession ('Rath Yatra'): 'Anyone sitting at home, sipping tea and reading the newspapers will say that it is obvious that a minority would never start a riot, we are too afraid that it had to be politically motivated'. [This shows that] [t]he selfish and petty politicians still play with the emotions of the young people like Javed and Babban, instigate them to create violence and use them for their own ends.

Bobby/Babban is brought in as a moderator between the fanatical Javed and the prejudiced Aruna Gandhi. If he has had sinned by saving an initiator of a carnage, Bobby absolves himself of more sins by trying to make Ramnik Gandhi see the pointlessness of interreligious hatreds and convincing Aruna Gandhi of the non-biased attitude of God. However, Oommen further adds:

> Bobby is ashamed of who he is and camouflages the Muslim name 'Babban'. Just as Bobby tries to turn Javed away from the violence of mindless rioting, Smita's outburst works against him. Bobby returns the audience to the fable. He picks up the

> Hindu idol to prove to Javed the absurdity of imaginary sacrilege and the senselessness of payback. [...] *Final Solutions* troubles the audience with a question from the past, of the sense of belonging, of strictures of inclusion and exclusion (352).

The chorus (shown by masks) plays a very important role in *Final Solutions*. If the title of the play, alluding to the Holocaust, hints at the brutalities and carnages as means frequently adopted for 'cleaning' societies, it also offers solutions to end the hostilities – the will of mind to rise above prejudices and refute the religio-political instigations and exploitations. The mob – wavering between Hindu communalists and Muslim fundamentalists – is both implicated for its role in spreading violence and exorcised by being shown the pointlessness of racial hatreds. The presence of the chorus/mob, who like in (Samik Bandyopadhyay's translated version of) Mahasweta Devi's *Mother of 1084* (Act VII) (*Modern Indian* 695-7), serve to suggest the atmosphere of impending massacres, takes the play to an expressionistic level. Prasad and Subhashini write, "The Mob/Chorus wearing and changing their masks (five men and ten masks on sticks) conveniently exposes the radical elements clinging to the externals of faith". Dattani's own note on the chorus must also be mentioned:

> Since *Final Solutions* is an experiment in time and space and relates to memory, it is a play, which involves a lot of introspection on the part of the characters in the play and thus induces similar introspection in the viewers. I have attempted to experiment with the chorus. It has been used in a style, which I would like to call 'realistic stylisation'. The chorus represents the conflicts of the characters. Thus the chorus is a sense is the psychophysical representation of the characters and also provides the audience with the visual images of the characters' conflicts. There is no stereotyped use of the characterisation of the chorus because communalism has no face, it is an attitude and thus it becomes an image of the characters.

Considering that the first Indian English play – *The Persecuted, or, Dramatic Scenes Illustrative of the Present Sate of the Hindoo Society in Calcutta* (1831) by Krishna Mohon Bandyopadhyay – began with societal depiction, Dattani has, in his *Final Solutions*, managed to keep the focus almost unwavering. In between, one may recall such societal, mythological and historical plays to have been staged as Michael Madhusudan Dutt's *Ratnavali* (1858), C.S. Nazir's *The First Parsi Baronet* (1866), D.M. Wadia's *The Indian Heroine* (1877), P.V.R. Raju's *Urjoon Singh, or, The Princess Regained* (1875), Ramkinoo Dutt's *Manipura Tragedy* (1893), Krishnamacharya's *Dasaratha, or, The Fatal Promise* (1901), A. Srinivasacharya's *Harishchandra, or, The Martyr to Truth* (1912), Krishna Iyer's *Lord Clive* (1913), P.P. Meherjee's *Dolly Persen* (1918), (the plays collected in) V.V. Srinivasa Aiyangar's *Dramatic Divertissements* (1921), the several plays of Harendranath Chattopadhyay, T.P. Kailasam, and Bharati Sarabhai.

The postcolonial phase in Indian English playwriting – the 'adept' phase identified after Barry (196) – which continues with Dattani's dramas, began with G.V. Desani's *Hali* (1950). Pratap Sharma followed it with *A Touch of Brightness* (1968) and *The Professor has a Warcry* (1970). The postcolonial dramatist Asif Currimbhoy's popular productions include *The Tourist Mecca* (1959), *The Doldrummers* (1960), *The Captives* (1963), *Goa* (1964), *The Hungry Ones* (1965), *Monsoon* (1965), *An Experiment with Truth* (1969), *Inquilab* (1970), *The Refugee* (1971), *Sonar Bangla* (1972), *Om Mane Padme Hum* (1972), *The Miracle Seed* (1973), and *The Dissident M.L.A.* (1974). Nissim Ezekiel contributed to the subgenre of Indian English plays with *Marriage Poem: A Tragicomedy* (1969), *Nalini: A Comedy* (1969), and *The Sleepwalkers* (1969). Girish Karnad produced *Yayati* in 1961 and *Tughlaq* in 1964; Dina Mehta *The Myth-Makers* and *Brides are not for Burning* respectively in 1969 and 1971; Gurucharan Das produced *Larins Sahib* in 1970, Cyrus Mistry *Doongaji House* in 1990, and Manjula Padmanabhan *Lights Out!*, *The Artist's Model*, and *Sextet* respectively in 1984, 1995, and 1996.

Dattani's plays are postcolonial in their employment of the Indianised form of the English language – something very necessary for the assertion of postcoloniality as Loomba understands (66) – and in presenting in a country that has been ravaged by the greedy English colonisers. The Hindu-Muslim diversions in *Final Solutions* are identifiably the results of the partition of India engineered the English imperialists in 1947. Though Santwana Haldar, in her *Mahesh Dattani's 'Final Solutions': A Critical Study* has focused on themes like communal riots in India, protest and anger, guilt-consciousness, presentation of pictures of Indian society, stagecraft and dramatic devices and symbolism, the theme of postcolonial identifiably dominates the three-act 1993 play. Prasad and Subhashini continue to extend their focus on the ravages generated by the partition of India by the English:

> Hard facts are glossed over in the evocative accounts of past violence in that such stories are circulated to construct a quintessential dichotomy and fortify crude ethnic particularities.' Increased communal polarisation is promoted by painting the other group as the real culprit. In an interview, Urvashi Butalia points out the grossly partisan role of rumours in stoking up bitter Partition memories: '[I]n individual and collective memory, inside families particularly which is where this history of partition is largely contained, it's very one-sided. You hear from families about their victimhood, but you never hear about their involvement in the violence'. In a context of intense political mobilisation religious support is sought to be consolidated by mounting a hate campaign against the rival communal group.

Dattani has Daksha to corroborate this point:

> He [Daksha's father] said that before leaving, they [the Britishers] had let loose the dogs. I hated to think that he was talking about my friend's fathers... But that night in Hussainabad in our ancestral house –when I heard them outside—I knew that they were thinking the same of us. And I knew that I was thinking the same, like my father. And as their voices grew louder, I blamed them more and more for my father's absence. The windows broke, one by one. My mother and myself, we hid in the pooja room. The stones came smashing into our home. I clung to my mother. My mother clung to the family idol of Lord Krishna'.

Deshpande, in his 'Introduction' to *Modern Indian Drama*, writes of the post-independence plays like Dattani's that such plays have had to be responses not only to the plays of the colonial period but also need to be modern. He hails such plays for 'announcing the end of imperialism' (*Modern Indian* xiv).

It may be stated in conclusion that Mahesh Dattani's *Final Solutions* not only tries to accentuate the efforts of the maintenance of peace and harmony as being undertaken by some conscious individuals, it also seeks of become one of the flawless specimens of Indian dramas in English. Chaudhuri has already identified the play as a 'turning point' in Dattani's dramatic career (39). One can only hope that the audience/readers grew more receptive to the social messages implied in *Final Solutions* and desist themselves from acting out violently as and when religio-politically motivated individuals lambasted people from other religions to them.

Works Cited

Barry, Peter. *Beginning Theory*. New Delhi: Viva Books Pvt. Ltd., 2008.

Chaudhuri, Asha Kuthari. *Mahesh Dattani: An Introduction*. New Delhi: Foundation Books, 2005.

Das, Bijay Kumar. *Form and Meaning in Mahesh Dattani's Plays*. New Delhi: Atlantic Publishers and Distributors Pvt. Ltd., 2008.

Dattani, Mahesh. *Collected Plays – Volume I*. New Delhi: Penguin Books, 2000.

Haldar, Santwana. *Mahesh Dattani's 'Final Solutions': A Critical Study*. New Delhi: Prestige Books, 2008.

Loomba, Ania. *Colonialism/Postcolonialism*. 2nd edn. London and New York: Routledge, 2005. Rpt. 2007.

Modern Indian Drama: An Anthology. Ed. Deshpande, G.P. New Delhi: Sahitya Akademi, 2000. Rpt. 2004.

Oommen, Susan. "*Inventing Narratives, Arousing Audiences*: The Plays of Mahesh Dattani". *New Theatre Quarterly 68* 17(4), November 2001: 347-57.

Sarkar, Sudhir Chandra. *A Dictionary of Mythology*. Kolkata: M.C.Sarkar and Sons Pvt. Ltd., 1958. Rpt. 1985.

The Columbia Encyclopaedia of Modern Drama, Volume – I. Eds. Cody, Gabrielle H., and Evert Sprinchorn. New York: Columbia University Press, 2007.

12

Marginalization and Identity Crisis in Mahesh Dattani's *Seven Steps Around the Fire*

Archana Bhattacharjee and Bhairaban Borah

> Man has created a very complex language called theatre. A language that has the ability to redefine the natural concept of time, space and movement. A language that goes beyond the verbal a movement that goes beyond the physical. Through this language of theatre he has been able to see himself for who he is what he has made of himself and what he aspires to be. (*JIWE*, Jan. 2002, 1)

This is the comment delivered by Mahesh Dattani at Ravindra Kalakshetra on 11 February, 2011 as part of the Krishi Festival plays to celebrate the 50th Anniversary of Bengali Theatre in Bangalore as he intended to achieve a harmony (that is missing). His desire is to have an identity of our own and:

> ...to form our cultural identities we need all three traditions, continuity and change. It is when we accept the need for all three in our theatre that we can truly have a theater movement that is inextricable linked to the development of cultural, social and individual identities. (*JIWE*, Jan. 2002, 4)

India has rich heritage of drama from the ancient time. Drama in India begins its journey with Sanskrit plays. A. L. Basham, a prominent historian expresses his view in this manner: "The origin of Indian theatre is still obscure. It is certain however that even in the Vedic period dramatic performances of some kind were given and passing references in early resources point to enaction at festivals of religious legends, perhaps only in dance and mime". Indian traditions are preserved in Natyashastra', the oldest of the texts of the theory of the drama. This play claims for the drama divine and a close connection with the sacred *Vedas* themselves. The origin of Indian English drama can be traced to the ancient rules and seasonal festivities of the Vedic Aryans. The dramatic performances of those times mainly included such events like depiction of events of daily life accompanied by music. Some members of the tribe acted as if they were wild animals and some others were the hunters. In such a crude and simple way was drama performed during the age of the Vedic Aryans. Later, difference episodes from the *Ramayana* (Ram Leea) the *Mahabharata* and the *Bhagavad Gita* were chosen and dramatized in front of the people. Drama in Sanskrit literature is covered under the broad umbrella of Rupaka which means depiction of life in its various aspects represented in forms by actors who assumes various roles.

Rise of Modern Drama

The rise of modern drama dates back to the eighteenth century when the British Empire strengthened its power in India. The modern Indian owed its first flowering to the foreign grafting with the impact of Western civilization of Indian life; a new renaissance dawned on Indian arts including drama. Furthermore, English education gave an impetus and a momentum to the critical study of Western drama. The Western impact awakened the dormant critical impulse in the country and to bring Indians face to face with new forms of life and literature and to open the way for a fruitful cross fertilization of ideas and forms of expression.

Unlike poetry and fiction which have flourished in speed, sustained by the fertile imagination and the creation talent of poet and novelist, drama in Indian soil suffered and lagged behind because of the want of dramatist and the conducive atmosphere facilitating its growth by thematic and effective dramatic derives. Of course, dramatists like Tagore and Harrindranata Charropadhyaya were there but with their own limitations.

Modern Indian dramatic writing in English is neither rich in quantity nor on the whole is of high quality. Enterprising Indians have for nearly a century occasionally attempted drama in English—but seldom for actual stage production.

The causes for such paucity in Indian drama are very many. Languages, dialogue, settings, stagecraft are some of the impediments in the way of Indian drama making its progress practically an impasse. The credit of rejuvenating Indian drama by infusing a new life into it goes to modern dramatists whose service is a sort of instant elixir to the staggering and slugging drama. Among the modern Indian dramatists Girish Karnard stands out by the singular sign he made by his feat diversely as a dramatist, director action on the stage, screen and TV media.

Dattani as a Modern Dramatist

While we talk about the true successor of Girish Karnard, of course Mahesh Dattani comes in front, who champions the true art, free from any theory, universal in taste and flavour appealing to all section of society never bound to any caste, class and creed. His plays emerged as fresh arrival in the domain of Indian drama in the last decade of twentieth century. Theatre, according to him, "Is a reflection of what you observe. To do anything more would be to become didactic and then it ceases to be theatre." What he observes can well be seen in almost all his chief plays where he has tried his best to assimilate both matter and manner. Although each and every play of his raises some prominent issues concerning the various maladies contaminating the healthy tissues of the society, he is never seen didactic and straightforward in his attitude. He knows the art of expressing the views through some powerful images, symbols, stage direction and other means of art. He himself observes that in his plays "everything is geared towards rasa." His plays deal with the contemporary issues. They are plays of today sometimes as actual as to cause controversy, but at the same time they are plays which embody many of the classic concerns of world drama. He moulds his subjects in such a way that it is both topical as well as appealing. He makes an abundant use of mythology rituals and traditions and contemporary problems. India is beset with but he elevates these themes to a higher level, touching the human chords that emanate love, happiness, sexual fulfilment and problem of identity. It is in the fitness of things that we make an attempt at evaluating the playwright's thematic concerns as well as his exploration of and experimentation with stage.

Mahesh Dattani's *Seven Steps Around the Fire*

Seven Steps Around the Fire shows Dattani a master of language and characterization. As a playwright he was not afraid to work within a relatively conventional dramatic structure to tell a story that was bold and powerful without ever being melodramatic. The stated play beautifully deals with the pathetic plight of the *hijras,* their ways of life, their ardent sense of individual identity in a callous and cruel atmosphere where a minister had the young *hijra* burned to death. Uma, the daughter of the Vice-Chancellor of Bangalore University is a postgraduate student of Sociology uncovers the truth behind the murder of a *hijra.* Unlike a sleuth, she uses uncommon means to discover the truth. She boldly goes to the locality of the *hijra's,* community and asks questions to them. Her attitude to the eunuchs is very friendly and sympathetic. Though her husband Suresh Rao is the chief of superintendent of police, he is unable to solve the knots of the mysterious murder of a *hijra*. Constable Munswamy who was tasked by Suresh Rao with keeping his wife out of danger, creates a sense of humour and makes the story more enjoyable. Kamala, a beautiful *hijra* eunuch has been secretly married to Sabbu, the son of a government minister. The minister got this *hijra* burned to death and arranged a marriage reception for his son to marry an acceptable girl of his choice. But the table is turned. At the wedding, all the *hijras* sing and dance and Sabbu in a fit of anger takes out a gun and kills himself.

Each one of us is marginal in a way, residing in a no man's land-between crisis and comfort zone-trying to belong to the comfort level while the crisis pulls us back. We are all in a midst of some momentous change waiting for something that will remake the boundaries of human existence, extends to the conception of sexual life. Whatever is lost, some new possibility opens up. The fragmentation of traditional social forms creates in which new innovations of intimacy can appear.

> Two things what I want to be and what I am not. My chest will never be huge. My legs are too thin. My nose is an old shape. I want what Man's health pushes. I want to be guy in Gillete commercials. (Dorothy E. Smith—1926)

Ideally Narcissus, in reality a college student, talks about his desire to the journalist, the same desire that instigate us to venture different things in life which are not necessarily/always sexual. It is the desire to be categorized to belong to a certain space so as to get others' attention. The flipside of this is that this desire, when promises to deviate from the given societal norms is strangulated by the society itself. This is what we find in the marginalized characters in Mahesh Dattani's plays. They are all standing in front of the mirror looking at their desiring self like this college students knowing fully well that they cannot be what they desire because their self-images/masks are manipulated by the society and which change from one situation to another as the other selves get prioritized over the other.

Dattani's technique is to pirouette around the identities located in the grey areas of the society and place discreet spot light on the section of people that comes into contact with both the orthodox (with their colonized minds) and the unorthodox (with their decolonized minds)-to hold "a mirror up to society". The characters are always searching for the fulfilment of their identity which they are unable to find in their partial identity.

Broadly speaking, the concept of marginality can be interpreted and used from two points of view – in the sense of 'not integrated into' and 'excluded from'. The former applies to a dualist view of society and refers to the people who are moving from one sector to the other and not yet fully incorporated into the latter like the homosexuals. Furthermore we must remember that the locus of heterosexual is a historical construct. As a matter of fact the first recorded use of the word "Homosexual" was in 1869 by Karl-Maria Kertben, with Richard Freiherr von Krafft-Ebing's 1886 book *Psychopathia Sexual* is popularizing the concept. The latter refers to those as marginal who are driven away from, or prevented from participating in the dominant culture and its institution which includes the *hijras* and the transsexuals. There are various references in Sanskrit as well as in Pali texts of Kliba, Pandaka, Tritiyaprakriti, or a more common Napumsaka providing historical evidence for the pre-modern (and pre-Islamic) concept of sexuality and the category of sexual thirdness in India.

Talking in an interview with Sudha Menon Dattani says: "being gay or lesbian is not right or wrong, it is the reality and we have to learn to accept alternate relationships and live with them." Homosexuality leads to a kind of homophobia as it is imagined as a threat to, and of, masculinity. This creates a short of sexual anxiety in others. Sexual orientation/instinct/desire is located in one's private domain which one is free to access publicly. A homosexual may not publicly acknowledge his orientation for the fear of being disintegrated. The complexity arises in the case of those who are easily identified by their physical attributes like the *hijras* who are simply excluded from the mainstream society.

For many Indian—both upper and middle class—*hijras* exist (and to some extent have always existed) at the periphery of their imaginaries, making themselves visible only on certain circumscribed ritual occasions. They are believed to be endowed with the power to confer fertility on newlyweds and newborn children ("traditional" ritual power) as Uma confides in *Seven Steps Around the Fire.*

> Perceived as the lowest of the low, they yearn for family and love. The two events in mainstream Hindu culture where their presence is acceptable—marriage and birth-ironically are the very same privileges denied to them by man and nature. (33)

It is not just Uma, who acknowledges the emotional upheavals in the *hijras'* interior domin; Dattani also makes them sexually attractive as Sabbu, the minister's son, weds the 'beautiful' *hijra* Kamala. But this does not suffice as an identity marker rather it is but an incident captured in a photograph (taken after Sabbu-Kamala's marriage) for the posterity. This reminds us of Pedro Almodovar;s film to do *Sobse in Madre* (English titled – *All About My Mother*) where Menuela does not keep one half of the photograph featuring her partner who happens to be a transsexual hooker. She is compromising herself with the society and does not want to reveal her son, Esteban, the hidden half of his birth which is otherwise 'tabooed'. The marginal is pushed to maintain that 'given' identity otherwise face the same fate as Kamala faced as she was burnt to death. The mystery behind the death is there in the police—politician—crime nexus which is a postcolonial development. The evidence is destroyed but the consciousness remains. Dattani's deconstruction of his own beauty parlance is a post modernist approach. "I scratched her face, hoping she will become ugly and Sabbu will forget her ...She was beautiful, very beautiful." That is why, Salim's wife put fire to her beautiful skin and burnt her to the other world. It seems to reflect the discourse of sub version and liberation against the politics of hegemony. Dattani's appears to be a reformist, with a setting both the traditional and modern, unable to find out any alternative solution. This genderless sub-group also constructs its mark of difference, its feminity by wearing saris.

As we can refer the term "Subaltern" to the marginalized group this "subaltern" in *Seven Steps around the Fire* is forced to maintain silence against oppression and injustice. Since the concept of marginality can be interpreted and used from two points of view: in the sense of not integrated into an excluded from." The former applies to a dualist view of society and refers to the people who are moving from one sector to other and not yet fully incorporated into the latter like the homosexuals. The latter refers to those as marginal who are driven among from, or prevented from participating in the dominant cultural and institutions which includes the *hijras* and transsexuals.

In the traditional society of India, the identity of gays, lesbian, *hijras*, and homosexual has not yet been organized. Dattani dramatizes the crisis of those relationships that are not rigidly demarcated in terms of socially accepted gender constructions. Dattani's play *Seven Steps Around the Fire* represents the voice of eunuch community who are not even allowed to show their faces in public. The play deals with the violence inflicted on the *hijras*, who are unseen and unheard in the society. The play expresses the identity crisis of the *hijras* and their heartfelt longing for being treated as a social being in an indifferent society.

Uma Rao, the sociology scholar, emerges, as the most powerful character of the play, the month piece of the playwright who fights to establish the identity of a eunuch. Kamala, during her research on the class and gender related violence and crime. It's justice in the nemesis of the play. A eunuch, a beautiful one, invited for marriage, and the final tragic death—all seem to be a misconstruction. But it happens. The mystery behind the death is in the police-politician-crime nexus. Uma Rao's research on this ancient tribe brings into focus the hypocrisy and repression that 'the big shots' are capable of because they are beyond the reach of law. The society accepts a *hijra* for gracing the ceremonies of marriage and birth but would not allow him to partake of such ceremonies. The author has ironically portrayed this aspect that would not have otherwise heart-rending story about a *hijra*, murdered simply because he fell in love with Sabbu, a young man with a status of importance in society, feels us with horror and sense of injustice. When the facts of her being a *hijra* are revealed to people, she is mercilessly murdered. Her deprivation in terms of essential feminity instead of arousing sympathy and a feeling of compassion in looked down upon; she is discriminated against and ultimately murdered. A sense of horror and injustice prevails for it is not by choice but by sheer misfortune that she is what she is. For many Indians—both upper and middle class—*hijras* exist at the periphery of their imagination, making themselves visible only on certain occasions.

We feel somewhat uncomfortable when they emerge out of nowhere in a public space, especially in the trains and malls, and we combat the advancing uncomforting situations with a meagre amount forcing out of our disgusted fingers. Do we repel due to their physical attributes or due to the mystery behind them? But why at all we feel repulsive of them? Again the notion of values comes in. That they are to be de-valued in the notion we grew up with, as if 'given' by the society. Yet there is a "yearn" as Uma says to be integrated into the society. This desire is partly actualized by their attributing mainstream relationship between themselves as Anarkali calls Kamala her 'Sister'. Even they try to establish relationship with those supposedly located in the centre as the following conservation between Uma and Anarkali suggest.

> ANARKALI (sympathically) Oh! (*Smokes*) If you were a *hijra*, I would have made you my sister.
> UMA: Oh! Thank you.
> ANARKALI: But you are not a *hijra*, no?
> UMA: No Anarkali, So you will not be my sister.
> *Pause.*
> UMA: Of course we can be sister!
> ANARKALI: Where are you and where am I?

Knowing full well their standpoint Anarkali could even feel the futility of Uma's desire which she herself acknowledges. "I do not have any power!" In a rare moment of privileged presence of Uma, Anarkali comes out of her marginalized self and articulates passionately in front of Munswamy. "We make our relations with our eyes. With our love! Look at him, he looks at me, and he is my brother! Look at you. You look at me and we are mother and daughter." But on articulating her passion in public she is confronted by the 'given' behavioural code and immediately puts her mask that we are accustomed to. Her conversion shows how the identity shifts, very clearly.

> ANARKALI ...Oh, brother, give me a cigarette, na.
>
> MUNSWAMY. Shut up. And don't call me brother
>
> ANARKALI. Just one na (Very sexual.) I will do anything for you brother. Give na.
>
> MUNSWAMY. Chee! Who would want to...(flustered) I-I don't smoke.
>
> ANARKAL. If you had a beautiful sister, you will give her a cigarette for a fuck, no?

A part of their identity is always marginalized but the other half comes out of the closet within them only. Dattani here questions the whole notion on tolerance. We claim to know about them, they are as Uma says:

> ...the invisible minority. Behind Russel market, knew where to find them, although I could not see any hizras on the street. They only come out in groups and made their presence felt by their peculiar loud hand claps.

Yet they make their presence felt residing in the closest with their loud hand claps accompanied by the dancing better on their feet, an oxymoronic symbol (of liberation and confinement). The loud hand clap becomes their identity markets. They rarely get the chance of getting acknowledgement publicly. Yet they have to survive in this otherwise hostile world.

Just now everybody wants to talk about identity. As a key wood in contemporary politics it has taken our so many different connotations that sometimes it is obvious that people are not even talking about the same thing. One thing at least is clear – identity only becomes an issue when it is in crisis. When something assumed to be fixed coherent and stable is displaced by the experience of doubt and uncertainty. From this angle, the eagerness to talk about identity is symptomatic of the post modern predicament of contemporary politics.

Without delving deep into the politics of marginal identify what we could form from Mercer's view is to, overcome the crisis an individual puts up different self images which are nothing but social masks. She/he adjusts the mask according to the need of the given situation.

Moments create self images and self images are the basic units upon which an identity is formed. Within the interactive sphere, an individual according to particular social situations forms his identity what Schlenker calls composite identify. If one can assume a self-image of a homosexual then translates it into an identity with the others/society and develops certain behavioral strategies to maintain that particular image in daily life thereby a new identity gets incorporated into an overall sense of self. The society determines the sexual orientation/instinct as the marker of one's identity in regard to homosexual.

But the self image of the transsexual like Kamala is constructed according to given circumstance which is a function of nature. With this self identity she fell in love with Sabbu a young man status of importance in society. When the fact of being *hijra* is revealed she is mercilessly murdered. Being a transsexual and her feeling of love is not right or wrong, but it is very much embarrassing that her deprivation in terms of essential femininity is looked down upon. A sense of horror and injustice prevails for each not by choice but by sheer misfortune that she is what she is. Obviously a question arises whether only the sexual orientation and the presence of genitals is marker of one's identity. In this crisis zone they are still surviving.

> Those who survive are those who do not defy the gravity of others. And those who desires even a moment of freedom, find themselves hurled into space, doomed to crush with some unknown forces.

The civilizations, the social structure, the theology, the laws, all regard heterosexuality as the only sexual activity. So, all other kind of sexuality is unnatural and thus they are perversion. So, judged against the touchstone of heterosexuality, homosexuality, transsexuality are perversion, a sin and an act of evil desire. Heterosexuality was established as a norm in the society in terms of sexuality. Anthropologists like Grayle Robin and feminist theorist like Luce Irigaray point to the capitalist mode of production in society as main sector of the prevalence of heterosexuality. There may be another very peculiar reason which can be thought one of the main factors that helped heterosexuality to come to the forces for reproduction. Reproduction is the basis of any given society and it is all the more true in case of capitalist mode of exchange.

So far as the historical background of a family is concerned, the patriarch or a group of patriarchs established the village community. In pre-civilized society, there was no system of ownership. The patriarchs were in want of social system for their benefit. And this benefit was computed in terms of good, in terms of economy. For this purpose, the patriarchs wanted labour. More labour meant for production. Demands for more population were increasing. The only way to solve the problem was copulation between men and women. Thus marriage between men and women was institutionalized. It was the only way to legalize the ownership of reproduction where the owner was always the male patriarch. This also explains why male patriarchs were permitted by the society or by the law, to marry women as they wanted. In such a scenario women were only commodities, a mode of exchange baby-producing machines.

Since then with this concept of family the society is running. The existing system propagates heterosexuality since society flourished because of family, not because of the people like Sabbu who prepared to enter into an union where reproduction is a farfetched reality and again the society runs in the terms of reproduction where heterosexuality is a kind of necessity rather than the activity of transsexuality which is mere an instinct of a transsexual like Kamala.

The reason why this stigmatization and perversion achieved was that transsexuality lacked an identify, the destiny of Kamala expressed nothing but an identity crisis of *hijras*, the process of union with Sabbu is a struggle of Kamala to jump from a crisis zone to a comfort zone. Of course, we have heard voice of a *hijra* which echoes with a heartfelt longing for being treated as a social being in an indifferent society. But this is the religio-political-social sphere under patriarchal dominance where people like the government minister seldom feel a qualm of conscience in getting a *hijra* burnt to death.

Conclusion

Dattani's plays do not end. They are simply preambles of the advancing complexities that are yet to be faced.

Mahesh Dattani's plays demonstrate different attitudes that society has towards anybody who is different or who is at the lower end of the political balance. These subaltern sexualities face threat or violence because of their position in the society that are often ignored in registering their legitimate claim through literature politically and socially disenfranchised groups without a voice to be heard. Dattani is narrating the counter claims of the 'subaltern sexualities' in a society that promises more in the name of democracy and liberty. His plays depict the social space of violence faced by 'subaltern sexualities' and theatrical validity gets transferred to legitimate social responses.

Works Cited

Dattani, M. (2000), *Collected Plays*, New Delhi, Penguin Book India.

______, *Preface to Collected Plays.*

Jha, Gauri Sankar, (2006), *Current Perspective in Indian English Literature*, New Delhi, Atlantic.

Mortimer, Jeremy, "A Note on the Play *Seven Steps Around the Fire, in Collected Plays*, New Delhi, Penguin.

Prasad, Amarnath (2007), *British and Indian English Literature: A Critical Study*, New Delhi, Sarup and Sons.

Spivak, G.C. (1995), *Can the Subaltern Speak? The Post-Colonial Studies Reader*, ed. Bill Asheroft, et. al.

www.hindu.com/../20050807001403OOhtml

www.literaryindia.com/../785.html

www.wikipedia.org/wiki/Mahesh_Dattani

13

Opening the Discourses on Incest and Child Sexual Abuse with Reference to Mahesh Dattani's *Thirty Days in September*

M.S. Raj Sree

Situating Mahesh Dattani's *Thirty Days in September* with in theatrical tradition of feminist plays in India, this article attempts to foreground the depiction of experiencing and witnessing trauma. Girish Karnad, Manjula Padmanabhan, Shiv K Kumar, Dina Mehta, Badal Sarkar, Vijay Tendulkar, and Mahesh Elkunchwa, K.N. Panikkar, Tripurari Sharma and Mahesh Dattani are among the most interesting and important playwrights writing in India today, and their work demonstrates the wide range of styles, philosophies, and issues being dealt with in the contemporary Indian theatre scene. Dattani can be considered the true successor of Girish Karnad and is remarkable for the revolutionary progression of Indian English drama.

Dattani's work probes tangled attitudes in contemporary India towards communal differences, consumerism, gender discrimination, violence against women, gender roles, construction of identities, etc. he rearranges the social fabric and depict the post colonial and gender dichotomy that exist in post colonial India. His major plays are *Dance Like a Man, Thirty Days in September, Bravely Fought the Queen, Final Solutions, Tara, On a Muggy Night in Mumbai.* All of which forms a brilliant contribution to Indian drama in English. His awards include Sahitya Kala Parishad for best production of *Dance Like a Man*(1997), Sahitya Akademi Award, in 1988 for book of plays *Final Solutions and Other Plays* in 2000 and Sahitya Kala Parishad for the best production of *Tara*. Dattani is also a film-maker and his films have been screened in India and abroad to critical and public acclaim.

The aesthetics of Mahesh Dattani's plays is embedded in his deft constructions of gender and class discriminations, familial affiliations and discords, communal politics and violence, as well as the dilemmas and tensions of the differently able, the transgendered, the gay and the lesbian. Mahesh Dattani writes in English, and takes as his subject the complicated dynamics of the modern urban family. His plays are also well known for the language he uses—Indian English. The plays of Mahesh Dattani are perhaps the first to challenge effectively the assumption that Indian drama written in English represents a disjunction between language and sensibility, material and medium. Dattani does not see his choice of English as arbitrary, as a 'postcolonial' gesture, or as an example of 'the empire writing back'. Dattani's plays signal a new phase in the naturalization of English as a theatre medium in India, and redress some of the inequalities outlined by post colonial writers in English.

His themes reflect upon the ordinary and everyday conflicts of urban people who may be living in transitional periods of history, caught between the firm undertow of tradition and modernity. His characters struggle for some kind of freedom and happiness under the oppressive weight of tradition, cultural constructions of gender, and repressed desire. His characters and plot reverberate with the reality of contemporary Indian society. He belongs to that tradition of avant-garde feminists who presents women as the centre of their fictive world. Not only Mahesh

Dattani but also other playwrights like Cyrus Mistry, Poile Sengupta, Dina Mehta and Gieve Patel view family as a source of oppression and the breeding ground for social prejudice and sexual violence. *Thirty Days in September* also depict family as a site of abuse and oppression in every sense if the term.

Theatre has the ability to redefine the natural concepts of time, space and movement. It goes beyond the verbal and the physical. As Tutun Mukherjee argues:

> drama and theatre are two cultural products, in which the bias of gender generics and sexual difference are in evidence as social and psychic reality. Placing the forms within the discourse of 'gender as genre' reveals the way [the] sex-gender system operates in the art and practice of drama and theatre and controls their cultural reproduction. (4)

Dattani makes use of this in a nuanced way, especially in *Thirty Days in September*. Translated in Hindi by Smita Nirula, and directed by Arvind Gaur, *Thirty Days in September* was presented by Asmita, a leading theatre group that stands committed to socially relevant theatre. A play about love and betrayal, *Thirty Days in September* interrogates the sensitive and generally taboo issue of child sexual abuse. *Thirty Days in September* is a play commissioned by an NGO called RAHI (Recovery and Healing from Incest) that helps survivours of child sexual abuse. *Thirty Days in September* endeavours to lift the veil of silence which surrounds child sexual abuse and addresses the issue unflinchingly. It builds on the trauma of Mala who lives with the haunting memories of her abused past.

How women's bodies have been constructed and politicized becomes a central question for contemporary Feminist theatre. In Judith Butler's words, "there is no reference to a pure body which is not at the same time a further formation of that body" (10). Indeed, the constructions of gender and embodiment found in women's performance narratives of violence draw important links between "the everyday body as it is lived, and the regime of disciplinary and regulatory practices that shape its form and behaviour" (Shildrick and Price, 8). Nevertheless the witnessing of women's bodily traumas and violence offered in the garish public space of the contemporary theatre are advents that herald the possibility of resistance and transformation.

A play about love and betrayal, *Thirty Days in September* treats the sensitive and generally taboo issue of child sexual abuse. Mala is the victim of abuse in the play. Her abuser who is her uncle subconsciously lives with her all the time, as part of her dirty reflections. He damages her natural growth, deters her from pursuing her love interests beyond the ominous 30-day period and scars her soul every now and then. As she comes to the stage of adolescence, she finds that the world is hostile and human relationships are sources of betrayal. She becomes hostile to the world around her and finds herself alienated from the same. She bears the pain of humiliation of her body but is not permitted to reveal the truth before the society. Her anguish becomes more painful on the realization that even her mother maintains severe silence. As Mala withers under the psychological pressure exerted on her by the abuser, her mother watches silently, living her own pain and suffering mutely. Adrienne Rich in *Of Woman Born* emphasized the absurdity of such a situation:

> Through motherhood is the experience of women, the institution of motherhood is under male control and the physical situation of becoming a mother is disciplined by males. This glorious motherhood imposed on women conditions her entire life. (45)

As motherhood was controlled and disciplined by males, Shanta was unable to face Mala's predicament. The pathetic situation is best expressed in Mala's lamentation:

> You know, I couldn't say anything to you. You never gave me a chance to. If only you had looked into my eyes and seen the hurt or asked me 'beta' what's wrong? Then maybe I would have told you...but ma, I did look to you for help, while you were praying your eyes avoiding mine, and I knew deep down I must have known that you will never ask me that question you already knew the answer. (53)

Exploring the painful problem, Mahesh Dattani raises valid concerns and structures a world of optimism where the wrongs can stand corrected and resurrection of brutalized faith is possible. But none of this happens without another man's willingness to help the two women bury their traumatic past and find ways of rejuvenating their present.

Deepak, Mala's boyfriend, becomes the agent of change here. He dares to unmask the evil, even at the cost of his love. He hits the women hard until they hit the rock bottom. Finally, there is no way but to come up—face the wrongs and dare to correct them, notwithstanding the challenges the process of correction entails. By marking a daring departure from norm, the play ensures that we, as a society, no longer take comfort in the routine of uttering word "incest" in gutless undertones. The play also brings us closer to the reality of abused children. Pleasure does form a part of their pain, but finally the consequence of dangerous games can only be dangerous. Our only way to fight danger is to recognize it and crush with generous doses of brutality lest we are ready to condemn innocence to lifelong death.

Caught as they are, in a repressed world of trauma, the survivours of child sexual abuse and incest, occupy a liminal position in our society. Their voices are stifled and silenced by the patriarchal society. The issue of incest and child sexual abuse can be tackled from the perspective of psychological theories. It wounds the mind and destabilizes language, consciousness and perceptions. Dattani so develops the plot that all through the play, Mala lives with the haunting memories of her past. Perhaps, without being conscious of it, the uncle has permanently damaged her development with the result that she cannot pursue her love interest beyond 30 days, psychologically hinted at by her underlining a particular date on the calendar. By his words and deeds, her uncle expressed a desire at once to annihilate and consume her, demanding that she metaphorically, if not literally, assume whatever posture he might devise to revitalize his waning sense of mastery. Her uncle's acts of sexualized violence assaulted not only the body of Mala, but also her psyche purveying incalculable injuries that merit consideration on their own terms. It was traumatic and left Mala emotionally crippled through out her life sexual assault is associated with greater psychological harm than other crimes. Mala's suppression of the pain of the abuse causes physical and mental disorders. She finds herself helpless and this helplessness gradually led to rebellion, aggressiveness to all kinds of humiliation, neglect and injustice.

Accounts of incest are quite common in Royal dynasties, mythology (especially Greek and Norse) and in various folklores. However, incest and child sexual abuse is politicized victimization and the trauma of sexual assault cause acute or relatively immediate reaction and long range effects on the victim. And their post traumatic life is characterized by an array of emotional and mental disorders which can be collectively termed as Post—Traumatic Stress Disorders. They repeatedly re-experience the torment and anguish of the ordeal in the form of flashbacks, memories, nightmares, or frightening thoughts, especially when they are exposed to events or objects that associated with or remind them of the trauma. The acts of violence render the victims helpless and they lose their sense of control, connection and meaning which is essential for a healthy life. These acts of violence leave the victims in a state of helplessness and thereby undermine their sense of personal efficacy, their relational capacity, and their ability to psychologically integrate the upheavals of life in meaningful ways.

In the play Mala is the victim in a state of helplessness. To watch her facial expression, living her own silent pain was indeed a rewarding experience for the audience. For instance, when Mala and her mother are blaming each other and Mala says to her mother, "Once we were talking about a rape case that was in the papers. You said something about children also not being safe...Then I told you about what happened to me. But you changed the subject...That time I wondered if it was I or did I imagine it all? Surely not. No, it did happen" (Dattani). The victims in India face two distinct problems—first, they have to convince their audience and readers and listeners that child sexual abuse and incest are widespread and is problematic to the social fabric. And the second one is the absence of an environment which will catalyses their inner healing. They find it difficult to make the society believe that it is real.

The mother knew all along that her daughter was being sexually abused but still chose to be silent. It is this silence of the near ones that makes the abused feel betrayed. Shanta instead of encountering the reality escapes the reality. Mala ends up accusing her mother; "Only person who can, who would have prevented all this is my mother. Sometimes I wish she would just tell me to stop" (18). Shanta as a method of defence seeks shelter in the picture of Krishna or compels her to eat parathas:

> Oh! Yes, you would remember that I always like the parathas because that is what I get whenever I come to you hurt and crying. Instead of listening to what I had to say, you stuffed me with food. I couldn't speak because I was being fed all the

> time, you know that? I began to like them. I thought that was the cure of my pain. (24)

According to Judith Herman, remembering and telling the truth about terrible events are essential tasks both for the healing of individual victims, perpetrators, and families, and for the restoration of social order. Both the cognitive and the communicative must be accomplished if subsequent generations are to understand and ameliorate the seemingly intractable racial and gender hostilities and violence that continue to afflict our society. But as Mala's mother, the society is so stubborn and just refuses to open discourses on incest and child sexual abuse.

"Forget all these bad dreams," says the mother. "Every time uncle visited us it would happen...whenever I told you, you always said eat well and go to sleep, the pain will go away... Yes it did go away but it always comes back" (Dattani). But traumatic experiences like incest and child sexual abuse upset the victims' perceptions about life and drastically shatters their world view. It creates a sense of alarm, fear, panic, apprehension and dread that will linger well beyond the actual experience of the traumatizing event. Trauma is the result of victim's adaptability to their experience of those events. Some develop resilience which enables them to carry on with life, and some find that their social, psychological, and biological stability is damaged. The victims of sexual assault fail to develop that kind of resilience and are emotionally scarred. Dattani unfolds the layers of butchered and tortured psyche of Mala who suffering has two dimensions—firstly, her struggle with her own inner self and secondly her discontent with her mother who maintains terrible silence to escape horrors of the reality of the situation. This status quo thrives as the common notion that aggression and violence are unquestionably male while submission and vulnerability are traditionally female is circulated by the media and other official discourses of power.

Trauma is highly contagious in the sense that hearing the truth evokes terror, rage and despair in listeners. And thus the children of the victims also suffer from the aftermath of abuse as the adult survivours implant their own emotional stability into their children's mental make-up. So it is necessary to protect the second generation too who are under the clutches of traumatic memories of the parental generation.

Child incest victims are often called 'secret survivors' as there is often no one to take their side or to listen to their shame, confusion, and self-loathing as incest is a taboo topic. Very often they end up blaming themselves. "I know it is all my fault really...It must be. I must have asked for it...Somehow, I just seem to be made for it. May be I was born that way; may be..." (26). In many cases of such incest the non-perpetrating parent supports the other parent or denies the other parent's perpetration, fearing the loss of the spouse. And hence the child does not have the other parent to turn for support. Parental incest is known to sometimes do severe psychological harm to a child, due to the child's physical, mental, and emotional dependence on a parent, due to total disparity in the power of authority, due to the disparity in emotional and physical maturity, and finally due to the fact that the incestuous relationship may damage or destroy healthy aspects of childhood development. Their traumatic existence is one of suffering that fragments the psyche and body's self-defense mechanisms, which leaves them with a variety of post traumatic stress disorders.

The dramatic conflict in the play develops through the unorganized and fractured conciousness of Mala. Action in the play moves through exclusive use of monologues and incomplete sentences echoing the fragmented psyche and inner conflict of

Mala. Dattani takes the family setting to reveal the ramifications of trauma caused by sexual violence. However, "the starting point for many of the greatest plays is family—from The Orestia to Hamlet, from Racine to Ibsen and Chekhov, from, royal concerns of Shakuntala to the tribal spectacles of Wole Soyinka, human relationships and the family unit have always been at the heart of dramatic representation" (John MacRae). Dattani deliberately chose an upper class family as the setting. He said in an interview:

> I would rather see the setting of *30 Days in September* as upper middle class. I chose this setting because I did not want them to dismiss sexual abuse as something that does not happen to people like them.

In India, reported cases on incest are less but on the other hand the actual number is alarmingly high. The patriarchal set up and even women who internalized those values refuse to admit the fact that incest is very much happening in our society. Irrespective of class distinctions it is quite common. Though Hinduism speaks of incest in highly abhorrent terms, it is rampant in various tribes and familial circles in Indian society. The harsh fact is that sexual violence remains a tool all too readily available for exploitation of women in modern warfare, whether in family or in the public space, be it real or metaphorical, domestic, civil, or international.

Narratives on incest and child sexual abuse should come up which must question the motives of the perpetrators, which would open discourses on the trauma that incest and child sexual abuse left behind and which would share the victims anger and indignation towards the society that does not provide a support network for incest. The narratives on incest and child sexual abuse will be helpful to thousands of victim all over India as they would be able to relate the tales of incest told by a few and can create a frame work within which to examine her own experience.

"Years of silence. Silence wrapped around life like a cocoon…" (Daniaca 77). In India women are reluctant to speak out about their abuse as it would invite social humiliation, ridicule and disbelief. Indian women are silenced by fear and shame. There was yet another most powerful scene when the mother tells her daughter what she had seen. "You were pushing yourself in the bedroom, you were asking him to kiss you, to touch you, to pinch you…: I also remember when your cousin came for his holidays...you wanted my brother and your cousin dancing around you. How can I forget?" (51). Here the victim is blamed for what has happened. Yet another beautiful sequence essayed with immense control is when the mother finally says, "Don't talk about it, forget the pain... try to forget the pleasure." "But the pleasure is part of the pain," says Mala.

The very silence of the victims gave more opportunities and license to every forms of abuse. In the play the financial assistance offered by uncle Vinay made Shanta silent. "He bought your silence so that you can never tell anyone what he did to your daughter" (52). Women should identify the sources of continued social pressure that keep them confined in the role of a victim. They should also identify their own socialized assumption and misconception which make them vulnerable to abuse. They should realize that what matters is their confrontation and disclosure while how the family and society reacts is immaterial. When the family responds with unyielding denial or fury, there must be a peer group or friends or other survivours or therapists who are always ready to support and validate the victim's testimony. Otherwise the child victims will not come out of the hard shell which bounds them. In *Thirty Days in September* Mala is silent because of various reasons, "I remained silent not because I wished to but I didn't know how to speak. I cannot speak. I cannot say anything my tongue was cut off…" (55).

Sexual violence is by definition beyond the blue, a topic that most of the people were content to leave unspoken. Given this cultural reticence, there existed no established language in which to narrate the experience of sexual trauma, and that absence itself circumscribed the possibilities for conceptualizing and representing any but corporeal injuries. This interpretation resonates well with Judith Butler's astute observation that the site of traumatization may be the very loss of what is narratable, hence, intelligible. Nevertheless, Dattani succeeds in bringing forth the pain and frustration of Mala in a pertinent manner with great success.

Exploring the painful problem, Mahesh Dattani raises valid concerns and structures a world of optimism where the wrongs can stand corrected and resurrection of brutalized faith is possible. But none of this happens without another man's willingness to help the two women bury their traumatic past and find ways of rejuvenating their present. Deepak, Mala's boyfriend, becomes the agent of change here. He dares to unmask the evil, even at the cost of his love. By marking a daring departure from norm, the play ensures that we, as a society, no longer take comfort in the routine of uttering word "incest" in gutless undertones. The play also brings us closer to the reality of abused children—pleasure does form a part of their pain, but finally the consequence of dangerous games can only be dangerous. Our only way to fight danger is to recognize it and crush with generous doses of brutality lest we are ready to condemn innocence to lifelong death.

Nevertheless Dattani deserves the praise and honour bestowed upon him as Merchant says:

> Mahesh Dattani's pathos-with-a-punch approach, picked with a dash of humour, makes him the perfect candidate for chronicling urban angst. His plays are peopled with city slickens

> wrestling with issues-in a manner-close to the modern psyche...change-the-world brand of range and impulsiveness, threatens to upset some apple carts... eager to understand mind contrasted by informed prejudices...character growing...build in conflict in marriage...collapse of certain stereotypes...prejudice holder forced to look outside the cosy community circle...

Works Cited

Butler, Judith. *Bodies That Matter: On the Discursive Limits of Sex.* New York: Routledge,1993.

Daniaca, Elly. *Don't: A Woman's Word.* San Francisco: Cleis Press, 1988.

Dattani, Mahesh. *Collected Plays.* New Delhi: Penguin Books, 2000.

Merchant, R. On Mahesh Dattani, in *India Today*, Feb. 14, 2000.

Shildrick, Margrit, et al. "Openings on the Body: A Critical Introduction." *Feminist Theory and the Body: A Reader*, Edinburgh: Edinburgh University Press, 1999, 1-14.

14

Speech Situations in Radio Plays: A Pragmatic Approach to Mahesh Dattani's *Seven Steps Around the Fire*

Umesh S. Jagadale

The radio play, *Seven Steps around the Fire* by Mahesh Dattani, is characterized with the typical radio-play features like the use of sounds, silences, pauses, voice-over, etc. The playwright sets the play in a stark reality of the socio-cultural ethos in the contemporary world. The play candidly uncovers the problems of gender identity of *hijra* community, their sexual exploitation and social isolation. The storyline of the play is developed, as the investigation of a murder mystery of the *hijra* person, who is married by the son of a minister.

The communication in general and the speech situations in particular in this play are obviously influenced by the theme of the play, as also by a whole lot of other components[1] of a radio play. The pragmatic perspective adopted here, for the analysis, facilitates to open up the communicational intricacies in the play. The analysis of the selected sample is done by using the following analytical model. The model of speech situations in drama, evolved in the researcher's Ph D thesis entitled *A Pragmatic Study of Speech Situations in Drama*, is adapted here as the analytical model.

The Analytical Model

1. AREA OF ANALYSIS

Message Transmission

Narrative	Conversational	Co-textual
(Stage directions)	(Utterances)	(Grammatical Level)

Message Reception

2. PARAMETERS OF ANALYSIS.

1. Addressers and Addressees

i) *Interpersonal*: Characters in Conversation

ii) *Ideational*: Author-addresser, Performing addressers, reader-addressees, audio—addressees, performer-addressees etc.)

2. Context

i) *Socio-cultural dimension*

ii) *Literary dimension*

iii) *Theatrical dimension*

3. Speech Acts

i) *Locutionary act*: (a) Phonetic; (b) Phatic: use of grammar; (c) Rhetic: semantic level;

ii) *Illocutionary act*: verbal and non-verbal ['kinesic, paralinguistic, and proxemic' (see Birdwhistell R.L. 1952)] forces;

iii) *Perlocutionary act*: verbal and non-verbal (kinesic, paralinguistic, and proxemic) expressions.

Seven Steps Around the Fire

A flashback opens the play, with a hint of some marriage situation, immediately followed by a scream of a dying person. The whole play develops in the context of the same flashbacked situation, and progresses to unveil the murder mystery, which after getting unveiled is veiled again, once and for all.

Subbu, the son of the minister Mr. Sharma, falls in love with the *hijra* person named Kamla. Despite the domestic and the social objections they get married; however, soon Kamla is brutally burnt alive by the men of the minister. The case is hushed up. Later on, Uma, the protagonist—who is a researcher in sociology, wife of Mr. Suresh, the police superintendent, and daughter of the Vice Chancellor of a University—investigates the same case, as a part of her thesis. She succeeds in uncovering the case with the help of a police constable named Munswamy and some *hijra* persons like Anarkali and Champa. However, when she shares the result of her investigation with Suresh, he and his senior authority take every measure to hush up the case once again and forever.

Uma's 'voice-over' used in the end of the play sums up the total episode with an exasperating note on the bitter and brutal reality.

The picture of such a dark and stark reality obviously influences all the speech situations in this play. A few of such situations are produced for the analysis in the following sample.

Sample

From *Collected Plays* by Mahesh Dattani (2000)

The following sample is the concluding part of the play. It throws light on the mystery of Kamla's murder. Uma's investigation succeeds with Anarkali's help. However, when she informs it to her husband Suresh, the police superintendent, he with his senior authorities does everything needed to hush up the case. In the end she sums up on the entire episode and the play concludes. The sample is produced below.

[sd1] ***Interior. Living room of Champa.***

([sd2] *Tinkle of bells as Uma walks in.*)

ANARKALI: [u1]Madam!

UMA: [u2]I am so glad you are here.

ANARKALI: [u3] I am not going anywhere. I am now the head hijra. Champa has retired. She is leaving to spend the rest of her days in her sister's house in Bombay.

UMA: [u4] Why didn't you tell me?

ANARKALI:[u5]Would you have believed me? Anyway, what is the use of all that? What does it matter who killed Kamala? She is dead....[p1] So many times I warned her. First I thought Salim was taking her for his own pleasure. When she told me about Subbu, madam, I tried to stop her. I fought with her. I scratched her face, hoping she will become ugly and Subbu will forget her. He wanted to marry her....[p2] I was there at their wedding....[p3] She gave me that picture to show to Champa. I saw the men coming for her. I told her to run....[p4]

([sd3] *Cries for a while.*) Here, madam, take this.

UMA: [u6] What is it?

ANARKALI:[u7] A special mantra is in the locket. Champa gave this to me for you. Wear it and you will be blessed with children. Sister! May you and your family be happy! Now go away, and do not come here again. Please go, sister! ([sd4] *Silence.*)

[sd5] ***Interior. The bedroom of Suresh and Uma.***

UMA:....[p5] [u8] The photograph was what Mr Sharma was after. A Polaroid picture that Subbu and Kamla had taken soon after their private wedding in some remote temple....[p6] A picture of Kamla as a beautiful bride smiling at Subbu with the wedding garland around him. The poojari probably didn't know that Kamla was not a woman. Of course Mr Sharma couldn't have it—[p7] totally unacceptable. So he arranged to have Kamla burned to death. But Salim had to tell him about the picture. Mr Sharma simply had to have that picture. He sent Salim to threaten Anarkali and Champa....[p8] He did get the picture eventually....[p9] after losing his son. What a price to pay! And now he will be arrested and tried for murder.

SURESH: [u9] I don't know....$_{p10}$ ([sd6] *Pause.*) how do you know all this?

UMA: [u10] I have my resources.

[sd7] ***Interior. The office of the superintendent of police.***

([sd8] *Whirring of fan.*)

SURESH:[u11] Sir, that is the truth. I have my resources to verify all this. Of course, they are all sworn to secrecy so.... $_{p11}$ And Mr Sharma's gratitude will be expressed in ways that will be, I am sure, more than adequate....$_{p12}$

([sd9] *Whirring of fan stays for a while.*)

UMA ([sd10] *voice-over*): [u12] They knew. Anarkali, Champa and all the hijra people knew who was behind the killing of Kamla. They have no voice. The case was hushed up and was not even reported in the newspapers. Champa was right. The police made no arrests. Subbu's suicide was written off as an accident. The photograph was destroyed. So were the lives of two young people.... $_{p13}$

([sd11] *Music.*)

Features and Observations

The sample includes four different speech situations distinguished by typical radio-play directions (see [sd1, sd5, sd7] and [sd10]).

Every situation has a distinct space, time and temporal set-up.

The typical radio-play features like the use of 'silence' ([sd4]), 'sounds' ([sd2, sd8] and [sd9]), 'pauses' ($_{p1\ to\ p13}$) and 'voice-over' ([u10]), which denote and establish the following aspects of the play:

The silence ([sd4]): *change of the speech situation;*

The sounds ([sd2]): *the movements, i.e. proxemic action, and* ([sd8] and [sd10]): *the place of action;*

The pauses ($_{p1}$ to $_{p13}$): *the various thoughts, transmitted non-verbally;*

The voice-over ([u10]): *the thought and the action of the play, summarized at the end of the play.*

Analysis of the Sample

1. Addressers and Addressees

(a) Interpersonally Operating

Anarkali (see [u1, u3, u5, u7; sd3;] and [p1 to p4]);

Uma (see [u2, u4, u6, u8, u10, u12; sd2, sd10;] and [p5, p6, p7, p8, p9, p13]); and

Suresh (see [u9, u11; sd6; and] [p10, p11, p12]).

The characters, i.e. the interpersonally operating addressers and addressees use various utterances, pauses and actions in the stage directions to process their communication. The frequent use of the pauses is specific to the radio performance of the play, since the radio performances are marked by the use of sounds and silences. In all 13 pauses along with 12 utterances and 11 stage directions not only impress the statistical ratio of these communicational variants but more significantly they emerge as the salient feature of the radio plays.

Findings: The pauses mark the strength of the non-verbal communication in the radio plays.

(b) Ideationally Operating

(i) Directly Ideational (directly from the author to the audience):

The radio directions ([sd1] to [sd11]) inform about how the author-addresser communicates his ideational address directly to the reader-addressees, the performer-addressees and the radio-addressees.

The address in the radio directions, although influenced by the features of the radio performance, displays certain features of the literary performance also.

The directions [sd1, sd5] and [sd7] inform about the various places of action (e.g. [sd1]:'Interior. Living room of Champa'), which are normally communicated by the use of music or some other techniques specific to the radio performance.

The use of the directions ([sd1, sd5] and [sd7]) is specific more to the literary performance than a radio performance, since the author uses these directions basically to inform the places of action more directly to the readers and the actors than to the listeners of this play.

In short, the author-addresser composes his directions variedly depending upon the varying demands of the various mediums of performance.

Findings: The author-addresser's directly ideational address is influenced by certain medium-specific demands.

(ii) Indirectly ideational (indirectly from the author to the audience, through the characters):

The four different speech situations in the sample communicate different indirectly ideational addresses. The author-addresser in every situation passes his message to the audience, indirectly through the characters' communication. A few of such instances are produced below:

(a) *Situation-1 (from [sd1] to [sd4])*

The characters communicate about the mystery behind Kamla's murder.

The author indirectly communicates the success of the protagonist-investigator.

(b) *Situation-2 (from [sd5] to [u10])*

The characters communicate about the murder investigation and in it the protagonist-investigator surprises her husband, the police-investigator.

The author indirectly communicates the failure of the police investigator.

(c) *Situation-3 (from [sd7] to [sd9])*

The characters communicate about hushing up Kamla's murder case.

The author indirectly communicates the injustice of the guards of justice.

(d) *Situation-4 ([sd10] to [sd11])*

The character communicates as the mouthpiece of the author and summarizes on the unjust practices used to hush up the murder case.

The author indirectly communicates to spotlight the ghastly picture of the power politics.

Although the above discussion probes into certain shades of the author's different messages from different situations, it doesn't claim to have brought full of the messages.

2. *Context*

i) Socio-cultural Dimension

The superstition in the following example operates as the socio-cultural dimension of the context.

> ANARKALI: [u7]A special mantra is in the locket. Champa gave this to me for you. Wear it and you will be blessed with children. Sister! May you and your family be happy!

The superstition of the bliss of mantra in the locket is a socio-cultural reality that functions as the context, in which Anarkali's communication gets certain meaning.

As this particular contextual dimension plays a decisive role to make the utterance meaningful, all the addressers' and addressees' shared knowledge of the same can facilitate the meaning making process.

ii) Literary Dimension

The use of [sd1, sd5] and [sd7] displays a literary technique into operation as the literary dimension of the context. The above-referred directions, as a literary convention, inform about the different places of action in the different speech situations. The use of this literary technique offers the context in which the speech in these situations becomes meaningful. The following example throws light on this operation.

> [sd7] ***Interior. The office of the superintendent of police.***
>
> SURESH:[u11] Sir, that is the truth. I have my resources to verify all this. Of course, they are all sworn to secrecy so.... [p11] And Mr Sharma's gratitude will be expressed in ways that will be, I am sure, more than adequate....[p12]

On the basis of the information shared with the audience in [sd7] the utterance [u11] becomes meaningful. Without knowing this information, it can be difficult to draw inferences on [u11]. Hence, the literary technique of using [sd7] operates as the context, in which the utterance [u11] becomes meaningful.

iii) Theatrical Dimension

The radio-specific technique of the voice over used in [sd10] functions as the theatrical dimension of the context. In the literary performance the information: 'UMA ([sd10] *voice-over*):', and in the radio performance its phonetic execution play the contextual role, which helps the addressees' interpretation of the utterance [u12].

Without sharing this context, it can be difficult for the addressees to process the interpretation of the utterance [u12] in isolation.

The use of sounds like the tinkle of bells ([sd2]) and the whirring of fan ([sd8] and [sd9]) establish the places of actions respectively, Champa's room and the office of the police superintendent. The further part of the action takes place in the context of these places of action.

The use of these sounds here operates as the 'contextual cues' (Kramsch: 1998: 27)

3. Speech Acts

(i) Locutionary Act

a) *Phonetic Act:* The phonetic act is discussed here with the help of the following examples. The phonetic execution of the utterances 'Madam!' in [u1] and *'Sir'* in [u11] is obviously influenced by politeness, whereas the utterance [u12], being a voice over, is influenced by the specific convention of its phonetic execution in the radio performance.

   So, the phonetic acts of executing [u1] and [u11] are influenced by the politeness principle and that of the [u12] is influenced by the performance-specific convention of the voice-over.

Findings: The variations in the execution of the phonetic acts are the results of the factors like the pragmatic principles and the theatrical conventions influencing the execution process.

(b) *Phatic Act:* As the phatic act of saying something is represented grammatically, the dashes indicating the pauses $_{p1}$ to $_{p13}$ strengthen the various locutionary functions of expressing something, what is not effectively expressed verbally alone.

For instance, in the following utterance, a particular use of the grammatical structure, with the pause $_{p10}$ between the two sentences, facilitates the performance of the phatic act.

Suresh: ^{u9} I don't know....$_{p10}$ (*Pause.*) how do you know all this?

The most vital aspect to be communicated by the above utterance is how Suresh is surprised not to know something, what Uma knows, and it is significant that the surprise is not effectively communicated verbally, as much it is communicated in combination with the use of the pause $_{p10}$.

Grammatically, the pause $_{p10}$ in the utterance ^{u9} connects a statement with a question, both of which independently do not communicate the surprise on the part of Suresh. The 'surprise' is expressed effectively, only with the use of the pause between the two sentences.

Like the two sentences, even the pause $_{p10}$ does not express the 'surprise' independently, but in combination with the two sentences only.

The composition of these two sentences, with the pause between them, has a certain grammatical structure, which helps the performance of the present phatic act of expressing the 'surprise'.

In this sense, the grammar proves to be 'complementary' (Leech: 1983: X) to the pragmatic operation of the locutionary (phatic) act, by facilitating the expression of the illocutionary force of the 'surprise' hereby.

Finding: Certain 'complementary' grammatical structures facilitate the performance of the speech acts.

(c) *Rhetic Act:* The act of performing [u12] is the performance of a rhetic act, as it employs the literary and the rhetorical device of effective narration. With the effective narrative technique used in [u12], the addresser summarizes the total action to conclude the play.

The perception of the message that the utterance [u12] communicates is semantically derivable and rhetorically facilitated.

As the semantically derivable message is facilitated rhetorically, the process of the perception operates pragmatically, since the rhetoric facilitation here performs an illocutionary function 'in' (Austin 1962: 120) communicating the message.

Findings: The rhetic act pragmatically operates the perception process of the message, which is derivable semantically and facilitated rhetorically.

(ii) Illocutionary Act

(a) *Verbal Forces:* e.g. The force of the success transmitted verbally in the utterance [u10] is discussed here.

> UMA: [u10] I have my resources.

The transmission of the above utterance is the transmission of the force of Uma's success in unveiling the brutal act of the social system (including her own family members) that tries to hush up the murder case of Kamla.

It is against the utter brutality of the act that the force of success strongly evolves from the utterance.

So, the intensity of the force of success is born out of the intensity of the force of brutality.

Precisely, the force is communicated against its anti-force. The greater the anti-force, the better the communication of the present verbal force. In this sense, both these forces are directly proportional to each other and operate in the opposite directions showing a centrifugal trend i.e. moving away from the center between them.

Findings:

1. Certain pragmatic forces and their anti-forces are directly proportional to each other in their operation.
2. These forces operate in the opposite directions showing a centrifugal trend.

b) *Non-verbal Forces* (kinesic, paralinguistic, and proxemic): The non-verbal illocutionary forces are discussed here with the functioning of the pauses in the sample, e.g. the pauses $_{p1,\ p2,\ p4}$ and $_{p13}$.

There is a non-verbal force of helplessness that emerges neither kinesically, nor paralinguistically, nor proxemically, but out of the pauses $_{p1,\ p2,\ p4}$ and $_{p13}$, as seen below.

1. 'What does it matter who killed Kamala? She is dead....$_{p1}$'
2. 'He wanted to marry her....$_{p2}$'
3. 'I told her to run....$_{p4}$'
4. 'The photograph was destroyed. So were the lives of two young people.... $_{p13}$'

All the four pauses above express the force of helplessness coming out of the situations, where the characters have no choices and they are seen at a point of no return. Considering the 'felicity conditions' (Grundi 2000: 273), it is found that the force becomes meaningful in the context of the utterance and the felicity conditions, and not by the expression of the pauses, in isolation. Precisely, the non-verbal forces operate in the context of the utterances and the felicity conditions processing their communication.

Findings: The non-verbal force of pauses functions not in isolation but in the context of the utterances and the felicity conditions processing their communication.

(iii) Perlocutionary Act

(a) *Verbal Expressions*: e.g. The utterance [u5] operates as the verbal expression of the perlocution delivered in response to [u4].

UMA: [u4] Why didn't you tell me?
ANARKALI: [u5]Would you have believed me? Anyway, what is the use of all that? What does it matter who killed Kamala?

The perlocution in [u5] operates as the response to the indirect speech act used in [u4] by Uma, who asks Anarkali to tell her something she wants to know. Initially the doubts in [u4] are responded to by the doubts in [u5], however later, the expected explanation follows.

The perlocutionary act in [u5] again shows here the expected and the unexpected responses operating in it.

Findings: The perlocutionary acts can have both the expected and the unexpected responses.

(b) *Non-verbal Expressions (kinesic, paralinguistic, and proxemic)*: The sample shows a few non-verbal expressions functioning as the perlocutionary acts. For instance, Anarkali's *'crying'* in [sd3] is a paralinguistically operating non-verbal perlocution to the utterance [u4].

UMA:[u4] Why didn't you tell me?

ANARKALI: [u5]Would you have believed me? Anyway, what is the use of all that? .... ([sd3] *Cries for a while.*)

Except for this example ([sd3]), the sample doesn't show any other paralinguistic, kinesic or proxemic operations of perlocutionary acts. However, some other examples of the non-verbal perlocutions are found in the form of the pauses, e.g. the pauses $_{p1,\ p2,\ p3}$ and $_{p4}$ operate as the non-verbal perlocutionary acts in response to the utterance [u4].

Findings: The form of the radio play evolves certain form-specific findings. The major findings from the above analysis are produced below.

1. The pauses mark the strength of non-verbal communication in the radio plays.
2. The author-addresser's directly ideational address is influenced by certain medium-specific demands.
3. The variations in the execution of the phonetic acts are the results of the factors like the pragmatic principles and the theatrical conventions influencing the execution process.
4. Certain 'complementary' grammatical structures facilitate the performance of the speech acts.
5. The rhetic act pragmatically operates the perception process of the message, which is derivable semantically and facilitated rhetorically.

6. Certain pragmatic forces and their anti-forces are directly proportional to each other in their operation.
7. These forces operate in the opposite directions showing a centrifugal trend.
8. The non-verbal force of pauses functions not in isolation but in the context of the utterances and the felicity conditions processing their communication.
9. The perlocutionary acts can have both the expected and the unexpected responses.

Key to Abbreviations and Symbols

Abbreviations

^{u} = Utterance

$_{ri}$ = Rising intonation

$_{fi}$ = Falling intonation

$_{p}$ = Pause

^{sd} = Stage direction

^{n} = Negation

Symbols

'/' = Rising intonation

'\' = Falling intonation

Works Cited

Anandlal. 2004. Ed. *The Oxford Companion to Indian Theatre.* New Delhi: Oxford University Press.

Austin, J.L. 1962. *How to Do Things with Words.* London: OUP.

Birdwhistell, R.L. 1952. *Introduction to Kinesics: An Annotation System for Analysis of. Body Motion and Gesture.* Washington D.C.: University Microfilms.

Dattani, M. 2000. *Collected Plays.* New Delhi: Penguin Books Ltd.

Grundy, P. 2000. *Doing Pragmatics.* London: Arnold.

Halliday, M.A.K. 1970. 'Clause Types and Structural Functions', pp. 140-165 in Lyons. J. Ed. *New Horizons in Linguistics.* Harmondsworth: Penguin.

_____. 1973. *Explorations in the Functions of Language.* London: Edward Arnold.

Hymes, D. 1972. 'Models of the Interaction of Language and Social Life' pp. 35-71 in Gumperz and Hymes. 1972. Ed. *Directions in Sociolinguistics.* New York: Holt, Rinehart and Winston, Inc.

Key. Mary R. 1975. *Paralanguage and Kinesics.* Metuchen: The Scarecrow Press, Inc.

Kramsch, C. 1998. *Language and Culture.* New York: Oxford University Press.

Leech, G.N. 1983. *Principles of Pragmatics.* Lancaster: Harlow: Longman.

Mohan, K. & Banerji M. 1990. *Developing Communication Skills.* Delhi: Macmillan India Ltd.

Searle, J.R. 1969. *Speech Acts.* London: Cambridge University Press.

15

Study of Gender Issues in Dattani's *Tara*

Yatri D. Dave

Dattani is a kind of dramatist who deals with the burning issues of the society in his dramas. His works mainly deals with the contemporary India towards communal defences, consumerism and gender bias. He represents the young generation of Indian English dramatists. His experiences are varied. He made its presences felt outside the country even.

In Dattani's plays he always tries to deal with the central idea of the society. He tries to present the society as if it is in the reality. Even in his subject matter he says that he writes about what he sees around and what concerns for common people. There must be reasons, which made him to take up the predicament of modern man as the theme of his plays. He is highly motivated by the fragile characters in the plays of Tennesse Williams who uses the same technique to depict the trauma of the character.

Mahesh Dattani's plays are set in contemporary society. He has examined issues of gender inequality, social exclusion, fundamentalism and the impact of dreaded disease like HIV/ AIDS on people's mind. What distinguishes him from other playwrights is his courage of conviction in depicting the innovative themes like portrayal of sex preferences by men and women which were until recently considered to be a taboo in Indian society. His realistic portrayal of human nature evokes both sympathy and empathy in the minds of readers.

In his most famous play *Tara*, Dattani focuses on the nature of typical Indian bious society. Tara is protagonist in the play. She is a victim of social prejudices. She has all the quality of an emerging new woman ready to defy age-old prejudices and compulsions. Here emergence as new woman is reflected in her ability to take decision and assert her identity. Chandan is Tara's twin brother. They are siamese twins conjoined as their waist. They are separated by an operation. He loves and cares Tara. He recognizes her identity and potential. He represents the new generation of male in our society. Bharati is the mother of the twins. She represents herself as traditional women in Indian society. She has inherited her father's property and arrogance. She is only one who is responsible for the pain through which Tara has to suffer. Her compensatory behavior to Tara prejudices her against her father Patel. Tara hates Patel because she has been made to think like this. Bharati's favor to Chandan makes her to develop guilt-complex, which results in her nervous breakdown and death.

Tara and Chandan are siamese twins separated physically when they were infants. Even after their unjustified and manipulated division which is done against the law of nature, they are emotionally united. Both of them share similar mental agony which is delineated by Chandan when he grows to be called as Dan. Dan, that is the older Chandan, explores his psyche / Tara's psyche after her death. She dies in a shock when she learns that it is her mother (whom Tara trusts more) who is involved in the conspiracy of her unfair separation from Chandan. Though Chandan physically survives this trauma, he could never lead a peaceful life and so, he migrates to suburbs of London, changes his name and attempts to create a new identity. He also tries to write his auto biographical play, though a futile attempt.

Patel is the manager of the company and he is a firm believer in old values. He has a fixed opinion regarding women's position. He is helpless and confused due to Bharati's dominating nature and her Father's interference. Next is Dr. Thacker who operates upon the Siamese twins of Patel and Bharati who are conjoined at their waist. He knew the result of the decision to transplant the third leg to Chandan. But his materialistic approach and ambition to establish the biggest clini in Bangalore made him perform this operation. Roopa is nextdoor neighbour of the Patels. She is 15 and is in tenth standard. She is curious by nature and belongs to the class where women are not in the habit of questioning anything. She is short-tempered and does not like to be made aware of her shortcomings. Dan (older Chandan) makes us to know the important past events in the lives of the Patels. Prema and Nalini is Roopa's best friend. They belong to the ordinary class of society. They are curious by nature. They are always ready to laugh at others. They are surprised to see Tara's artificial leg. This is about all the characters which make the play much intresting.

Tara is a riveting play that questions the role of a society that treats the children of the same womb in two different ways. Dattani's *Tara* is a poignant play about a boy and a girl who are joined together at the hip and have to be separated surgically, which will mean the death of either of the two. The fact that the injustice perpetuated by the victim's own mother whose preference is to the male child, makes the play more powerful suggesting that it is woman who continues the chain of injustice. Tara is not just the story of the protagonist of the play *Tara,* but it is the story of every girl child born in Indian family whether urban or rural. The situation is aggravated if the girl is physically challenged or there is any other physical or mental deformity in her. It is a bitter example of child abuse present in the Indian societies. Every girl child born in an Indian family does suffer some kind of exploitation and if there is a boy child in the family, the exploitation is very much visible as the privileges are consciously or unconsciously propounded to the son.

The scene opens in London with Chandan, now a play wright, reminiscing about his childhood days spent with his sister Tara. Tara and Chandan are two sides of the same self rather than two separate entities and that Dan, in trying to write the story of his own childhood, has to write Tara's story.

The play revolves around the Siamese twins, chandan and Tara Patel, an operation to separate the twins at birth, leaves Tara crippled for life. Chandan, the privileged brother wants to turn his anguish into drama on his sister's childhood. Throughout the play we can feel that she bears some kind of grudge against the society. She seems to have some kind of aversion with the outside world and her world consists of only her parents and her brother whom she was ever close to. The play explores besides exposing the typical Indian mind set which has from time immemorial preferred a boy child to a girl child. It looks at the triumphs and the failures of an Indian family, comprising father (Patel), mother (Bharati) and two children (Chandan and Tara) coping with the trauma of disability. Tara, a feisty girl, who isn't given enough opportunities as were given to her brother eventually wastes away and dies. Chandan escapes to London, changes his name to Dan and attempts to repress the guilt he feels over his sister's death. His sense of trauma and anguish is so intense that at the end of the play, we see Chandan apologizing to Tara in the most moving of all the lines: "Forgive me, Tara. Forgive me, for making it my tragedy."(Chapter 3)

Tara's life is full of hollowness. The wor itself suggests that she is stuffed with some kind of thoughts which makes her one of the most emotional character in this play. At a same time Tara is over ambitious and enthusiastic girl. She is also full of zest and spark of life. She is just like a bright and shining star which has a source of cheerfulness and happiness of the family. She wishes that if has a ball with which she can fulfil her desires. She once says to Chandan that "I'd probably have a ball, that's what I would do. Having both mummy and daddy dancing around me. 'Yes Tara!' 'No Tara!' 'Anything you say, Tara!'." (333)

Tara is physically not well. She knows this fact nicely. It is also expensive to keep her alive. She thinks that it is better to use the money for some good cause instead of wasting for her existence. She has a true desire to work with Mother Teresa for missionary work. Tara's zeal is exemplary. Despite her physical limitations, she is brave enough to fight with this world and accept the challenge of the life. Her determination, dedication, courage and spirit makes her most memorable. Dattani used the stream of consciousness. When the play begins, Chandan is Dan and at present a writer who is writing about the story of Tara's life and suffering. He firmly believes that he is only one who is responsible for Tara's tragic and troublesome life. He is the true representative of the young generation, ready to recognize and respect the women. He believes in giving them freedom to choose their career. He has a faith in Tara's ability to choose her career. He does not appreciate Bharati's worry for Tara's career and future.

Chandan's love for Tara is reflected in his statement when he tries to comfort his mother. Bharati is extremely worried about Tara's future. Like a typical Indian women she thinks that the problem will grow with each passing day, but Chandan says that he is here for Tara. Chandan has got balanced nature. He can judge a thing in its proper perspective. He has an impartial nature. This quality of his nature is seen in his opinion of his father. In her bid to cope with her guilt-complex, Bharati tries to prejudice Chandan against his father. She says that her father should be concerned with Tara's career also as he is with his career. But Chandan does not find his father lacking in concern for Tara.

Chandan has a healthy sense of humor. He never misses a chance to crack jokes. This he just does to lighten the serious mood of his parents and is twin sister Tara. Sometimes he jokes throw light on Dattani's concerns. At a same time Chandan is intelligent and knows how to utilize particular situation to teach someone a lesson. He does not believe in categorization of the work. He does not find anything wrong when he helps Bharati knit. But Patel is angry to see this and scolds Bharati for not raising the children properly. Chandan cannot think of doing anything without Tara. He does not want to go the office with Patel but he says that he would go it Tara also goes there. He refuses to join college if Tara does not. He pleads with his father to understand his feeling for Tara. But here once again Patel think like typical Indian father who gives importance to his son's career over daughters.

Chandan represents new values. He is different from his father's this respect. He believes in women's potential and gives equal treatment to Tara whereas Patel is a firm believer in old values. He cannot think of associating Chandan's going to the office and college to Tara's going to the office and college. Chandan's query about Tara's share in his grandfather's will also reflects his values and respect for a girl's right. He is surprised and shocked to learn that learn that there is no reference to Tara's share in the will, but Patel considers it quite natural. His reaction is that of typical Indian male having old values.

> PATEL: He left you a lot of money.
> CHANDAN: And Tara?
> PATEL: Nothing.
> CHANDAN: Why?
> PATEL: It was his money. He could do what he wanted with it. (360)

Chandan has no qualms about accepting the fact that Tara's views are more mature than his. He even says, "Women mature faster!" (371). He accepts unhesitatingly Tara's views that there is no difference between a boy and a girl whereas his parents are guided by age-old values. Bharati denies Tara her right to the third leg and Patel is concerned with Chandan's career only. But Chandan is different from them. He always tries to make up for the loss she has to suffer. Thus we can say that Chandan is young, sensitive, sensible, liberal, flexible, intelligent, and concerned for those he loves the most. His feelings for Tara are pure and innocent. He cannot live without her. He is always there for her. He respects her potential and wants them to be utilized. Thus after the death of Tara he goes to London and there he start writing about Tara's lif and suffering. In this way this seems that Chandan's life also suffers the most after his sister's death. Patel represents the attitude of the old generation. He does not appreciate Chandan's generous and happy-go-lucky attitude towards everything particularly Tara. He wants that he should behave like a male child. So, he proposes that Chandan should accompany him to office till his college starts. He does not spare even Bharati, whom he thinks responsible for spoiling Chandan.

Chandan is not ready to go to office particularly without Tara. Unlike Patel he has full confidence in Tara's potential and respects her instinct to win. But Patel cannot think even of talking Tara to the officer. He is firm in his decision. Patel has traditional attitude wherein a male is cut out to work outside to earn for the family and a female is made to look after the family, rear children, bring them up, obey her husband and remain inside the house. His view is reflected when he expresses his disapproval of Chandan helping Bharati with her knitting. He holds her responsible for making Chandan like this. He says that Tara should learn household work. But Chandan does not like his biased opinion.

Patel is bitter to think of Bharatri's exhibition of her love for Tara. He is aware of the truth, which makes Bharati behave that way. He is pained to think of his helplessness regarding the decision, which was taken to favour Chandan. He repents for his weakness. He gets the opportunities to make Tara and Chandan know the reality when Bharati is in hospital following her nervous breakdown. He did not want that Bharati should get the satisfaction of either confessing her guilt or asking her children biased. One more thing is there, which cannot be overlooked. It is his urge to express his wounded and suppressed feelings to his children. He narrates the whole story, from his marriage to Bharati to her final nervous breakdown, his orthodox family's refusal to approve his marriage, his compulsion to accept his father-in-law's superiority, his hatred for his property even, his denial to allow Bharati to get the 'Satisfaction of confession'. He has the convection to accept that he is also responsible to some extent, "I suppose we were both to blame. Your mother and I/ and your Grandfather". (337)

Though Patel appears to be stern, traditional, partial and stubborn, there is a father in him who craves for his children's love and proper understanding of his concern for them. So he is hurt to see Bharati prejudicing his children against him. He becomes aggressive when she to realize her mistake and accuses him of being partial. Here he seems like very typical Indian father, who often opposes the circumstances of his personal life. He with the development of the play makes his character very obvious and tragic because by the end of the play tragedy happens not only with Tara but also with Patel thus he suffers the most in his whole life.

Patel is hurt to see the way Tara is made to form a biased opinion of him. He is tense to see Bharati's possessiveness and her compensatory behavior. He is helpless in this respect. Moreover it is Bharati who is responsible foe Tara's suffering, but on the face of it Patel is painted as the root cause of all the problems. This makes him helpless and lonely. He accuses of making Tara delicate and weak. He has a soft heart, which has been hardened by the situations he had face. His helplessness to prevent the operation, his being kept out while taking decision, his failure to avert his wife's nervous breakdown and her death, Tara's death, Chandan's decision to leave the country and settle abroad are responsible for the mental and emotional suffering he has to undergo. Patel feels a bit light to confess his helplessness and confusion before his children. Thus his life has been a life full of suffering but not allowed to complain. This is the most tragic part of his character.

Bharati represents the old generation of Indian women, who used to stay at home managing the house, rearing children, and preserving the family tradition. Her old values make her decide in favor of Chandan. She takes her Father's help to get it executed. Dr. Thakkar is there to accomplish the work. But this operation of separation proves to be a curse for the twins. Here Chandan suffers emotionally the most. He has a felling that he is responsible for Tara's suffering. Bharati develops guilt-complex., which reflected in her compensatory behavior with Tara. Dattani had presented Bharati's concern for Tara's career and future. The women of new generation have come out of the shadow of the old generation when they gave importance to physical beauty. Today's women give importance to intelligence and confidence because these are the qualities, which make them lead their life meaningfully and respectfully.

Here Bharati is not a villain of the play, but she is most sensitive character of the play. Just her nature makes her partial for her son's future. She is also having her Father's support for her decision. She was inherited by her father's property. This makes her little bit proud and superior to her husband. She is not healthy enough to understand the repercussions of her constant effort to see beyond her own guilt-complex. She tries to confess when she is in hospital following her nervous breakdown. Her mental illness does not allow her to see beyond her own guilt-complex.

Bharati has a fear complex also. She always fears that Patel might disclose her past; this scars her. She knows that she is responsible for Tara's suffering. She is hysterical when Patel asks her to express her love for Tara following their quarrel. Bharati and Tara are two bodies and one soul till Tara comes to know the secret, which Bharati wants to divulge and Tara comes to know from her father. The revelation of the past proves fatal for their love. Tara has bitterness and hatred for her which she speaks out in following words: "And she calls me a Star!" (379)

Dattani here presents the character of Bharati as a dominating and haughty lady determined to win at all costs. But her death following her nervous breakdown makes her another tragic character in the Play. Roopa is not an important character in the play. She doesn't have her influence on the movement of the play. But Dattani has introduced her quite early in the play and she is presented till the end of the play. She has been presented as a contrast to Tara so that the difference between their characters may come out. Her importance lies in the fact that she throws light on the importance of the play. Roopa helps Dattani shed light on Bharati's attitude to bribery. This seems to be one of the concerns of Dattani in this play. Roopa is there to highlight the qualities of both Chandan and Tara. Her attempt to use Chandan just for fun highlights Chandan's ability to teach anybody a lesson, and her endeavour to prove Tara inferior brings out Tara's ability and confidence to teach her a lesson by making her aware of her uneven tits. She also tells her that she would never think to be an imbecile like her, that she never minds being one-legged, that she can live on her own, that she wants to have a meaningful life, that she is interested in her own identity, and she is not a weak girl.

Roopa represents Dattani's concept of a common, insensitive, opportunist and short-tempered girl. These three characters represents general society, who are not able to behave normally with the abnormal people. Dr Thakkar is the responsible for Tara's pain and her eventual death. His materialistic approach is responsible for Tara's suffering, Bharati's nervous-breakdown, and Chandan's sense of guilt. He doesn't listen to his conscience. He is not listing to it make him more helpless. Dr Thakkar doesn't appear on the stage. Dan's conversation with him makes the audience know about him. Dan is recollecting the past events.

The attitude of parents and society to girls is the main concern of Dattani's *Tara*. A girl child is always made to sacrifice. In the case of Tara we also find the same thing. He believes that Tara does not got what she deserves. She has been denied her right both by her parents as well as nature. Dan's real importance lies in his reflections on incidents, which have not been mentioned in the play. The audience are not made to witness either Tara's or Bharati's death. They come to know from Dan's present time conversation with his father. Dan is upset to know about Bharati's death. He shows his inability to come back to his father. He doesn't feel like coming back when neither Tara nor Bharati is there to welcome him. He requests Patel to settle abroad because that is the only way left to be with his son.

The play ends with Dan's and Dr Thakkar's last conversation. Dan is unable to control his emotion. He breaks down and asks Dr Thakkar to go away from his life. He pines for the love of his mother, father and sister. He even tries to find Tara among the stars in the sky after the death of Tara. He seeks forgiveness for what has happened. Both of them are seen on stage. They are without a limp. This is what Dattani expects the world to be, free from pain and suffering. The different characters of the play deal with the different kinds of problems of their own life. They show the hollowness not only of their life but also of their relations with their existences. *Tara* is a play which shows the predicaments of his characters with variety of subject matters.

Works Cited

Dattani, Mahesh. *Tara: In Collected Plays*. New Delhi: Penguin, 2000.

— Contemporary Indian Theatre and Its Relevance, *Journal of Indian Writing in English*, Vol. 30, No. 1, Jan. 2002.

Iyengar, K.R.S. *Drama in Modern India*. Bombary: The P.E.N. All India centre, 1961.

Styam, J.L. *The Elements of Drama*. London: Cambridge University Press, 1960.

16

Decrypting Symbols: A Symbolic Reading of Mahesh Dattani's *Ek Alag Mausam*

M. Anjum Khan

Literary artifacts are fertile with intellections and visions generating social response. There are signs and symbols embedded in text require unfolding of layers of meanings wrapped around them. Deciphering symbols is one of the best ways of interpreting literary texts. Sometimes, it is remarkable that the symbols delineated in a literary framework can intersect new avenues of cerebrating and bring in light the unexplored spheres. According to Barton and Hudson, a literary symbol designates "an object or a process that not only serves as an image itself but also refers to a concept or abstract idea that is important to the theme of a work".

World is inhabited with numerous symbols and signals in every walk of human life. Michael Ferber asserts: "After all, anything can be a symbol... ". A symbol is an object, person or a place suggesting more than the literal meaning attached to it. Sometimes the literal meaning of a symbol is absurd, so that the symbolic meaning overrides and annuls out the literal meaning. Symbols are concrete objects or explicit acts that retain their real nature while standing for ideas or values that do not have material existence. A symbol may have more than one meaning or multi-layered meanings. As a matter of fact, it is observed that the most significant symbols do convey an indefinite range of meanings. Symbols in a literary structure refer to concrete and abstract ideas as well.

Irrespective of the genre of literature, symbols are employed in all literary works to invoke ideas and provoke innovative resolutions. Drama is one such genres which applies symbols which signify implicit ideas on and off stage. Mahesh Dattani is contemporary play wright articulating vibrant themes through his plays. John McRae appreciates Mahesh Dattani's craftsmanship: "There is no substitute for this kind of craftsmanship, as working with any major playwright will confirm". Through the genre of drama, Dattani sets a platform to contemplate on various contemporary and indispensable issues.

Mahesh Dattani's *Ek Alag Mausam* is a sensitizing play articulating the unheard voices of HIV positive patients and prejudiced society. The play projects emotional, psychological medical and social ordeal of patients infected with HIV. The plot of the play whirls around the protagonist, Aparna who is in crisis, emotionally paralysed and disillusioned at one of the happiest moments of her life. She is traumatized by sudden kibosh of her motherhood and terror of approaching death. Besides Aparna, there are other characters enduring the approaching death and impending misery in form of physical ailment.

The play, *Ek Alag Mausam* furnishes two columns of people, one representing the HIV positive patients and the other representing the inanely biased people. The rehabilitation hospital which is more likely an asylum is accommodated delineating the microscopic view of medically helpless and socially marginalized folks. The stark reality resonating in the emotional quandaries of the sufferers render the disintegrating and crumbling lives of individuals. The social rejection of these ailing individuals elucidates the lack of awareness and narrow-mindedness of society. Beena Agarwal comments: "Dattani conceives the structure of drama *Ek Alag Mausam* with a socio-philosophical canon".

There are various symbols encrypted in play running parallel to the explicit motif presented. There are few objects, characters and places symbolizing notable themes and contemporary ambiance. Objects furnished in *Ek Alag Mausam* render various meanings and the characters limned in the play represent ideas as well. These symbols assist in decrypting the engrained themes in the play.

The character of Aparna symbolises numerous ideas latent in the play. She stands for unanticipated metamorphosis of happiness into misery. She in her prime months of pregnancy discovers that she is at the brink of life clutching desolation and desertion of her husband. Initially, she refuses to accept the reality that she is HIV positive and tries to back away from the ruthless verdict of kismet. She reaches Jeevan Jyoti under the pretext of volunteering her services for the HIV positive and when Dr. Machado shows that he is already been informed about her infection, she says: "Maybe I should leave. I have a headache" (490). However, she reconciles with her concentrated terrors and wake in a dawn of hope. She symbolises weakness. She is scared of death and so many other things in life. She says: "I am afraid of a lot of things". (490)

George represents rare kind of people who live cheerfully, selflessly and bravely fight back the pangs of approaching death. He symbolises courage, straight forwardness, service and social alienation. He is very courageous and seems fearlessly leading his life. He, unlike Aparna, accepts his syndrome in public and to his family. He diligently serves the cause of HIV posistive patients at Jeevan Jyoti and due to his intimacy with it, he is estranged by his friends and by his own parents.

There are many other characters representing some ideas. Rita symbolizing motherhood, prostitution and humility. Suresh representing defeat and betrayal. He stands for hopelessness and says, "How can I help when I am dying too" (482). Dr. Machado representing hope, service and life. Every character seems representing some idea or some phase of life. Paro represents young blossom which is tendered and nurtured with mother's affection. She is protected by her mother in spite of her mother's bodily and moral decomposition. She symbolises a sense of normality in Aparna's life. She brings up the girl and prepares a normal life for her. She is brought back to normal routine by the responsibility of bringing up Paro for life.

Social hostility, prejudice and lack of awareness are symbolised through characters in the play. Sukhvinder representing ignorance, lack of awareness and social prejudice. George's fellow villagers represent collective social prejudice against the HIV positive patients. His parents stand for filial estrangement and antagonism. His parents turn him out in order to avoid contamination and social humiliation: "You may live for another seven years. But you have killed us before we have entered our graves. What face do we have left in this village? Don't come back. Leave. Go George!". (537)

Truck is usually considered as a symbol of conveyance and movement. George's truck in *Ek Alag Mausam* symbolises conveyance of death. George explains to Aparna that as even municipality vehicles refuse to transport the corpse of a HIV positive, his truck performs the task. He says: "Who do you think takes the bodies for cremation? The municipality van won't even enter the compound" (497). George truck stands for mobilization and freedom for George. He adoringly declares: "I like driving the truck, Mother. I like to move. I am most happy when I am moving" (536). It is a symbol of economic independence as well. George earns his bread and of which his mother is very proud.

The truck is a symbol of rescue. It rescues the sufferers from pangs of humiliating and painful life. Moreover, it rescues the establishment of Jeevan Jyoti by availing adequate financial security. George's truck symbolises economic security for Jeevan Jyoti in the moment of crisis: "Don't you know? He sold all his trucks and his godown to pay for the lease agreement on Jeevan Jyoti" (544). George's truck signifies joy and glee for the children who eagerly wait for him. When they hear the horn of the truck, "The children suddenly get some life in them". (502)

Car is an icon of, luxury and mobility. Aparna's car represents economic luxury and independence. George's truck scales his position in society as a truck driver belongs to lower-middle class strata of society, whereas, Aparna's car renders a high position in the social ladder and other characters addressing her as Memsahib bonafides this idea. It is a rare privilege for Indian women driving cars and Aparna enjoys one such privilege which attests for her independence in life.

Aparna's car symbolises her mobility to and fro from Jeevan Jyoti. It facilitates a movement in her life which seems stagnated by traumatic assaults. She recognizes the visits to Jeevan Jyoti as means of escapades from her own frustrated panoptic living. she tries to rummage through the wreckages of other HIV positive patients life in order to identify her own invisible ruins. Her car smooths the progress of her reconciliation with abrasive truth. The car symbolises a means of run for Aparna. She refuses George's proposal of love and accelerates her move: "Aparna backs up the car and speeds away". (520)

Travelling and movement are recurrent symbols in *Ek Alag Mausam*. As Aparna is limned driving her car all through the play and George is shown moving on his truck, the movement of life can be interpreted in these moving action. Life is a journey moving forward and marching towards progress. This inevitable movement indicates life, some travel long and some are destined to travel brief. So is life, some people live long and some live short. The lives of Aparna and George are measured in terms of travelling and stopping by Dr. Machado. Dr. Machado observes: "You two are travelling in different trains. Here is travelling non-stop to the final destination and yours is stopping at all the small towns. Besides... has it ever occurred to you that she is travelling first class and you...". (530)

AIDS is another major symbol embedded between the lines of the text signifying a contemporary theme, the term 'Acquired Immune Deficiency Syndrome'. It is caused by the virus HIV. AIDS is a disease of disorder of the body's immune system. Immunity is body's natural resistance to fight against germs and resist diseases. The body of AIDS infected person stops producing natural defences against diseases, so victim often dies from cancer or other infections that it cannot fight.

AIDS is regarded as a symbol of death, terror, humiliation, contamination, hopelessness, misery, discrinimination and marginality in the society. The AIDS patients are fatal sufferer anticipating their doom which comes quickly over them with humiliation and shame. As there is no stable remedy for AIDS, death is the only solution of the misery endowed by this ailment. The persons infected with HIV suffer from social humiliation, marginalization, emotional wreck and physical deterioration.

Ek Alag Mausam unfolds the life of few of the HIV positives whose lives are eclipsed with contempt and misery. AIDS travels fast but carefully choosing the one who are not cautious and pursue the course of forbidden. Besides, there are victims who are forced to rot by others. Aparna is a healthy married woman until she gets HIV infection from her husband who is guilty of betrayal, lechery and murder. AIDS seems ever tolling the knell for the sufferers: "How can I forget? It is there! Written in our medical reports. Our death warrant". (533)

The wooden soldier toy is an iconic fillip of comfort and encouragement. Soldier is an epitome of braveness, courage, resistance and defence. Whereas, a toy is a symbol of joy, recreation, comfort, solace and contentment. The wooden soldier in *Ek Alag Mausam* fulfils the requirements of a soldier and that of a toy. Suraj intakes doses of valor from the toy soldier to retaliate the fangs of approaching death. He clings on it when his death seems gaining over his life.

Suraj is delineated as a cheerful young boy laughing over the humility and negligence which he is bound to receive from society. He is told, "Live like a soldier, die like a soldier" (506). He musters strength from the dummy soldier to defend his ailing bodily constitution from the virus. When ever, he falters in his resolution, he is reminded by the small icon of soldier that death should be bravely fought and heroically encountered.

The tape recorder is a twentieth century invention amusing people with music and is an apparatus of education as well. *Ek Alag Mausam* presents the tape-recorder as a symbol of pleasure, amusement and abundant joy for the children who are segregated from the mainstream of life. George uses it to entertain the children and Aparna uses it to test her credentials. The children dance enchanted to the tune played by the tape and urges Aparna to play it again, when it is switched off: "Aunty. Play the music" (503). It proves a symbol of improvement and progress in life.

The colored pills represent hope and longer chase of death. Dr. Machado is a medical doctor and the proprietor of Jeevan Jyoti. He imports some pils from America in order to slow down death and increase life span of HIV positive patients: "I smuggled some in from America. They will help them live just a little longer" (489). These pills imported from America shows India's poor medical supplies and doctor's jubilant efforts to sustain life. The pills are brought by diligent efforts by the doctor to append at least one day in an individual's life. George beams at the sight of the pills: "GEORGE (smiling). Aha! Looks like some of the children will just have to live a couple of years longer! (542). The dearth of pills symbolises death receding life among the patients.

The card game is a symbol of recreation and sportiness. In *Ek Alag Mausam*, the card game represents a hope for success and a tool for mocking death. The patients play with a dying patient to ease his pain and make him feel distract him. The dying man is Ramnath who clings on to the cards in spite of his paralysed efforts. Ramnath is engaged in playing card game in his death bed and building a sense of success. Manoj says: "You can't beat death. But you can beat us. Try!". (492)

Soap bubbles appear in the play twice, once in Jeevan Jyoti and the other time on hills in Panchagani. The soap bubbles are dallies enjoyed by the children who cherish the colorful and attractive pattern it leave in the air. The bubble symblises short-lived life. Life is like a soap bubble which pops out and stay very briefly on earth and the lives of HIV positive is comparatively shorter. As a soap bubble is savoured and relished by the on lookers, so should the life be relished and enjoyed utterly. Life is colorful and attractive like a soap bubble hanging in the air for brief moment. The span of a bubble varies from one to another and so as human life's span. The stronger bubbles manage to live little longer than the weaker ones, "Paro is blowing bubbles. We

follow the bubbles till they all break except for a few strong ones" (557). However, all bubbles break and it symbolises that death is inevitable.

The breaking of glass filled with water awakes Aparna from her dream and bring her into the reality. The dream succeeding the break of glass scars Aparna as she sees herself playing the card game with the dying man and she loses it. It shows her panick-stricken psyche. The broken glass symbolises the shattering of her dreams of being a happy life with her baby and her husband. The glass filled with water stands for the life which had happiness. However, the glass tumbles, breaks and the content is spilled. So is, her happiness snatched and her life is disintegrated.

Football game is a sporting activity involving stamina, pleasure and spirit. George entertains the children with a tale that day and night are consequences of a foot ball match which God plays. He says: "God is playing football with the sun. He always scores a goal" (518). This tale relating God's football match symbolises life is a series of matches containing subsequent defeats and victories. The football signifies a new day and so the rolling of the ball means the passing of days.

The symbol of Jeevan Jyoti is very remarkable setting representing an asylum for the discarded persons in society it is a symbol of ghettoic life. The HIV positive individuals seek comfort and refuge. Jeevan Jyoti hospital which literally means light of life symbolises the same. It supplies light in utter darkness for people lost in it. It offers light to those who seems lost in darkness and fret for death. It supplies medical assistance, emotional support, recreation, and moral support to go on in life which is anchored by the hooks of fear and uncertainty. The children of Jeevan Jyoti muster courage to live vibrantly and improve on: "We wanted to find ways tc keep this place running to help the children. Now the children are keeping this place running with their shows so that we can be happy". (541)

The hospital of Jeevan Jyoti is a symbol of segregation and sequestration as well. The people are neglected and dumped like trash in a corner of society. The municipality vehicles refuse to come near the place fearing infection from the air and people frequenting Jeevan Jyoti eventually become hostile to social standings. Sukhvinder detests George for attending the requirements of Jeevan Jyoti hospital and so his villagers despise him and eventually expel him from his own village. George warns Aparna that she will lose social footing, if she keeps coming to the hospital. Obviously indicating, that Jeevan Jyoti is a prohibited ghetto in the society which is regarded as a symbol of contamination and contagious suffering.

Jeevan Jyoti symbolises mutual trust, symbiosis and fuel for life. The children cheer each other and live helping each other overcome their emotional and physical impediments. The card game played at the bedside of a dying man is purely an act of recreation and easement for the sufferer. The doctor in charge, who renders his service as a tribute to his late son attempts his best to orient the socially mislaid and traumatized people at the moment of crisis in their lives. He facilitates medical relief, food, shelter and vigor to live. Besides rendering medical services, he bestows emotional stimulations by group therapy. He cheers his wards: "So let us all say together—'I am alive, this moment, this day!'". (486)

TV is another wonderful modern invention used as a means for entertainment, information and education. *Ek Alag Mausam* furnishes a TV which symbolises hope, happiness and a striking mirage. TV is an appliance which forms a bridge between the real world and the world of illusion. It presents fascinating things which are dubious and seldom practical. In the play, Rita watches her daughter on TV and she gets a glimpse into the future that her daughter will be spared from the miseries and will live a happy life. she sees her daughter, Paro performing, "Rita is so thrilled she rushes to the TV and kisses it" (540). She foresees a glowing future and visualizes her daughter as a little princess: "Oh! My little Paro came on TV! She looks like a little princess". (540)

The unborn baby is a symbol of approaching motherhood in *Ek Alag Mausam.* The unborn baby of Aparna symbolises the unattained happiness and her fall into the abyss. Aparna is very hopeful and happy to welcome her baby in her life. The baby symbolises dream of every mother and Aparna yearns to tend her dream. The baby is a symbol of promises and happiness for her future. When the doctor says, "Aparna... I would strongly advise you to.. give up your baby" (478). Somehow, they mean symbolically that Aparna should abort the prospect of happiness in future. The abortion of the baby indicates the crumbling image of her happiness which to a great extend relied on her motherhood. The doctor's advice to give up her baby seems the end of her world to Aparna and the illusion of happy life fades away into gravity of world.

The flask of orange juice conveys a symbolic meaning latent in emotions and actions of the characters. Aparna fills up a flask of orange juice for their journey to Panchagani by car. This orange juice symblises rejuvenation and refreshment. The flask of juice in the play, is a symbol of a parcel of happiness which Aparna tends for Paro. She gives Aparo the flask to drink in the happiness which awaits her way in near future. When, Paro intakes a ship of happiness from the flask, Aparna demands a swig from the flask to: "I'd like some of that too" (474). This can be interpreted that Aparna longs to rejuvenate her life and wish some happiness as well.

The admission letter for the boarding school in Panchgini is a symbol of new prospects and promising tomorrow. Aparna intends Paro to pursue her higher education in boarding school with educational hierarchy and academic perfection. The admission letter symbolises reappearance of elapsed happiness. The matron of the boarding school neglects and disregards Paro and Aparna, when she learns that they have not brought the admission letter with them. The absent letter seems symbolizing carelessness and irresponsibility on Aparna's part from Matron's point of view. She rebukes Aparna: "Not a very good example to your ward, are you? (551). However, the letter is found later on the car seat and thus resuming the course of happiness and hope for them. The letter, when rediscovered in the car elevates Aparna's joy and so does the reappearance of George impart happiness. Parma in the past has been lackadaisical with George's affection and looses it temporarily. However, the reappearance of George brings her back hope, prospect, and elapsed happiness.

Each symbol encrypted in *Ek Alag Mausam* divulges few very substantial and salient themes. The symbols employed in the play enumerate different purviews. There are various relevant themes conveyed through the conveyance of these simple and complex symbols. Sudden transformation for good or worse in life; emotional trauma caused by the fear of death; social estrangement and marginalization; the sturdiest tread from illusion to disillusionment; are few of the many ideas implicit in the play.

An analysis of these symbolic means elucidate various phases of life and different roles of the society. The adoptational problem encountered by HIV positives is mended by the selfless and caring services of an establishment, Jeevan Jyoti. The characters representing the aura of suffering and emotional devastation expound the premise that life is not always secured and gleeful.

There are different seasons in one's life ranging from desolate winners to joyous summers. One such season occulted by misery has befallen on few individuals' lives. However, blossoms can be tended in this bleak season as well with hope of some miracle: "While waiting for that cure to be invented or discovered, let us not forget—that miracles are known to happen." (556-57)

Motivation intertwined with tenderness can spam away the anxieties of approaching peril. The play culminates with an optimistic note presenting ceasefire between apprehensions and qualms. Awareness of AIDS in the mainstream society recruiting social norms against discrimination, marginalisation, subversion and estrangement of HIV positive patients underscores the ending note of the play. Tout ensemble, a symbolic reading of *Ek Alag Mausam* assists in decrypting the underlying themes in the text buried under the motifs of hope and despair; dream and disillusionment; endurance and annihilation.

Works Cited

Agarwal, Beena. "Ek Alag Mausam: Silence, Suffering and Sun Shine." *Mahesh Dattani's Plays: A New Horizon in Indian Theatre.* Jaipur: Book Enclave, 2008. pp. 138-151.

Barton, Edwin J. and Glenda A. Hudson. *A Contemporary Guide to Literary Terms.* Boston: Houghton Mifflin, 1997. pp. 191-193.

Dattani, Mahesh. "Ek Alag Mausam." *Collected Plays.* Vol. 2. New Delhi: Penguin, 2005. pp. 473-557.

Ferber, Michael. *A Dictionary of Literary Symbols.* New York: Cambridge UP, 2007. pp. 1-7.

McRae, John. "We Live in the Flicker: Reflections in Time on the Plays of Mahesh Dattani." *Mahesh Dattani's Plays: Critical Perspectives.* Angelie Multani Ed. New Delhi: Pencraft International, 2007. pp. 53-66.

17

Gender Discrimination and Social Consciousness in Mahesh Dattani's *Tara*

Grishma Khobragade

In the present paper, it is proposed to study mainly the dramas of Mahesh Dattani with reference to the gender bias and social consciousness in Indian social system. Contemporary Indian English drama portrays images of protagonists confined to rigid tradition and orthodoxy. The plays produced after independence show that Western culture has been partly assimilated by Indians.

In this study, therefore, an attempt is made to scrutinize Mahesh Dattani's drama to show how he is conscious of the social system that have come up in the contemporary India. The study is based on the hypothesis that his drama effectively depicts the gender discrimination and social consciousness of modern India.

Today's modern Indian drama highlights some current social issues and real life problems. The purpose of paper here is to discuss Mahesh Dattani's *Tara* (1990) and *Dance Like a Man.* His plays deal with the social and contemporary issues, the marginalized sections of our society, women, gays, and hijras (eunuchs). His plays raise questions of discrimination, including, gender discrimination and homosexuality. They not only bring up gender issues and the liberty fixed to women in a patriarchal society, but they also deal with gender biases and prejudices which influence the lives of girl-children even amongst middle class educated society.

Mahesh Dattani is one of leading and contemporary playwrights in English. A director, actor, and writer, in 1986, he produced first play *Where There's a Will.* There are several plays written by him as *Tara, Night Queen, Final Solutions, Dance Like a Man* and many more. His plays deal with the social and gender issues. One of his films *Dance Like a Man* has won the award for the best picture in English awarded by the "National Panorama". His plays focus on actual life problems and sometimes cause a controversy. His plays are about the marginalized sections of our society: minorities, women, gays and hijras. He once said:

> The function of the drama, in my opinion, is not merely to reflect the malfunction of the society but to act like freak mirrors in a carnival and to project grotesque images of all that passes for normal in our world. It is ugly, but funny.

Tara deals with the theme of gender discrimination and social consciousness in modern society. It is not only the story of the hero of the play, but also the story of every girl child born in society, whether urban or rural. Tara is a touchy play which shows the partiality towards the male child in highly educated and an upper middle class Bangalore society. The story of the play is about the twins who are born with three legs; blood supply to the third leg is from the girl baby. The parents of the twins and doctor decide to fix the third leg on to the male baby's body so as to make him complete. The decision is taken to make him physically fit and complete, not on the basis of medical ground but influenced by the grandfather, a politician. Male domination is reflected in the role of the grandfather who donates all his property and wealth to the male child. In our society, a male child is considered as an asset an a female child a liability. This is mainly due to certain misconceived religious beliefs and the problem of dowry. This discrimination against the girl child by family member shows the attitude and mentality of the society. It is tragic that the mother also supports in the act of attaching the third leg to the boy's body. It is our cultural heritage that a boy is always superior to a girl. The common method of obtaining higher death rate for girl children than boys is neglecting the girl child during early childhood.

Tara is a play that raises questions to the society that treats the children of the same womb in two different ways. It is a play about two children, joined together at the hip. One is a boy and the other is a girl, and they can be divided only surgically. The partiality and injustice starts here. It shows that a woman herself is the enemy of women. The mother prefers the male child and thus strengthens the chain of injustice. The first thought behind selecting the male child is, he will carry forward the family name. It is an example of child abuse prevalent in the Indian society. a girl is an unwelcome intrusion, the cause of sorrow when she is born, a burden for parents who have to amass dowry. Every girl child born in an Indian family suffers from some kind of exploitation, and if there is a boy child in the family, the mistreatment is very much noticeable as consciously or unconsciously all the privileges are offered to him. This is because getting dowry is regarded as a male privilege. Erin Mee rightly points out:

> Dattani sees *Tara* as a play about the gendered self, about coming to terms with the feminine side of oneself in a world that always favours what is male.

This play raises a few questions of discrimination, i.e., religious prejudice, gender discrimination. This play not only deals with gender issues and the treatment of girl child in a male-dominated society, but also with gender biases and prejudices which still affect the lives of several girlchildren even amongst educated, urban families. *Tara* is a play in two acts. It is set in London with Chandan, a dramatist, who is remembering his childhood days in the company of his sister Tara. He wants to write a story about his childhood but he has to write Tara's story. Chandan wants to twist his grief into drama by writing about his sister's childhood. Even after their unjust and manipulated partition, which is made against the law of nature, they are emotionally united. They share the same agony, which Chandan tries to describe by writing an autobiographical drama.

The root problem of discriminatory treatment being meted out to girls lies in the status of women in society. Dattani has presented the strange reality of women playing a secondary role to man. Males are seen as the providers and the role of the girls is neglected. This dirty practice is still present in some part of India. The drama also suggests supremacy of Patel when he insists that proper division should be made in the gender roles.

Tara's parents are educated, even then they have made such discrimination. Bharati's father can also be considered responsible for this catastrophe. She had been influenced by her father's decision. She is scared about the prospect of her daughter; she says:

> It's all right while she is young. It is all very cute and comfortable when she makes witty remarks. But let her grow up. Yes, Chandan the world will tolerate you. The world will accept you—but not her! Oh! ...when she sees herself at eighteen or twenty, thirty is unthinkable and what about forty and fifty! Oh God! (349).

She also tries to show her love by the act of donating her kidney to Tara, which ultimately turns useless. Dattani establishes that the mother and daughter relationship proves secondary to the orders of patriarchy. Mr. Patel represents male prejudice and domination.. He holds the supreme position in decision making in the family. Bharati has to follow his decision. She has to accept whatever is given to her. She had favoured Chandan at the time of operation. Patel makes her responsible for everything and finds an escape from his responsibilities.

The doctor represents a supreme position in the play. He operates the twins, but he has done an unjust operation under the pressure of Bharati's father. Dr. Thakkar, the God-like, 'life giver', he knows the reality. Tara is deprived of leg. Dattani appropriately shows that in this society it is an annoyance to be a girl. In India the male species is considered and treated as the first sex. This is reflected worldwide phenomenon. Dattani highlights the real face of our political leader. Manipulation for monetory consideration or at times due to political influence has ceased to surprise many. There is a gross negligence of child patients in India. Tara realizes the real story of her physical disability during her lifetime. Even though she is more intelligent, is discouraged from the beginning of her life. Parents do not give proper support to Tara. This makes her lose interest in life. Further, she refuses to go to college. It is significant that discrimination with Tara continues, even after her death. Chandan, who is fascinated with writing a story about his own tragedy, as Dan he apologizes to Tara for doing this, "Forgive me, Tara.Forgive me for making it my tragedy." (380).

Mahesh Dattani reveals the issue of gender discrimination in this play. The social norms, economic values and cultural elements have been answerable for the inequality against the girl child. Tara is a victim of this social system, which controls the minds and actions of the people. In Indian society, the woman is variously presented as a mother, wife, daughter and sister even goddess. *Manusmruti* and *Dharmashastras* have laid down specific rules for the conduct of women. The women were relegated to secondary position in all walks of life. The literacy rate of women has improved. Nowadays, they are given secondary status in household, offices, social and public places. women are exploited and harassed in Indian society. They are subjected to violence and harassment everywhere.

Works Cited

Dattani, Mahesh. *Collected Plays*, Penguin, New Delhi, 2000. p. 288.

Roy, Elizabeth. Freak Mirror and Grotesque Image. *The Hindu.* 15 March 2002.

18

Political Exploitation through Communalism in Mahesh Dattani's *Final Solutions*

R. Manjushree

The play *Final Solution* was first performed in 1993, which is about the communal issue of India. People of India and Pakistan were divided before the independence of India. The partition of India and Pakistan was not only the geographical division, but also Hindus and Muslims were forced to go to their respective lands, Hindus to India and Muslims to Pakistan. Thus, the play *Final Solutions* is about the cultural hegemony of how Hindus suffer at the hands of Muslim Majority like the character of Hardika/Daksha in Hussainabad, and how Muslims like Javed suffer in the set-up of the majority Hindu community. It disturbs the normal social life and also is hindrance for the national progress.

Chorus is the special technique introduced by Mahesh Dattani which is a symbolic way of expressing our own hatred towards another community. Another way of narration of the communal issue is also an innovative technique as the young girl Daksha who will be reading the diary which she wrote long back related to the communal riot, and immediately the young girl changes into the old Hardika. But there is no much difference between olden days riots and the present days riots as both have the same bloodshed, same intensity of violence.

Daksha closes her diary and then Hardika appears on the stage. In the living room of the Gandhis, Aruna, Ramnik Gandhi's wife, enters with her daughter Smita. Aruna is a God-fearing woman who strongly follows each and every ritual, being a Hindu, Javed and Bobby on the other side who represent Muslim community. But at the end of the play, the writer wishes to stop this hatred and communal tension.

The 'Divide and Rule' policy was adopted by the British during the colonial rule. Due to that there arose many differences between the communities. The result was communal hatred and many of them migrated to different places, which was completely new for them. Hindus migrated from Pakistan to India and Muslims from India to Pakistan. This migration was forceful and even after so many years people were not able to come out of the shocking events caused by migration. In the play *Final Solution* we find one such family to specify it's a character by name Daksha/Hardika. Even after independence people of both the nation were prejudiced by the past communal riots. The feeling of insecurity and confusion rose. People belonging to this age had to confront many strange issues as they settled in a new land and problems increased. The birth of religionalism, disputes in national identities and decline of human values—these disorders led to linguistic, ethnic and caste identities.

> For the Indian, the most important battle for the establishment of a distinctive identity within a territorial location lay in the partitioning of India. National identities were conceived and took shape in accordance with the ideologies that formulated these on the basis of religions identities. The gruesome rioting and communal/religious disharmony that took seed in 1947 has continued to throw up countless such incidents in independent to secular India. Such incidents and communal violence in India between Hindus and Muslims was underscored emphatically by the brutal bloodshed in Gujarat

> in 2002. These were some of the issues that Dattani had actually dramatized in the form of *Final Solutions* earlier, dealing with the recurring rhetoric of hatred, aggression, the monetary and political exploitation of communal riots, in chauvinism and parochial mindset of the fundamentalists, in the context of the India of the 1940s interspersed with the contemporary India. In confronting and negotiating responses to the post-Babri Masjid demolition and the post Godhra Hindu Muslim communal violence in Gujarat, through varied discursive frames of history and theatre, Dattani subsequently explored issues of identity, memory, suffering and loss... within the larger political context through the various productions of this play (*Final Solutions*). (Asha 77-78)

The play presents different shades of the communalist attitude prevalent among Hindus and Muslims in its attempt to underline the stereotypes and clichés influencing the collective sensibility of one community against another. This play is different from other plays as it is neither sentimental nor simplified in its approach. Mahesh Dattani won the Sahitya Akademi Award for *Final Solutions* in 1998. In the play there is clash between traditional and modern life and discussions on class and communities.

Dattani has showed how these communal problems in the society affect our family relationships:

> As Kenneth Pickering has rightly observed that "the problem play is that 'which explores a particular social problem, raising many questions about it and provoking the audience into finding answers. Such plays, sometimes known as, 'thesis plays' because they mount and work out an argument, may be tragic or comic in essence but their ideas constitute some issue of deep concern to the dramatist with which he wishes to engage the minds and consciences of the audience. (Kenneth 70)

The outburst of a riot is like a chain reaction. The play opens with Daksha reading from her diary. Then the young girl immediately changes into the old Hardika. "I opened my diary" (167). Daksha is the grandmother of the Gandhis. She closes her diary and then appears as Hardika on the stage. She feels things have changed a lot. In her family Ramnik Gandhi, her son, and Aruna daughter-in-law and granddaughter Smitha are there. Daksha is represented as a fifteen-year-old newly married young girl, writing her diary; this may be considered as the past and sometimes as Smitha's grandmother in her late sixties in the present. So, Ramnik and Aruna also come under the present but Smitha, Bobby and Javed may be considered as representatives of the future. Daksha always tells Smitha that "those people are all demons", which is not liked by Ramnik.

It is clear in the play that cultural hegemony can be noticed as those who are in majority rule over the minorities – at present Bobby and Javed are the victims and sufferers under Hindus as they are Muslims, that is in the present. But when Hardika reads the diary, in the past in the communal riots they were minorities and her father burnt a Muslim's shop. Javed here is a young man, who becomes a terrorist and is exploited by politicians in the name of 'Jehad'. He is sent to Hindu Mohalla where a 'Rath Yatra' is taking place. He is in the mob and he so overwhelmed that he throws the first stone on the 'Rath' causing chaos, ending up in the killing of the 'pujari' and the crashing down of the 'Rath'. Bobby who is close friend to rescues him from the violent mob and takes him to Ramnik's house to take shelter that night. But there is a discussion for the cause of Hindu-Muslim hatred and many terrific secrets are revealed.

Mahesh Dattani has introduced the chorus and mob in *Final Solution*, which helps to know, what is the intension of either the Muslim or the Hindu. And the mob gives awareness about what is going on between the two communities. Through their slogans they convey the message that they want to convey to their respective communities. It brings out the feeling of each community.

Stage setting plays on important role in the play as it helps the audience to experience the shift of time.

> Within the confines of the ramp is a structure suggesting the house of Gandhi's with just wooden blocks for furniture. However, upstage, perhaps as an elevation, is a detailed kitchen and a pooja room. On another level is a room with the roll top desk and an oil lamp converted to an electric one, suggesting that the period is late 1940's. This belongs to the young Daksha, who is in fact the grandmother, also sometimes seen as a girl of fifteen. There are several instances when Hardika, the grandmother, and Daksha, the young bride, are on this level, at the same time, although they are the same person. Hardika should be positioned and it is such way that entire action of the play is seen through her eyes (FS 165)

> When the curtain rises, we find Daksha, the newlywed bride, going through her diary dated March 31, 1948. Considering her diary as her sole friend in the new environment of her in-laws, she is sharing her secrets, experiences and views with her diary. The diary begins with the shattered dreams of a young girl who wanted to be a singer like Noor Jahan, but who has been married and confined to four walls of her in-law house. This suggests how most of us have to live a life of unfulfilled desires. This is a very lengthy monologue of Daksha but is written in the style of a spoken dialogue. She is narrating the horrible incidents of the partition, which are still haunting her mind ever after one year. (Gill 2010)

Hardika gives details about her father and how they suffered being minorities.

> We... gained independence. You should have seen it. Everyone was awake waiting for midnight-like children on the last day of school, waiting for the last bell of the last class before vacation. And their rushing out and screaming and shouting

> and fighting.... My father had fought for that hour. And he was happy when it came. He said he was happy we were rid of the Britishers. He also said something I did not understand then. He said that before leaving, they had let loose the dogs. I hated to think that he was talking about my friends' fathers. ...But that night in Hussainabad in our ancestral house –when I heared them outside –I knew that I was thinking the same of us. And I knew that I was thinking the same, like my father. And as their voices grew louder, I blamed them more and more for my father's absence. The windows broke, one by one. My mother and myself, we hid in the pooja room. The stones came smashing into our home. I clung to my mother. My mother clung to the family idol of Lord Krishna. (FS 166-167)

Hardika advises Aruna, her daughter-in-law: "Be careful I said. The dogs have been let loose"(168). Even after receiving education and instead of so many developments there are no changes in thoughts. Hardika and Javed have experienced the bitterness of the minority community. The selfish politicians exploit young people like Javed and Babban for their selfish ends. Hardika's father was murdered because they were member of the minority Hindu community in India. Javed has become a terrorist because he is from the minority Muslim community in India. He explains to Ramnik his reasons for involving himself.

> It is a terrible feeling;
>
> Being disillusioned. Don't we all have anger and frustration? Am I so unique? Now that I am alone .... I hate myself. It was different when I used to attend the meetings. I was swayed by what now appears to me as cheap sentiment. They always talked about motherland and fighting to save our faith and how we should get four of theirs for every one of ours. Babban never came to any of these meetings. He was busy trying to forget his faith. (FS 205)

Javed answers Ramnik questions that both Bobby and himself long to be amongst the majority section of the society.

> Javed: It must feel good
> Ramnik: What?
> Javed: Being in the majority
> Ramnik: Yes, I never thought of it.
> Javed: After feeling good you are in the majority?
> Ramnik: No, about being the majority.
> Javed: But Sir, it is in your every move. You must know. You can offer milk to us.
>
> You can have an angry mob outside your door. You can play in civilized host. Because you know you have peace hidden inside your armpit (RS 192).

Javed narrates his horrible experience and reveals the story of the 'Rath Yatra', what happened to him and how he became the victim of that situation. Bobby gives a picturesque description of what happened to them in that mob and gives the reason as to why Javed was violent. "I clung to him, putting my arms around his waist trying to hold him back. I was dragged by his force.... I pushed him aside, just as the chariot began to keel over, we escaped in the panic and confusion" (FS 207-208). Aruna, Ramnik's wife, is a staunch follower of Lord Krishna. But Javed who is against idol worship and against Hinduism, picks up the idol and grasps it in his hands: "You can not remove my smell with sandel paste and attars and fragrant flowers because it belongs to human being who believes, tolerates, and respects what other human beings believe that is the strongest fragrance in the world"(FS 225).

Aruna gets hurt by this act of Javed, taking Lord Krishna's idol in his hand and blaming the Hindu religion and the rituals associated with it. Then realizes that she feels sad and he tries to convince and console her: "The tragedy is that there is too much that is sac red. But if we understand and believe in one another nothing can be destroyed.... And if you are willing to forget. I'm willing to tolerate" (FS 225). Aruna is a religious lady and expects the same from her daughter, Smita. She trains Smita on how to perform pooja and other rituals. Smita follows all. She meets Bobby and falls in love with him but later Bobby is engaged to Tasneem, her friend. Smita is disappointed; she is not interested in her work. Just mechanically she performs everything. Mahesh Dattani brings out the conscious level of thinking. That after all these years Smita opens up and says that "I never could express my feeling as well as you do. May be my religion oppressed me for more". (FS 213)

> Communalism being the worst form of materialism divorced from being anything that is sacred and oriented towards worldly wealth and power, can truly be combated by a higher form of the sacred that combines the secular ideal of human equality, democratic awareness, identification with the suffering alleviation of by poverty to resistance to a deep inner inquiry and belief in the holiness of all forms of life, those who turn religion as mean to attain state, power and world status are indeed the most irreligious of all, for they profane the most hallowed on usurp even the last refuge of the spirit from a world where the best lack all the conviction and the worst are full of passionate intensity by joining the ignorant armies that class might. (Satchidanand)

Finally Ramnik confesses that his father had burnt the Muslim shop in an earlier riot and took possession of it. He regrets for that action, and her mother being sensitive, immediately reacts to this conversation. Ramnik explains to his mother Hardika the background of their gaining control over a shop, and things become clear at this point as the reality is revealed.

> HARDIKA: (*crushed*). Why didn't you tell me? All these years.
> RAMNIK: You have to live with this shame only for a few years now.
> HARDIKA: Do you think... do you think those boys will ever come back?

RAMNIK: If you call them they will come. But then again – if it's too late – they may not. (FS 226)

Abbreviation

FS Final Solution

Works Cited

Dattani, Mahesh: *Collected Plays*. New Delhi: Penguin Books India, 2000.

Gill, Dr.S.S.: *Critique of Violence: Mahesh Dattani's Final Solutions*. Chandigarh, posted on oct 31, 2010.

Kumar Das, Bijay: *Form and Meaning in Mahesh Dattani's Plays*. New Delhi: Atlantic, 2008.

Kurian, Anna: *Texts and Their Worlds I Literatures of India An Introduction*. New Delhi: Foundation Books Pvt.Ltd, 2005.

Kuthari Chaudhuri, Asha: *Contemporary Indian Writer in English: Mahesh Dattani*. Delhi: Foundation Books, 2005.

Malgonker, Manoher: *A Bend in The Ganges. Delhi*: Oeriental Paperback, 1994.

Pickerning, Kenneth: *How to Study Modern Drama*. London: Macmillian, 1998.

Prasad, Amar Nath: *Indian Writing in English: Tradition and Modernity*. New Delhi: Kanupriya Sarup and Sons, 2006.

Sharda Iyer, Natesan: *Final Solution and Other Plays Mahesh Dattani Musing on Indian Writing in English: Drama*. New Delhi: Sarup and Sons, 2007.

19

Tragic Elements in Mahesh Dattani's *Tara*

Sophia Jaychandran

Mahesh Dattani's *Tara* is an absorbing play which questions the role of a society that considers deformed twins (male and female in the context of this play), as a burden. In fact, his plays have been considered a weapon against trauma inflicted on individuals due to orthodoxy and stagnation of the society. His plays take up a lot social issues and discuss societal concerns at length. *Tara* is an emotional play about a boy and a girl who are joined together at the hip. Their predicament is that they have to be separated surgically, which will mean the death of either of the two. Injustice is promulgated by Tara's own mother, Bharati, whose preference is to the male child. This issue makes the play more compelling signifying that it is woman who perpetrates preferences. Tara, apart from being the protagonist of the play, is also the centre point of thought-provoking discussions and deliberations. The physical deformity of Tara is a matter of grave concern. As far as the Indian society is concerned, girls are not placed on a higher pedestal in the social structure. The girl child, eventually, is a victim of biased attitude in every respect. The play *Tara* brings out this discrimination which has marred the life of Tara.

The scene opens in London with Chandan, now a playwright, recalling his childhood days spent with his sister Tara. He loves his sister and is in a state of despair when he feels that

Tara deserved a "fair share" bur was not granted the same. Throughout the play, we get an impression that Tara and Chandan are the projections of the same self rather than two disconnected beings. As the play progresses, it is clear that in writing a story, Dan is infact, incorporating Tara's pathetic circumstances.

> This isn't fair to Tara. She deserves something better. She never got a fair deal. Not even from Nature. Neither of us did. May be God never wanted us to be separated. Destiny desires strange things. We were meant to die and our mortal remains preserved in formalin for future generations to study. Our purpose in life was may be that. Only that. But even God does not always get what he wants. Conflict is the crux of life. A duel to the death between God and Nature on one side and on the other – the amazing Dr. Thakkar. (*Drama: Contemporary India*, 238)

Owing to the operation to separate the Siamese twins, Tara becomes crippled for life. Chandan, the privileged brother, wants to turn his anguish into drama on his sister's childhood. Throughout the play we can feel that he bears some kind of resentment against the society. Such is the case even with Tara. She seems to have some kind of repugnance with the outside world and her world consists of only her parents and her brother to whom she is more attached.

Besides exposing the Indian way of thinking, the play also delves into the success and the failures of an Indian family. Tara's father, Patel, mother Bharati, brother Chandan and Tara herself deal with the trauma of disability. A high-spirited girl, Tara is not provided enough opportunities as her brother Chandan. Eventually she dies. Such a tragic treatment again is evidence to the fact how girls are perceived in the Indian society. Chandan could not come to terms with the death of his beloved sister and ultimately escapes to London. Having changed his name to Dan, he attempts to overpower the guilt he feels over his sister's death. His sense of distress and torment is so powerful that at the end of the play, we see him expressing regret to Tara in a heart-rending manner:

> "And those who desire even a moment of freedom, find themselves hurled into space, doomed to crash with some unknown force. (Pause) I no longer desire that freedom. I move. Just move. Without meaning. I forget Tara. I forget that I had a sister—with whom I had shared a body. In one comfortable womb. Till we were forced out—and separated.
> (A spot fades in – empty.)
> But somewhere, sometime, I look up at a shooting star—and wish. I wish that a long-forgotten person would forgive me. Wherever she is.
> "Forgive me, Tara. forgive me, for making it my tragedy."
> (*Drama: Contemporary India* 238)

Dattani has exhibited his skill by employing themes like gender identity, discrimination, middle-class life, revelation etc. He has beautifully shown the excruciating pain of a girl placed in a typical Indian society. He has lent scope to a great deal of experimentation on the stage. For a dramatist, theatrical conventions hold a paramount significance. The discrimination between a male and a female and the repugnance towards a female has been projected circumspectly by him. The intermingling of theatrical techniques along with thematic considerations brings the tragic element of *Tara* to the fore. He makes full use of the stereotypical gender roles. This can be exemplified in the scene when Tara explains the father-son conversation to Roopa:

> The men in the house were deciding on whether they were going to go hunting while the women looked after the cave.
> (*Drama: Contemporary India*, 237)

Dattani's farsightedness lies in the belief that an individual cannot endure in seclusion but one has to make unending effort to synchronize his 'determination' with the system of nature and society. In the play *Tara*, the customized setting and conflict of familial relationship is portrayed. The plot of *Tara* is arranged around domestic relationship where each individual has to bear the burden of social values which eventually brings helplessness and despair in their lives. After the marriage of Mr. Patel and Bharati, Mr. Patel is forced to leave his parental home because this relationship is not accepted by his parents. He has a painful realization about his own struggle in the early years; however, it is his from his family that he receives agony. With the insecurity of the separation from parents and consequently the birth of the Siamese twins, he finds himself secluded. He is pressed to decide upon the surgery of kids for their separation. In this surgery, a tragedy is about to happen. After the surgery, Tara becomes a cripple, Bharati goes insane and Mr. Patel becomes aggressive. He demonstrates apathy towards Tara and doesn't care for the complications involved in her treatment. As gender prejudices and discrimination emerge to the forefront, the tragedy that grips Tara makes the play more pathetic and dismal in nature. Bijay Kumar Das remarks:

> Unlike Girish Karnad who lays emphasis on history, myths and purans, Dattani concentrates on contemporary society and reality in the fast-changing world. He is a playwright on contemporary urban India and his plays are topical dramas. The question he addresses in his plays are those of gender, sex, religion, communal tension, feminine identity, same-sex marriage and above all, gay and lesbian relationship. Hence, his plays appear to be revolting, sometimes, outrageous.
>
> (Das 4, 2008)

In the play, Dattani contemplates the emotional dilemma of Chandan, hence the action is almost internalized. All the major characters in *Tara*, Bharati, Mr. Patel and Chandan suffer from an uncompromising sense of remorse and in the course of the play, it is evident that everyone seeks a means to vent their guilt and contribute their share in Tara's suffering. The psychological turmoil of all the characters is laid bare and we can have a glimpse of their anguish. In order to compensate for his loss, he distances himself from the societal ambience. Mr. Patel's sadistic attitude towards Bharati is a frantic endeavour to run away from the trauma of parental responsibilities. Even Bharati is tense about Tara's future. We need to comprehend that her concern Tara is a reflection of her insecurity. This trepidation surfaces owing to the patriarchal conventions and the disability of Tara. It is a bold attempt on the part of the playwright to bring to the limelight such burning issues.

In this rigmarole, Tara's bold stance and her outlook towards life is more appealing to us. She maintains a stable position by neither brooding over her dilemma nor extracting sympathy from her dear ones. Her confidence is supreme and so is her sense of humour. She does not get vexed when her friend "stared at her leg, felt it and knocked on it". She describes herself as "Strong, Healthy. Beautiful." Both Tara and Chandan proudly show their legs to their neighbours without manifesting any inhibitions. They are intellectually smarter as compared to other children of their age. Even though Tara is required to undergo a kidney transplant, she exhibits a bold disposition. Dan is not able to come to terms with Tara's untimely death and has severed all ties with his own family. After her death, he learns that their separation was inevitable. The doctor who operated them believes that the greatest challenge was to keep the girl alive. Patel tells Chandan that the twins had three legs. The third leg was fed by the girl's blood system. The chances of the leg's survival were greater with the girl. But Bharati and her father decided to give the leg to the boy. With this shocking disclosure, we come to know that Bharati's love for Tara was an outcome of her guilt consciousness.

Though a change comes over Bharati's behaviour towards Tara, Patel remains unchanged. Chandan considers that he was responsible for Tara's tragedy. He vehemently believes that as he was a male, he snatched away the possibilities of a healthy life from Tara. Dr. Thakkar is also one of the wrongdoers as he was involved in Tara's operation. Dan tries to overcome his agony by scripting a play "Twinkle Tara" and dedicating it to her.

> To masticate my memories in my mind and spit out the result to the world in anger. *(Picking up the sheet he has typed.)* My progress, so far, I must admit, has been zero. But I persist with the comforting thought that things can't get any worse. I keep staring at my typewriter everyday wondering how best to turn my anguish into drama. All I find every day, without fail, is one typewritten sheet with the title of the play, my name and address, and the date. Nothing changes – except the date.
>
> (*Drama: Contemporary India* 232-233)

Tara is, no doubt, a victim of the tragic consequences that keep happening around her. Adding to her misery is the attitude of the society towards the physically challenged. Thus, the tragic element is accentuated to a great extent. Nobody befriends Tara, owing to her disability. Bharati has to bribe Roopa with cosmetics and other such stuffs to make her come close to Tara. Yet, Roopa has a hidden dislike for the freaks. Towards the end of the play, there is a verbal war between Tara and Roopa. As a result, Roopa places a poster with a slogan "WE DON'T WANT FREAKS" against a wall in the area. This demoralizes both Tara and Chandan. They are shocked and are afraid of meeting new people. The element of tragedy incorporated in the play speaks volumes of the playwright's concern for the disabled. To quote Bijay Kumar Das:

> Mahesh Dattani frequently takes as his subject the complicated dynamics of the modern urban family. His characters struggle

> for some kind of freedom and happiness under the weight of tradition, cultural constructions of gender and repressed desire. Their dramas are played out on multi-level sets where exterior and interior become one and geographical locations are collapsed – in short, his settings are as fragmented as the families who inhabit them. (Das 7, 2008)

Family tensions also augment the impediments of Tara. Thus, Dattani embarks on a mission to voice the sufferings of the handicapped and reaches out to the multifarious issues associated with the same. He has also delved deep into the concerns that plague the society. The play *Tara* vouches for the much-needed acceptance that society needs to extend to individuals like Tara. The conversation between Tara and Chandan shows how the twins are connected to each other. They know each other very well and have a deep understanding of their predicaments as well. The comments made in a lighter vein, jokes, curt replies to Roopa and debates over choices and preferences, all go on to prove that both can't do without the other. That is the reason why Chandan's approach changes dramatically when he realizes the truth about the separation. He is the only character in the play who expresses grief towards his beloved sister's death. Though the play exposes the tragedy of Tara, it focuses equally on the tragedy of Chandan (Dan) as he now understands that the future is bleak for him and life, absurd.

Works Cited

Das, Bijay Kumar. *Form and Meaning in Mahesh Dattani's Plays,* New Delhi: Atlantic Publishers & Distributors (P) Ltd, 2008.

Mee, Erin B. *DramaContemporary India,* New Delhi: Oxford University Press, 2002.

20

Spivak, Subalternity and Mahesh Dattani's *Final Solutions*

Sanjeev Kumar

This paper seeks to investigate representation of subaltern in Mahesh Dattani's play *Final Solutions* in the purview of postcolonial theory particularly from Gayatri Chakravorty Spivak's interrogation of the voice of subalternity. Dattani is one of the distinguished contemporary playwrights, asserts Radha Ramaswamy in his "Introduction" to the play in question, experimenting with both—technique and thematic issues while encompassing "brilliant use of a variety of spoken Indian English not heard on the English language stage before" (*Final Solutions* vii). While highlighting multifaceted vibrations of contemporary psyche and its distortions, especially in the postcolonial set-up, Dattani unearths how the subaltern seeks to speak against a background of multiple oppressions—religious, social, familial, gender and, more importantly, psychological. While exposing the communal conflict in *Final Solutions*, the playwright highlights how the subjugated and maltreated voice protest in an attempt to affirm themselves.

The term 'subaltern', taken from Antonio Gramsci's *Prison Notebooks* (1971) where "subalterno" euphemistically designate a class of inferior rank, i.e. proletariat, has become all inclusive in the hands of Spivak, Guha and other postcolonial scholars, and includes people who are browbeaten, subjugated and marginalized by the oppressive forces in the society. Spivak's concerns for the subalternity demonstrates a post-structuralist, Marxist, feminist, and psychoanalytic critique of the power that tends to throw the unvoiced and battered mass to the periphery of the system thus turning them into *others*. She emphasizes, observes Elleke Boehmer, that the "so-called subaltern consciousness is a product of elite discourse, not a concrete entity in the world; it is construction of socially authorized language, not a self or subject that can will itself to speak" (*Literary Theory and Criticism* 354). Ranajit Guha uses the term "as a name for the general attribute of subordination in South Asian society whether this is expressed in terms of class, caste, age, gender and office or in any other way." (*Subaltern Studies* vii) Subaltern Studies, as a result, attempts to "allow the 'people' finally to speak within the jealous pages of elitist historiography and, in so doing, to speak for, or to sound the muted voices of, the truly oppressed." (*Postcolonial Theory* 2)

It is with this perspective and meaning of 'subaltern' that this paper analyses *Final Solutions* as a critique of various subaltern groups in the contemporary India challenged by myriad forces within its territory. Dattani has meticulously mapped out several strands of subalternity which basically include two major religious divisions—Hindu and Muslim. Within these two groups, nevertheless, there are multiple classes that have been nullified and thrown to the periphery—women, literate and illiterates, and young and old.

The play sets off with Daksha writing her diary on 31 March 1948 and translating her thoughts to the personified diary. She is a young girl, she writes, who "does not matter to anyone outside her home." (4) What she also mentions is the objections of her in-laws to her singing. She admits, "All my dreams have been shattered." (4) She is conscious of her being a marginalized woman unable to find anyone to share her thoughts except the diary. She seems to show no resistance to her subjugation and repression at fifteen and remains silent. She is the *other* who remains weak and fails to speak.

Daksha also gives glimpses of the trauma of partition and the violence associated with it. Partition, she says, was "a most terrible thing" that happened to her country. (4) When her father tells her that the English, before leaving the country, "had let loose the dogs," she dislikes it. She, then, throws light on how the communal riots in the streets spoilt the charm of Indian independence:

> The windows broke, one by one. My mother and myself, we hid in the puja room. The stones came smashing into our home. I clung to my mother. My mother clung to the family idol of Lord Krishna. I could see the fire they were carrying, reflected in the broken glass lying around us. (5)

This episode highlights the communal violence turning the dominant religious group into subalternity not only by physical power but also by psychological force. What we find here is the *othering* of a religious group by the outraged other religious ethnicity. Subaltern here represents, in the words of John Beverley, "a subordinated *particularity,* and in a world where power relations are spatialized that means it must have a spatial referent, a form of territoriality." (*Subalternity and Representation* 2)

Initially based on politic and economic study, we should not forget, Subaltern Studies group of historiographers now covers religiosity, castism, rumours, and even myth rather than hegemonic cultural forms only. In the later subaltern studies, asserts Prem Poddar, "where colonial power is understood as a diffuse force circulating through the entire body politic, the subaltern is not an independent entity and is located only within elite discourses. The subaltern cannot, therefore, simply speak" (*Encyclopedia* 427). The focus of Subaltern Studies within the gamut of postcolonial studies has increasing shifted away from the 'subaltern' toward 'community' as the critique of the nationalist project has proceeded. This fragmentation of subalternity, in the context of Indian society, is centralized under the rubric of the colonial and postcolonial state and must be widened, recent scholars have added, to include a critique of Enlightenment rationalism and secularism.

Final Solutions encompass many of these strands within the range of subalternity. The religious outrage, even after 40 years, lingers on. The old Daksha as Hardika sadly admits, "Yes, things have not changed that much" (6). The choruses, representatives of Hindu mob, verbalize it loudly and furiously after the Hindu chariot was broken and the priest was murdered by the Muslims:

> Chorus 4, 5. Why did they? Why did they today?
> Chorus 1. How dare they?
> ...
> Chorus 1. It is in their blood!
> Chorus 2, 3. It is in their blood to destroy!
> ...
> Chorus 1 (*pounding with his stick*). Send... them... back.
> ...
> Chorus 2 (*pounding with his stick*). Drive... them... out.
> ...
> Chorus 3. Kill the sons of swine! (6-7)

The rage and resentment of the chorus represents the common fanatic Hindu ready to rise against the religious coercion by the other religious extremists. This is open resistance and protest of the Hindu community having no religious tolerance against the Muslim minority. The bombing on the Muslim girls' hostel is a case of retaliation which shows their enraged religious outburst.

The choruses, wearing the Muslim masks now, seem to contradict the apprehensions of the Hindus who think that the Muslims would attack them. They rather object to the charges of Hindus:

> Chorus 3. They say we razed their temples yesterday.
> Chorus 2. That we broke their chariot today.
> Chorus 1. That we'll bomb their streets tomorrow.
> Chorus all. Why would we? Why? Why? Why would we?

The choruses having put on different masks at different times create impressions of two subaltern classes that, with the change of place and time, become oppressive powers and then the oppressed minority simultaneously. They show their resistance and emotional hatred based on religious animosity.

This raises questions on Spivak's assertion that the subaltern cannot speak. It, nevertheless, is a movement away from her argument that the West has always looked down upon the East and writes in a way that carries its submissive voices. These submissive voices are not genuine as they carry the weight of hybrid consciousness. Spivak, on her way to deconstruct historiography, interrogates Marx's suggestion that man must endeavour toward self-determination and unalienable practice. She also questions Gramsci's proposition that "the lower classes" must "achieve self-awareness via a series of negations" (Quoted in *Elementary Aspects of Peasant Insurgency* 28). Her point of departure rests upon the argument that the subaltern can speak only when they have erased the forced ideology of the power system which they have imbibed unconsciously while living under duress for a long period. She argues that a subaltern consciousness is "not consciousness-in-general, but a historicized political species thereof" (*Subaltern Studies IV* 338). The 'subaltern,' therefore, does not appear without the thought of the elite or the power system that has marginalized them and has reduced them to *others.*

When Spivak considers the 'margins,' i.e. the silent or silenced centre of the circuit marked out by the epistemic violence, men and women among the illiterate peasantry, the tribals, the lowest strata of the urban subproletariat, he argues that they are not heard: "on the other side of the international division of labour from socialized capital, inside *and* outside the circuit of the epistemic violence of imperialist law and education supplementing an earlier economic text, *can the subaltern speak?*" (*Marxism and the Interpretation of Culture* 257). She adds that for the 'true' subaltern group, whose identity is its difference, there is no unrepresentable subaltern subject that can know and speak itself (*Marxism and the Interpretation of Culture* 257). In other words, the oppressed and silenced cannot, by definition, "speak or achieve self-legitimation without ceasing to be that named subject under neo-colonialism." (Raman Selden 234)

For Spivak, Stephen Morton maintains, the term 'subaltern' is "useful because it is flexible; it can accommodate social identities and struggles" (such as woman and the colonized) that do not fall under the reductive terms of strict class analysis (*Gayatri Chakravorty Spivak* 45). As she asserts in an interview published in the US journal *Polygraph*:

> I like the word 'subaltern' for one reason. It is truly situational. 'Subaltern' began as a description of a certain rank in the military. The word was used under censorship by Gramsci: he called Marxism 'monism, ' and was obliged to call the proletarian 'subaltern.' That word, used under duress, has been transformed into the description of everything that doesn't fall under strict class analysis. I like that, because it has no theoretical rigor. (*The Post-Colonial Critic* 141)

Moving from the West perception to the subaltern within the array of the East, the Subaltern Studies highlights that whatever is subalternity in the Western mind may not be so in the East. In other words, whatever is the subaltern ideology in the West may become a force and an oppressive tool in the East. The Hindu minority, for instance, is subalternity when looked from the Western point of view but a majority that represents power within India. Another point here that must be considered is that the subaltern class, based on religious count, at times, becomes a force, takes power in its hand and turns the otherwise power of majority into a minority one. Who is the subaltern in these two classes then? Does it entirely depend on circumstances, time and place? Is it more than that and has other dimensions?

Leela Gandhi raises similar issues in her noted book *Postcolonial Theory: A Critical Introduction.* Supporting Spivak's assertion that we may not touch the consciousness of the subaltern even if we investigate their politics, Gandhi authenticates Spivak's questions:

> How can the historian/investigator avoid the inevitable risk of representing herself as an authoritative representative of subaltern consciousness? Should the intellectual 'abstain from representation?' Which intellectual is equipped to represent which subaltern class? Is there an 'unrepresentable subaltern class that can know and speak itself?' And finally, who—if any—are the 'true' of 'representative' subalterns of history, especially within the frame of reference provided by the imperialist project? (*Postcolonial Theory* 2)

Final Solutions, when scrutinized from aforesaid curious perspectives, seems to relate to some of the arguments. As the play moves, we find things changing and taking curious turns. Dattani provides us a peep into the mind of people engaged in practices of communal violence and oppression. Hardika (the aged Daksha) complains, "They don't want equality. They want to be superior" (11). Her numerous responses toward the Muslims show her prejudice and contempt particularly toward the two young Muslim boys—Bobby and Javed. We also find that these two boys are interrogated, rather menaced by the chorus representing the Hindu community. They take refuge in Ramnik Gandhi's house where his daughter Smita recognizes them as her friend Tasneem's brother and his friend. The rest of the play is enacted in the house with the queries, comments, disgusts, anguish and resentment of different characters.

Hardika is afraid that her family will be hated for protecting the two boys. She is also afraid of the pride in the Muslims' eyes that she had witnessed during her youth. She says:

> I know their wretched pride! It had destroyed me before and I am afraid it would destroy my family again! (*Pause.*) They don't want equality. They want to be superior. (11)

She also narrates how she, when young and married, was denied sternly to visit the Muslims and get mixed up with them. She remembers what happened when she returned from Muslim's house one day and got rebuked by her husband Hari.

> I did not touch their food! (*Recoils as if she has been hit.*) Ah! Don't hit me! (*Angrily*) Don't do that! I swear I didn't eat anything! Aah! Stop that! Stop it! All right. I won't go there again. (71)

She is a silenced woman in the family, an 'other' who has no voice to speak. We find here echoes of Spivak's argument that within the effaced itinerary of the subaltern subject, the track of sexual difference is doubly effected. She adds that it is not the question of female participation in insurgency or the basic rules of sexual division but both and "the ideological construction of gender keeps the male dominant. If... the subaltern has no history and cannot speak, the subaltern as female is even more deeply in shadow." (*Marxism and the Interpretation of Culture* 287)

Even in her old age Hardika remains an oppressed class. She is, at the same time, an enlightened soul who has come to an understanding that the Hindu fanatics are not a part of her community. They are unreliable people who give air to the fire of communal violence. She says, rather ironically, "Where were our own people when we needed them?" (33) The time when "they" were needed reminds of the time and place where her community was minor and the Muslims were a majority.

Another female subaltern is Aruna who has little substance in the play as she is also put to periphery in the family. Nobody attempts to really listen to her which nullifies her being. She is mocked at by her daughter and Javed. He disrupts her religious ceremony and perturbs her mentally and religiously. Smita also joins Bobby and Javed and does not care for what her mother says. What Dattani highlights through the creation of Hardika and Aruna as subaltern women is the fact that a postcolonial woman becomes a subaltern when seen through the lenses of male-dominated society or of imperialism. The subaltern woman, Robert Young writes in connection with Spivak, is "rewritten continuously as the object of patriarchy or of imperialism" (*White Mythologies* 164). It is imperative to quote Spivak in full here:

> Between patriarchy and imperialism, subject-constitution and object-formation, the figure of the woman disappears, not into a pristine nothingness, but into a violent shuttling which is the displaced figuration of the 'third-world woman' caught between tradition and modernization.... Such would be the property of repression... repression functions well as a sentence to disappear,

> but also as an injunction to silence, affirmation of non-existence; and consequently states that of all this there is nothing to say, to see, to know. (*Marxism and the Interpretation of Culture* 306)

If Hardika and Smita are representatives of traditional Hindu women, Smita represents modern outlook little mindful of the superstitious religious matters. If she has never spoken of against these empty religious ceremonies relating to untouchability, she says, it is because she did not want to hurt the feelings of the elders. When her mother states that it is good to have progressive ideas but not at the cost of *sanskars*, she bursts:

> How can you expect me to be proud of something which stifles everything else around it? It snifles me! Yes! Maybe I am prejudiced because I do not belong. But not belonging makes things so clear. I can see so clearly how wrong you are. (57)

Hardika and Smita are representatives of two different generations. When Hardika, in her youth, attempted to resist the Hindu caste ideology, she faced brutality from her husband. Her resistance vanished and she surrendered herself before the patriarchal forces that would turn her into a subaltern. But Smita does not surrender before such forces and has the ability to uncage herself from the chains of familial oppression. She says to Bobby, "Maybe we should all run away from home like Javed. For five minutes every day. So we can quickly gulp in some fresh air and go back in." (67)

Smita's assertion of her individuality, nevertheless, remains weak as she has to live with her parents and abide by their desires and expectations. Spivak maintains that through similar instances of territoriality and:

> ... the communal mode of power, the figure of the woman, moving from clan to clan, and family to family as daughter/

> sister and wife/mother, syntaxes patriarchal continuity even as she is herself drained of proper identity. In this particular area, the continuity of community or history, for subaltern and historian alike, is produced on... the dissimulation of her discontinuity, on the repeated emptying of her meaning as instrument. (*Subaltern Studies IV* 362)

Smita is merely an instrument in the play who represents females in a family who empty their own meaning in the face of patriarchy.

Ramnik represents patriarchy but with an open and sane mind. He is not opinionated and does not force his ideas on others. He seems to represent the playwright and becomes a vehicle, through Bobby and Javed, in unfolding the crucial events in the play. He does not have any case to be a subaltern in .the play and hence needs no further discussion.

Bobby and Javed remain central to the full understanding of the play. Babban changed his name to Bobby because his college friends would call him Baboon that reveals how a person has to change his name on account of his friends' jokes and mischief. Javed is rather an interesting character as it is he who offers serious and combating resistance to the power that tries to oppress him. At the same time, he invites our sympathy for being misused by the Muslim fanatics for their selfish motive of spreading religious agnosticism. The astounding fact is that he knows that he has been used and abused. He knows that the Hindu and Muslim vagabonds spreading communal violence are alike. In his yearning to raise his voice in remonstration, he was swayed by "cheap sentiment," he says. (50)

Javed is a confused minority who could go to any extant to assert his existence before the majority Hindus. When he heard the chanting coming from the Hindu precession, something snapped, something broke in him and he got ready to use violent means to assert himself. In his trance or frenzy of communal hatred, he shouted and abused them, started pelting stones at the procession and finally attempted to kill the priest. The priest, nonetheless, was killed by another Muslim frantic. The chorus, wearing a Muslim mask, speaks:

> Must we lose our identity? Is that what they want? Must we tolerate more? Does our future lie in their hands? Is there anyone more unsure, more insecure than us? Oh, what a curse it is to be less in number! (54)

The Muslim minority feels menaced by the Hindu majority and faces psychological oppression. The play also throws light on how some selfish Hindus would burn the shops of the minority creating conditions to sell the shops very cheap.

The consciousness of the groups and individuals in the play, to bring Spivak back, is not the consciousness of the class of the general consciousness. Spivak terms it 'self-consciousness' and asserts that it is in this particular instance only that Gramsci's notion of an "ideological *coherent,*" "spontaneous philosophy of the multitude" is reasonable and compelling. (*Prison Notebooks* 421) She argues:

> For class-consciousness does not engage the ground-level of consciousness—consciousness in general. 'Class' is not, after all, an inalienable description of a human reality. Class-consciousness on the *descriptive* level is itself a strategic and artificial rallying awareness which, on the *transformative* level, seeks to destroy the mechanics which come to construct the outlines of the very class of which a collective consciousness has been situationally developed.... The task of the 'consciousness' of class or collectivity within a social field of exploitation and domination is thus necessarily self-alienating. (*Subaltern Studies IV* 342)

This is how the subaltern in *Final Solutions* fail to find voice of their own and speak in multiple voices which, as a matter of fact, echoes the oppressor of the power people/system. They, nevertheless, remain on the periphery of the system—marginalized and *others.*

Final Solutions provides no solution to the complex problems it highlights. Yet the play represents multiple facets of subalternity who suffer pangs of being either members of a minor community or being females. Even within a certain community we find strata of different categories. Some of them offer resistance to religious, familial, emotional and psychological oppression from the powers that tend to marginalize and subjugate them. While a select numbers are heard, others remain at the periphery and cannot speak and remain *others.*

Works Cited

Beverley, John. *Subalternity and Representation: Arguments in Cultural Theory.* Durham: Duke Uni. Press, 1999.

Boehmer, Elleke. "Postcolonialism." *Literary Theory and Criticism.* Ed. Patricia Waugh. New Delhi: OUP, 2006.

Dattani, Mahesh. *Final Solutions* with "Introduction" by Radha Ramaswamy. New Delhi: Penguin, 2005. All citations from the play are included in the text in parenthesis.

Gandhi, Leela. *Postcolonial Theory: A Critical Introduction.* Delhi: OUP, 1999.

Gramsci, Antonio. *Prison Notebooks,* tr. Quintin Hoare and Geoffrey Noel-Smith. New York: International Publishers, 1971.

Guha, Ranajit, ed. *Subaltern Studies 1: Writing on South Asian History and Society.* Delhi: OUP, 1982.

Harasym, Sarah, ed. *The Post-Colonial Critic: Interviews, Strategies, Dialogues.* New York: Routledge, 1990.

Morton, Stephen. *Gayatri Chakravorty Spivak.* London: Routledge, 2003.

Poddar, Prem. "Subaltern Studies." *Encyclopedia of Postcolonial Studies.* Ed. John C. Hawley. Westport: Greenwood Press, 2001.

Selden, Raman, Widdowson, Peter and Brooker, Peter. *A Reader's Guide to Contemporary Literary Theory.* Delhi: Pearson, 2006.

Spivak, Gayatri Chakravorty. "Can the Subaltern Speak?" *Marxism and the Interpretation of Culture.* Eds. Cary Nelson and Lawrence Grossberg. Urbana: U. of Illinois Press, 1988.

_____. "Subaltern Studies: Deconstructing Historiography." *Subaltern Studies IV: Writing on South Asian History and Society.* Ed. Ranajit Guha. Delhi: OUP, 1985. 330-363.

Young, Robert. *White Mythologies: Writing History and the West.* London: Routledge, 1990.

21

Tara: The Other Side

M.K. Rukhaya

Mahesh Dattani's *Tara* comes across as a play that deals with twin aspects which are two sides of the same coin. It also presents the conflict between illusion and reality as echoed by the multi-level set. The house of the Patels are as kept in memory. The only realistic level is the part of the wall covered with faded wallpaper that has the writer writing the play in which he appears to the audience. In this sense, the playwright presents metatheatrical aspects as he talks of distancing oneself from the experience and writing about it.

The Doctor as portrayed in the set, stands in contrast as the omnipotent Author with the Author-God like stance. It thereby underlines the clash between the subjective and objective author. Chandan discovers that even distancing himself physically "in a seedy suburb of London thousands of miles away from home" hasn't done the trick. He attempts as much as possible to alienate himself from the script, but suffers from a writer's block and everything remains stagnant on his paper just as his life is. Just as in his life, nothing changes but the dates. And the greatest irony is that Indo-Anglian literature isn't worth toilet paper in his own country. He neglects his own personal history to get over his guilt with what happened to Tara. Just as the lowest portion occupies a major portion of the stage, the memory of guilt haunts and dominates Chandan's personality. It is to deny this that he creates his alter-ego Dan. His being a Diaspora, this causes another divide in his self: the identity of the Diaspora caught between his native culture and foreign culture as signified by Chandan and Dan.

> Our culture is so rich with tradition, and that's a great advantage and disadvantage a swell..(321)
>
> The desperate immigrant (Mimes removing yet another.)(324)
>
> The mysterious brown with the phoney accent. The last being the hardest to drop having spent two whole years in acquiring it. And what remains is what I intend making capital of. (324)

The title 'Tara' is symbolic of a shooting star that is a temporary guest of a small fraction of time as the protagonist is. The idea also brings to mind the concept of the binary star systems that consist of two stars that "are gravitationally bound, and generally move around each other in stable orbits. When two such stars have a relatively close orbit, their gravitational interaction can have a significant impact on their evolution." Just as the Siamese twins in this case have an interwoven identity; and has a great impact on each other, mentally and biologically in their evolution. They are spiritually inseparable. With the demise of Tara, Chandan experiences a sense of identity crisis.

The inseparable twins very evocatively remind us of the celebrated pair Rahel and Estha in Arundhati Roy's *The God of Small Things* who are forcibly separated by choice. Just as they emerge from a zygote they get back their revenge on society as they go into a taboo method of fusion towards the end of the novel. The twins in the prescribed play are born as 'inseparably fused'—hugging each other emblematizing their emotional coherence at the very outset. Chandan envisages their reconciliation towards the end of the play as they get together in a tight embrace, back to their former fused form. They stand for two sides of the same concept. For instance, gender. How man and woman complement each other, and how one is incomplete without the other:

> TARA: And me. Maybe we still are. Like we've always been. Inseparable. The way we started life. Two lives and one body, in one comfortable womb. Till we were forced out...(325)

Dattani sees *Tara* as a play about the gendered self, about coming to terms with the feminine side of oneself in a world that favours always what is 'male'. The quality of being effeminate is a reason for shame in India (320). The playwright also seeks to portray science and nature in a similar manner. How Science and Nature complement each other. However Science cannot conquer everything and has its own lapses as Nature does. This is signified by the twins with impaired legs as they form a mirror image of each other. The play depicts how Science cannot always conquer Nature as the leg attributed to the boy is rejected by the body in a brash attempt at disregarding both Nature and God. Dan hits the nail on the head when he asserts "Conflict is the crux of life. A duel to death between God and nature on one side and on other –the amazing Dr. Thakkar (330). This explains the God-like stance of the Doctor, who is seated with a seeming omnipotent presence representing Advanced Technology.

> Behind, on a higher level, is a chair in which Dr. Thakkar remains seated throughout the play. Although he doesn't watch the action of the play, his connection is asserted by his Sheer God-like presence. (323)

The drama has two sides to it with respect to the time frame-the past and the present. It also reflects the virtual and the real. An utterance sometimes refers to two different time frames with respect to time, occasion and the statement applicable to different characters. The following lines hold true for both Bharati and Dan as they are distant in time and space:

> If at all they must know, it will be from me. Not from you. (345)

The twins, especially 'Tara', are repeatedly referred to as "freaks". The term 'freak' has been conventionally used to refer to person who has something unusual regarding their appearance or behaviour. The older usage of the word 'freaks' refers to the state of being physically deformed, or characterized by rare diseases and conditions. The word was utilized to suggest 'sideshow performers'. In such an instance, the word 'freak' represents the state of women, who are marginalized. The female race who are not congenitally deformed but are so as society forces the handicap upon them. Just as it is presented in concrete terms in the play: Tara's leg is callously separated from her to render her twin brother normal, defying the tenets of Nature. It echoes Simone de Beauvoir's dictum: "One is not born a woman, one becomes one."

A natural freak refers to a genetic abnormality, while a made freak is a once normal person who experienced or initiated an alteration at some point in life (such as receiving surgical implants). Here both the terms can be used to describe Dan and Tara. But Tara is less of a natural freak; as Nature was more in her favour. "Freak" has also been employed to describe genetic mutations in plants and animals, i.e. "freaks of nature." "Freak" used in the verb form, implies: "to become stressed and upset". Here, the twins are in a state of depression owing to their predicament but utilize a curtain of sarcasm and wit to shield the same.

Man cannot accept the woman's intellect, and gets intimidated by her intelligence. Tara's victory at the card game is seen as thorough cheating and Chandan is ashamed to admit her victory. He sees her as a good business woman as she cheats at cards; not attributing it to her business acumen, but to her shrewdness. Tara gets hurt at the remark as it holds no truth value. Even Patel ignores her future prospects and the need to engage her in any meaningful endeavour. She is forced to conform to the stereotype of the Indian woman—devoid of any intellect, deemed fit only to perform mechanical household chores. In other words, a domestic animal, which can be cared for, but not regarded with respect.

Tara quips at this: "The men in the house were deciding on whether they were going hunting while the women looked after the cave" (328). She highlights the plight of women who were presumed to be suitable for the domestic domain only. The play as a whole thus depicts the relegation of the relevance of the Woman, and her upper edge whenever it does assert itself in a male-dominated society. This is why the Grandfather and the Mother who represent tradition prefer the male over the female; the Male is the archetypal successor or prototype of cultural progeny. This explains why the author names the play after the female child whose identity is demoted otherwise; in order to invert the dialectical pair male/female. The woman has always been hailed in philosophy, but in practice she is treated as an object to be overlooked. As Virginia Woolf asserts in her *A Room of One's Own*: "Imaginatively, she is of the highest importance; practically she is completely insignificant. She pervades poetry from cover to cover; she is all but absent from history."

In the prescribed play, though Bharati dotes on her daughter Tara, she insensitively attributes a piece of her daughter to the son. The conflict between illusion and reality is yet again echoed here. What is actually a public display of attention on part of the mother is actually a screen to shield her guilt. The context also serves as a satire on the self-sufficient Indian male, for whom, to accept anything feminine is beneath his dignity, and an indelible question mark on his masculinity. Even Dan acknowledges the same, as he writes the play. Though the craft of the play is his, he has to borrow the material from Tara. Aristotle had declared that "the female is female by virtue of a certain lack of qualities" and added that "we should look upon the female state, as it were, a deformity, one which occurs in the ordinary course of nature. On account of its weakness it quickly approaches its maturity and old age since inferior things all reach their end more quickly" (*Generation of Animals* trans. Peck). In *Tara*, the deformity of the Woman is caused by the Man, and caused in order to complete the Man. The playwright utilizes the motif symbolically as well. This is the reason why Tara approaches her end more quickly, and it is not owing to her inferiority. The handicap also symbolizes the predicament of girls in Indian families who are made to forsake their chances of getting educated as the edification of the boy becomes a priority.

There is a reference to the Lady of Shallot, who is imprisoned within a building made of "four gray walls and four gray towers." It runs parallel to the plight of Tara who is jailed in her handicap and the constraints of tradition. Just as the Lady of Shallot foresees her impending doom in the mirror, Tara senses her end too in the mirror represented by the expressions of her closest relatives. Both Tara and the Lady of Shallot, find a release from their predicament only in death.

The death of Tara has a more powerful impact than her existence. Just as the death of the Star gives way to the Black Hole.

The Black Hole stands for the God in the World of Physics, it being linked to the Male Gods in Hinduism like Shiva, Krishna, Rama etc. who are black. Religion has also been predominantly patriarchal. Christianity professes: "Men are God's stars." (Genesis 15: 15-18.) By naming his female protagonist as 'Tara', Mahesh Dattani puts it otherwise.

Works Cited

Dattani, Mahesh. *Collected Plays*. New Delhi: *Penguin, 2000.*

de Beauvoir, Simone. *The Second Sex*. New York: Vintage Books, 1973.

Woolf, Virginia. A Room of One's Own. New York: Harcourt Brace & Co., 1989. 53

22

Tara: The Star That Never Shines

Sanchita Das

All the world's a stage,
And all the men and women merely players:
They have their exits and their entrances;
And one man in his time plays many parts.
(Shakespeare, *As You Like It* 266)

Mahesh Dattani takes on what he calls the 'invisible issues' of Indian society in his plays. By pulling out taboo subjects from under the rug and placing them on stage for public discussion, he challenges the constructions of 'India' and 'Indian' as they have traditionally been defined in modern theatre. He is known for bringing into the open those issues which the Indian society and culture tends to brush into the garbage pail, because they are uncomfortable, has written and produced the play *Tara*, which has several entry points.

The play can be approached through the issue of simple man-woman relationship, or it can be responded to in terms of the disabled children's struggle against a variety of odds, which have been put in their way by nature, or chance, or accident of their birth. Or one can respond to the text through the positioning of the girl-child in Indian culture and society.

The man-woman relationship is dramatized through the interactions between Mr. Patel and his wife Bharati. He is shown to be often rude and authoritarian, when it comes to dealing with her and taking decisions. He turns out to be a caring husband, too, in his looking after Bharati during her bouts of depression. His words about Bharati reveal his concern: "Maybe I'm expecting the worst. It may never happen—no. Things are getting out of hand. I must worry about her. Yes, I am worried—about my wife" (Dattani 330). But at the same time, he exhibits a streak of harshness, even heartlessness towards her. His admonition to Bharati not to give one of her kidneys to Tara who needs a kidney transplant, is not the result of his concern for his wife's health, but is the product of his cruel attitude towards her. When questioned by Bharati why he is against it, his answer is in keeping with his overall treatment of his wife: "Because I do not want you to have the satisfaction of doing it" (Dattani 344). This quite negates his professed concern which he talks about when Bharati is in the throes of depression. Similarly, he deprives Bharati of the chance to confess her sin to Tara which she has committed towards her (Tara). That would have relieved her guilt and possibly her malady, but it seems that he does not want relief for her. His words sound heartless: "No. I don't want to give her the satisfaction of confessing" (Dattani 377). His summary dismissal of Bharati's opinions as inconsequential and not paying heed to her expostulations on behalf of Tara represents him as a typical overriding patriarchal husband. It is another matter that we come to know later why Bharati was rapidly trying to champion Tara's case—it is not for the sake of Tara that she does it. However, with Bharati's underlying motive for her effusions of love towards Tara becoming clear, the play does not linger on intensively on the unequal relationship between the husband and wife. This, therefore, is not the central strand, determining the progress of the plot.

The theme of odds faced by the physically challenged children in society no doubt comes through. Tara's artificial leg, the ridicule she is subjected to by her peers at school and in the neighbourhood (by Roopa, Prema and Nalini— the last two do not appear on the stage) and the limp caused by the artificial leg which symbolically serves as the marker of a disadvantage compared to others are indicative of the playwright's interest in this issue. Roopa's words about Tara are representative of the attitude of Prema and Nalini, and possibly of the society at large: "She is a real freak of nature all right" (Dattani 342). But in this case, too, we find that this disability does not pose an insurmountable challenge to Tara, who has the capacity to laugh at it herself, and laugh at the imbecility of those who consider it great deprivation and a subject of pity or ridicule. She is very much capable of holding her own and making the best of her life, with all its givens. This,too, therefore, does not frame the whole of the play, demanding detailed attention.

I would, therefore, like to use the last prism, that is, the positioning of the girl-child in Indian society to enter the text and raise the following questions: Who has killed Tara? And why? I would like to argue in the course of the essay that it is not one individual who has killed Tara. It is the socio-cultural system which is responsible for her death. The beliefs, the attitudes, and the prejudices that are deep-rooted in the collective Indian cultural psyche become instrumental in taking Tara's life. It is a complex play. Issues of class and community interplay to weave the plot of the play and bring about the climactic moment of reversal of expectations. This reversal of expectations in the matter of Bharati, Tara's mother, who sympathized with Tara, actually is not the central point the play makes.

Coming to the question who has killed Tara, it is proper to know who Tara is, what her background is, in what sort of family, neighbourhood and society she is born and lives and dies. She is a Siamese twin, born to the Patels— Mr. Patel and Bharati, his wife. Born conjoined as one body with her brother Chandan, she is separated by a complicated, technologically advanced surgical operation by Dr. Thakkar who is visiting India from London. The discrimination against her begins right from the process of surgery. I would revert to it later, but I would like to mention in passing the three levels on which Tara is deprived of what is her due:(i) at the hands of Nature, which makes her weaker and reduces the chances of her survival. In Dr. Thakkar's words: "Our greatest challenge would be to keep the girl alive. Nature wanted to kill her. We couldn't allow it" (Dattani 376), (ii) At the level of society whose attitude is reflected through her peers— her classmate in class nine, Roopa and her friends Prema and Nalini, who find amusement in her wooden leg, (iii) At the level of family, especially at the hands of her mother and maternal grandfather—they deprive her of one of the two healthy legs. Briefly going over the three levels of discrimination, we find that it is the last which would need detailed consideration:

1. Discrimination against her by nature is accidental. Generally, born as single children, girls have better chances of survival than boys. But in this case, Tara happens to be the weaker of the two twins.

2. As far as discrimination by the society is concerned, Tara is not overly disturbed what others think of her infirmity. Therefore, it is almost insignificant.

3. Discrimination by the family is a serious matter, as it is conscious and is the result of a conspiracy against her. At the time of surgical separation from her brother, a conspiracy is hatched against her by none else than her very own mother, Bharati, who has conceived and produced her, her grandfather (maternal) and Dr. Thakkar. She gets

> deprived of one of the two healthy legs. The Siamese twins had three healthy legs. One of the healthy legs had greater chances of survival on the girl child as the blood supply to it came from the girl's body. But Tara was not given her due. She was deprived of what was hers because Bharati wanted to have a healthy and able son. So, Chandan was given the two healthy legs. This conspiracy needs to be commented upon in the light of what happens to the girl child in Indian society. There is no specific and clear answer because there cannot be one. No one individual is responsible for what happens to her, because this has to do with the positioning of the girl-child in the Indian society.

The point I am trying to make is that all types of discrimination Tara faces at the hands of her family members are the consequence of their being prisoners in the hands of collective unconscious that constitutes their psyches. The sources of this collective unconscious are the cultural/religious texts which determine Indians' attitude towards women. What happens to the girl child in the Indian society? She faces infanticide and if by chance she is born, she is abandoned either to die, or to be picked up by an orphanage or by a needy couple and or compassionate couple who just want a child. More often than not, the abandoned girl child dies. Ironically, this happens in a society, which has a mythology, with goddesses being worshipped as Kali and Durga (shakti), Saraswati (as wisdom) and Lakshmi (as wealth). Indian society which seeks to occupy high moral ground through its belief in the concept of 'vasudhev kutumbkam' does not hesitate in exterminating its daughters by short term or long-term means.

There are two pointers in the play which make me believe that Dattani also wants us to interpret it along the lines of the social system being the culprit in the matter of cruelty to girl children. The following conversation between Chandan and Roopa serve as one pointer:

> CHANDAN: What would you do if you had to choose between a boy and a girl? Who would you choose?
> ROOPA: I think it's more civilized to drown her (girl) in milk. (Dattani 365)

Chandan and Tara's maternal grandfather was a wealthy man. He was in politics and came very close to becoming the Chief Minister. His will is a testament of the kind of treatment that is meted out to girls in Indian society. Mr. Patel and Chauhan are talking:

> PATEL: He [grandfather] left you a lot of money.
> CHANDAN: And Tara?
> PATEL: Nothing.
> CHANDAN: Why?
> PATEL: It was his money. He could do what he wanted with it. (Dattani 360)

The worst part is that this conversation takes place in the presence of Tara. No consideration whatsoever for her feelings! Tara is the victim of this collective social system.

Having been successfully separated from her twin brother, her ordeal continues. We have talked about the conspiracy of her own mother against her. Her father, Mr. Patel, is not much different from his wife, though Bharati is guilty of a more serious crime/sin against Tara. He continuously and doggedly favours Chandan when it comes to giving him higher education abroad, and a career. Tara is discouraged openly, notwithstanding her feelings in the matter, even though she is more intelligent, sharp and witty and would perform well if given opportunities in life. It is only when Chandan refuses to go to college without her, Patel thinks of sending Tara, too, to college. Bharati supports Tara in the matter of higher education and in some other cases, but her support is tainted. It is the product of the guilt and cannot be interpreted as fighting the systemic odds in Tara's way.

Economic and religious/cultural factors have been responsible for the antipathy against and inferiorization of the girl child. A boy helps in contributing to the family income, whether by working in the field, or elsewhere. It is through him that the *vansh* (clan) continues, because of the patriarchal system which requires the members of the family to carry caste names, coming from the father (male side). Parents can attain *moksha* only if a son does the *kapaal kriya* (breaking of the skull while being cremated). So, either girls are killed at birth, or abandoned. The medical and technological advances have made it possible to detect the sex of the fetus. This has given an impetus to the killing of the girls. All this factors combine to create the social system in which the girl child has to live and die.

Tara is killed by the social system, which controls the minds and actions of people. The trauma of coming to know the role her mother had played in her life, and the discrimination she faces at the hands of her father and grandfather become too much for her. And why is she killed? Tara is not wanted. Girls are not wanted. They are irrelevant from the points of view of religion and economics. They are dispensable.

It is noteworthy that discrimination against Tara continues even after her death. Chandan, who was always interested in writing, and who has come to England for higher studies, has transformed into Dan. He turns the story he writes into his own tragedy. It is only incidentally that he has to tell Tara's story, too. Dan apologizes to Tara for doing this: "Forgive me, Tara. Forgive me for making it my tragedy" (Dattani 380). It is quite another matter that it becomes Tara's tragic story also. But that is only incidental.

The play presents a mirror to the Indian society to see its true face. It tries to shock the society out of its grooved thinking. Through racy dialogue and bare minimum stage-setting (by just picking out the characters through cross fadings of light) the playwright effectively portrays the interactions among the characters. The authenticity of the play is established by making Chandan (Chandu at home and later called Dan after his arrival in England) as the narrator/writer of the play. He is one of the Siamese twins (the other twin being Tara, his sister) and nobody could know better than he does.

Works Cited

Dattani, Mahesh. *Tara* in *Collected Plays.* New Delhi: Penguin: 2000.

Katyal, Anjum. "Of Page and Stage: An Interview with Mahesh Dattani." *Seagull Theatre Quarterly.* (December 1999).

Shakespeare, William. *The Complete Works.* Oxford & BH Publishing Co. Pvt. Ltd.: New Delhi, 1980.

23

The Significance of Play within Play: A Study of Mahesh Dattani's *Brief Candle*

Nidhish Kumar Singh

The use of play within play has a very clear design in the dramatic structure of *Brief Candle.* Dattani, with the help of this dramatic device, indicates to his audiences that suffering, tragedy and death are inescapable human conditions but there is a possibility of reducing the sting and pain of these with the help of art, which in this case is dramatic art. The play within the play makes it possible to look upon suffering and eternal death through an artistically philosophical vision. One of the notable characteristics of the dramatic construction of Mahesh Dattani's *Brief Candle* is the fact that it contains a play within the framework of the main play. Perhaps, Dattani has used this device, a play within a play, to give a comparative view of life. Dattani endeavours to show that life is not as bland as people usually think it to be. Life is full of joy and variety. The device helps Dattani in the representation of these two aspects of life.

Dattani is not the first to use this device. Probably, Bhavabhuti was the first dramatist who had used this device. He used it in his celebrated play *Uttam –Ramacharita* (eighth century). The English audience got the chance to see a play within a play in the sixteenth century, about eight hundred years after

Bhavabhuti's *Uttar-Ramacharita*. Probably, the first dramatist of England who had used this device was Thomas Kyd. He tried his hand at making a play within a play in his renowned play *The Spanish Tragedy* (1587). Later Shakespeare and others made use of it. Shakespeare used it in *The Taming of Shrew*, *Love's Labour's Lost*, *A Midsummer Night's Dream* and *Hamlet*. Contemporary Indian English drama is not lagging behind in the use of a play within a play structure. The pioneers of contemporary Indian English drama Vijay Tendulkar and Grish Karnad have used this device very effectively. Tendulkar has used it in his celebrated play *Silence! The Court Is in Session*, Karnad has used it in *Naga-Mandala*. They are not the only playwrights who have used it but there are some others, one of them is Rushmi Ruth Devadasan. But the playwright who inspired Dattani with his play is Madhu Rye, a Gujrati dramatist. Datttani admits:

> I guess I was influenced early in my childhood by Madhu Rye's play *Koipan ek phulnun nam bolo to* (Tell Me the Name of a Flower), which was the first play I remember seeing and that had a play within the play.

A play within a play is a dramatic device in which one play is performed during the action of another play. Jonnie Patricia Mobley defines the device as "A brief play presented during the action of another play". An inner play is used to reveal something, satirize views, disclose the background of characters, acquaint the audience with the process of making a play, demonstrate something, give a comic relief, make a comparison, give a comparative view, provide an outlet to the characters' longing, or to tell a story. The device is used not only in drama but also in the other genres of literature and arts where it is denoted by different terms: story within a story, narrative within a narrative, show within a show, film within a film and painting within a painting etc.

An inner play is often closely related to the outer play and serves as a means of achieving something as in Shakespeare's *Hamlet.* Hamlet, the hero of the play, shares the belief that guilty people witnessing a play have been so deeply moved by the forceful performance that they have confessed their crimes. Therefore, he makes a plan to make the players enact before his uncle a scene resembling his father's murder in order to get more convincing proof than the words of the ghost. Similarly, Vikas, the hero of *Brief Candle,* has a motive behind writing the play. Firstly, he wants to get deliverance through his play. Furthermore, he wants to provide a chance to his fellows to live their dreams. Besides, the dramatic device serves the function of reiterating the two aspects of life mentioned in the early part of the article.

The main play deals with the bland life while the inner play represents the more joyful and colorful life. The main play is set in a hospice named Avedna Cancer Research Hospital and Hospice. Hotel StayLonger, the play within the play, is set in a hotel of the same name. The main play, *Brief Candle*, is a tragedy whereas the inner play, Hotel Staylonger, is a comedy. Dattani has used these two distinct forms of drama "because the play is about death but at the same time about the comedy of living a full life".

There are six characters in the main play out of which four are suffering from cancer. They are Vikas Tiwari, Amol Ghosh, Amrinder and Shanti Venkatraman. The fear of losing something that they have and never think of the possibility of losing that and the fear of approaching death make their lives dull, heavy and weary. Life is bland not only for these four but also for those two characters, Mahesh Tawde and Deepika Dev, who are not the victims of cancer. What makes their lives bland is the fear of losing. It is necessary to analyze the characters in the play within the play in order to see how they enact the comic aspects of the basically tragic flavours of life.

Vikas Tiwari, the hero of the play, is a "victim of cancer as a result of AIDS" (47). He is a drop out of medical college. He and Deepika were pursuing their MBBS from the same college. They were classmates. They loved each other. When Vikas decided to be a dropout, their ways were separated. Vikas became a "free-thinking, free-moving writer" and Deepika became a doctor in Arvedna Cancer Research Hospital and Hospice. When he succumbed to Cancer, he embraced his end and "wanted to live and die there, where I [Vikas] felt loved" (40). But one day he woke up with a dream to see her face, to kiss her, and to greet her goodbye. Therefore, he chose to come to the hospice. He strains his senses to feel her love and worm touch during his eight months stay in the hospice. Deepika opines:

> He chose to come here. He had very high expectations of me. I failed him and so he wrote this play. (26)

Yes, he has written the play because she fails him, but not for vengeance. When he dies, he expects her presence. He wants to see her for the last time, wish her goodbye and to swap those 'three magical' words with her. Mahesh comes to fetch her but she denies by saying "There is nothing I can do! Let me know when he is gone"(21). Consequently, he doesn't get deliverance. He says, "You refuse me to let me go" (12). Probably he had conjectured what was in Deepika's mind and also about the end of his life. Therefore, he planned to get all those things for which he craved till the end of his life through his play. So he writes the play to give her another chance to meet his expectations. He tells Deepika:

> One day you will act in my play. There is a role in it for you. I will touch you with this play of mine. From the dead. (16)

This is not the only reason why he writes the play. "He was a passionate man with strong views on everything and everybody" (22) at the same time "He was a good counsellor" (22). He is easily moved by the suffering of others. He is cognizant of their sufferings and knows they have suffered much more than one can imagine. Therefore, he longs to do something for them. First of all he gives what he has to those who are really in need of that. For instance, he pays for Amol's stay in the hospice. Moreover he does a lot for them through his play. He provides them a chance to live a life which they want to live in their lives but they cannot. This is why each character of the inner play has a great resemblance with the characters of the main play: Mr. Kulkarni resembles Mahesh Tawde, Mr. Sengupta resembles Amol Ghosh, Mr. Malhotra resembles Amrinder, Miss Unnikrishnan resembles Shanti Venkatraman and the Hotel Manager resembles Dr Deepika Dev.

Mahesh is a wise, meek and helpful ward-boy. He dreams of becoming a rich man so that he can buy a private plane for his visit to 'four Dhams' with his grandparents. Besides he loves Deepika and wants to win her, but there is a vast gap between their strata: she is a rich doctor and he is a poor ward-boy. He can't be a doctor but he can be a rich man. Vikas promises to help him out: "you are wise and wonderful. For that my friend, I will make you a rich man" (20). He keeps his word and creates a character, Mr Kulkarni, in his play that is a clone of Mahesh's dream. Mr. Kulkarni is a rich man of Kolhapur and has a private plan. He falls in love with Hotel Manager. He tries to impress her in the course of the inner play. Finally he wins her heart. The victory of Mr. Kulkarni not only wins Deepika for Mahesh but also for Vikas. Vikas feels her touch and swaps those 'three magical words' with her through the character of Mahesh.

Amol is also a victim of cancer. He is not rich enough to take care of the expenses of his treatment and stay in the hospice.

Moreover, he doesn't have his own house. His father has thrown him and his mother out of the house because Amol's step-mother does not want to share either her husband or her house with them. They are told by a man that "our father had married that man's sister and now it was her house" (37). He yells with frustration "Help. Somebody help us, please. Both of us without a home" (37). Then he goes to his Neelima Mashi to share her house. There he falls in love with Rose and gets married to her. He says, "Finally I spy Rose, Rosalynd. We danced, we made love, we married. The happiest time of my life. Until, until, one day" (37) life takes a U turn. Everything changes suddenly. Cancer has been detected in him and he is admitted to the hospice.

Mr. Sengupta is the avatar of Amol Ghosh. He is a middle-class man and a drunkard. He is looking for a room with a Bloody Mary in his hand. He is asked to share a room with Mr Kulkarni because the hotel is full of passengers. Flights have been cancelled because of bad weather and passengers are requested to stay in Hotel Staylonger. He doesn't get a room for himself from the beginning to the end of the play and the Hotel Manager has the last bottle of Bloody Marry to offer him. "The airline is paying for only one night" (10). If the flights do not resume from the next day, the passengers would have to pay for their stay. Mr. Sengupta doesn't have money with him. It is a constant source of worry for him. He asks the Hotel Manager "Where do I go? What do I do?" (10). Thus Mr. Kulkarni is in need of another bottle of Bloody Marry as Amol needs another bottle of blood. Both are lacking money and accommodation. Amol is also aware of this:

> I know somewhere that I was part of his inspiration. (Laughing.) I just love the bit where he is drunk from all the Bloody Marry and doesn't know which room he is in! Right till the end, he doesn't have a place to stay in Hotel Staylonger. (25)

Amrinder is another male character who suffers from cancer. Probably, he is a victim of carcinoma of prostate. When it is detected in him, doctors remove his prostate. A part of his body that makes him 'a real man' has gone. It puts him to dilemma 'to be or not to be'. He knows that his further life will not be easy. He will lose control over his urinary system which means urine can dribble down his pants without his notice. Moreover he can't have sex. However, he has to make a decision and he decides to live with every thing that he has because he shares the belief that it is better to live and face the embarrassment, adversity, or pain like a brave man than to kill himself or turn his back on life like a coward. Nobody understands his predicament except Vikas:

> AMRINDER. He understood what I was going through. Far better than you [Deepika] did. May be because he was a man. No, not true. My urologist is a man and he doesn't understand what is going on in my mind. Vikas knew. He knew the moment he saw me. (22-23)

Amrinder inspires Vikas to make the character of Mr. Malhotra. The Hotel Manager's statement tells us that Mr. Malhotra is a playboy: "And if you think you are going to score with Miss Unnikrishnan you have another thing coming" (11). Mr. Malhotra asks the Hotel Manager to set him with Miss Unnikrishnan for the night. He wants to propose to her but before that he "want her to know how good I [Mr. Malhotra] am in. . . how good I am at... you know-a real man" (11). But there is a problem; he needs Viagra before having sex. It means that he has some problem with his sex organ. It might be the result of erectile dysfunction. However, both Mr. Malhotra and Amrinder have problem with there sex organs and both are unable to satisfy their women. Amrinder's resemblance with Mr. Malhotra gives him a chance to review his judgment. He admits:

> That is why I want to do this play. To take a good look at myself... whether I choose not to have the surgery and die. Or live without really leaving. (33).

Shanti is a patient of breast cancer. Therefore, she has to get rid of her one of breasts. She loses a part of her body which she had hardly felt and seen herself even when she was taking a bath. Vikas ruminative comment candidly exposes Shanti's as well as other characters' dilemma:

> It is the fear of losing something that you have and did not even think of the possibility of not having. But now when there is a real danger of losing it, you begin to understand its true worth. And then you are afraid you will have to live without it for the rest of your living moments. (24)

The fear of losing fosters a desire in Shanti. Now she wants to be a complete woman once again. She yearns to feel and see the part of her body which is gone. Vikas provides her a chance to live a life of a complete woman through the character of Miss Unnikrishnan. Though Miss Unnikrishnan is married, she uses the title Miss which misleads Mr. Malhotra. Mr. Malhotra thinks that Miss Unnikrishnan is a spinster; therefore, he plans to propose to her. Besides, she flirts with him. Probably, she does this out of hate for her husband. She states "And even if you are my husband I don't love you" (43). The reason why she hates her husband is not mentioned in the play. Probably, like Shanti, she is not happy with her husband. But Shanti has some reasons. He wasn't with her when she needed him badly. When she came out of operating-theatre, she expected her husband and her sister to help her out. But they were not present during her operation. Moreover, her husband was rude to her. It was Vikas who offered her his shoulder. Probably, this is another reason for her doing this play. Vikas gives her one more reason for doing this play.

Shanti wants to be a film-maker. Vikas writes a script for her first film/play and asks her to direct it. Shanti acts and directs his play Hotel Staylonger. In other words the inner play benefits her twice: first it gives her a chance to live the life of a normal woman, secondly she becomes the director of the play.

Similarities between Deepika and the Hotel Manager are not many. Their similarities can be seen due to the fact that both are responsible for the others' comforts. Being a doctor Deepika has to take care of her patients' needs and comforts as the Hotel Manager has to. Deepika has her own reasons for doing this play which are a bit different from others. She does the play because she is asked by the committee to do something new and she has no choice. She does not act in the play to live her dream but to prove herself that she is not regretting and lamenting over the death of Vikas. She proclaims:

> I am not mourning! I am not suffering in silence! I can live through his absence like I can live through the absence of any of the ones who don't make it! (27)

Her veneer of hardness begins to crack in the course of the main as well as the inner play. The inner play brings the characters of the main play closer to each other. Consequently, they share their views with each other. Their views about Vikas change Deepikas perception. Finally she "gives in and allows Vikas to caress her" (26) and in the end she admits: "I just want the person to know that I love him very much" (48). This is what Vikas needs in order to get deliverance.

Thus, the inner play provides an outlet to the emotions and feelings of the characters of the main play. It lessens their "burden of stress, emotional turmoil, guilt or whatever it is that is adding to all that baggage"[5] that they carry around. Dattani succeeds in representing the two aspects of life: first, life is bland and the second, life is full of colors. The device and the resemblance between the characters of the main and the inner play help in this. Both, the characters of the main and the inner play, have similar problems but their ways of living are different. The characters of the main play are of the view that life is bland. The characters of the inner play are a group that lives a colorful life despite of all adversities. Thus the inner play and the main play are closely related. Mahesh Dattani is, of course, masterly in the use this dramatic device.

Works Cited

Dattani, Mahesh, Interactive Sessions With Mahesh Dattani, Department of English & Modern European Languages, University of Allahabad, Allahabad. 18 Dec. 2010.

______. A Note on the Play, *Brief Candle: Three Plays*, by Dattani, New Delhi: Penguin Books, 2010, 3.

______. *Brief Candle: Three Plays* (New Delhi: Penguin Books, 2010). All the citations of *Brief Candle* are from this edition and have been given in parentheses.

______. Personal Interview. 19 Dec. 2010.

Patricia, Jonnie Mobley, *NTC's Dictionary of Theatre and Drama Terms*, Lincolnwood: NTC Publishing Group, 1998, 114.

Index